Dog Grooming Simplified

STRAIGHT TO THE POINT

Jodi Murphy

National Certified Master Groomer, Certifier
Master Pet Stylist, Meritus

Jodi Murphy Enterprises, LLC
PO Box 598
Stanhope, NJ 07874

Copyright©2014 Jodi Murphy

ISBN: 978-0-9839720-1-3

All rights reserved. No part of this book may be reproduced or transmitted in any form or by any means, electronic or mechanical, including photocopying, recording, or by any information storage and retrieval system, without permission in writing from the Author/Publisher. No part of this book may be reproduced for educational institutions.

All product names and brand names discussed in this book are trade names, trademarks or registered trademarks of their respective owners.

Most show dog photographs courtesy of In Focus by Miguel unless otherwise specified.
www.infocusbymiguel.com

Skeletal drawings by Mackensie Murphy.
Diagrams, color charts by Devin Murphy.

Printed in the United States of America.

The information within this book is based upon the author's opinion, experiences, preferences and interpretation of the breed standards. Techniques discussed within this book are only to be utilized by experienced professional groomers. We are not responsible for misuse of tools, products and/or equipment causing injury to any pet.

Book Interior Design by Laura Jaeger: ljartdesign@gmail.com

Book Cover Design by Shane Davison: www.supradesign.net

Acknowledgements

I have been extremely fortunate over the years to be blessed with so many very talented mentors. They were there for me, as a new groomer, helping me to understand structure and the breed standards. A special thank you to Sally Hawks, Chris Pawlosky, Laura Heidrich, Denise Pippin, Pam Lauritzen, Kathleen Putman and the late Lynn Carver. I am forever grateful for the time that you have spent with me and for all the knowledge that you have shared. Meeting all of you in the early stages of my career gave me a solid foundation to build upon.

A special thank you to Miguel Betancourt for your beautiful photography. Your photos will give groomers the vision that they need to execute beautiful pet trims! I can't thank you enough for taking on this huge project. Together we made this book happen. It was a pleasure working with you and watching you in action.

To Dave, my best friend, significant other and confidant who is always there to push me and encourage me to reach the goals that I have set for myself. For the past four years I have poured every waking moment into this book and I cannot thank you enough for your patience, encouragement and support. . . . I thank you with all my heart.

To my good friend, Sally Hawks, for always sharing your knowledge with me. I can't thank you enough for our countless discussions. You have known me since I was a very new groomer and have been a huge influence in my career and a great inspiration . . . . Thank you!

A special thank you to Laura Jaeger for all your hard work. Your attention to detail is just phenomenal. Thank you for your dedication to this project. I enjoyed working with you into the wee hours of the morning! You are truly a gifted designer and I am so thrilled that our paths have crossed.

Thank you Mackensie Murphy for jumping in and drawing all the skeletons for *Straight to the Point*. And Devin Murphy for all your hard work with all the diagrams and color charts. I know how busy you were in college, Devin, and yet you found the time to take on this huge project. I look forward to seeing you excel in graphic design. You are so talented! You both did a fabulous job and I am so proud of both of you. You have grown up right before my eyes.

Thank you to my good friends, Diane Betelak, Maria Hetem and Denise Pippin, for always being there to listen to my thoughts and ideas. I can always count on your support and honesty.

Thank you to my long time graphic designer, Shane Davison, who is always there for me when we are pushing a deadline. I can always count on you to deliver top quality work! You are the best!

Thank you Renee Christensen and Linda Verhoest for taking great photos of my client dogs. I truly appreciate all the time and effort that you gave me but most of all I enjoyed spending time with you both!

I would like to thank several groomers who have been nice enough to supply me with photos as well as arrange to meet me for photo shoots. Thank you, Lindsey Dickens (Bichon Frise, the infamous and my beloved "Zoe" aka the wonder dog), a long-time mentor; Ann Martin (wavy Portuguese Water Dog). Veronica Frosch (Poodle/Sporting Trim), Diane Betelak (Poodle head photo), Jennifer Lee (Kerry-

Poodle), Mackensie Murphy (Poodlington), Nicole Kallish (Black Poodle), Jose Rojas (Pom-Poodle), and Lisa Correia (Bichon-Poodle) for allowing me to use photos of your dogs for this book. You are all fabulous groomers and I am honored to have featured your work in *Straight to the Point*.

Over the years I have met some of the most knowledgeable breeders and handlers throughout the United States. A special thank you to Margery Good, Sarah Hawks, Genea Jones, Laura Heidrich, Rae Mason, Leslie McCrackin, David Ramsey, Barbara Hopler and so many others who have helped me to understand their breeds. I can only hope that groomers will take advantage of talking to people like yourselves. You are all a wealth of knowledge. Thank you!

I would like to thank all the participating parent breed clubs that granted permission to quote parts of their breed standard in *Straight to the Point*. Your cooperation in aiding to the education in the pet grooming industry will greatly assist the reader in grooming these breeds to the breed standard.

In the end, it is the dogs that we are thankful for. Their beauty and unconditional love is what touches our souls. When I look at each and every one of these photos it just brings a smile to my face. Dogs are awesome creatures and I am so fortunate to be a part of this industry.

About the Author

Jodi Murphy I have been an animal lover my entire life, growing up with Poodles and Pointers from a very young age. My mom loved her toy Poodles and my dad was an avid bird hunter, so he always had at least three Pointers at one given time. I remember going to field trials as a child and found it fascinating to watch the Pointers hunt. My dad loved to work his dogs in the field and still does. I am the youngest of three children and the only one who took after my dad and his love for animals, but it wasn't until later in life that the idea of grooming ever crossed my mind.

As an adult I fell in love with American Cocker Spaniels. I bought my first dog when I moved out on my own at the age of twenty-one. Very shortly after that I added another Cocker Spaniel to our family. In 1995 my family was transferred to Dallas. I was having trouble finding a groomer in the area. My dogs had the same groomer their entire life in New Jersey and they were having a hard time adjusting to the change. I finally became so frustrated with their grooming experiences that I called a local grooming shop to see where I could go for training. I was told that I could apprentice under them; however, I was required to work as a bather for a year first. I began to work on Saturdays as a bather for three groomers. Holding this position for one year gave me the experience and confidence that I needed with handling different breeds. Once the year had passed I apprenticed for three months.

After the first year of grooming I attended my first industry trade show. I was in awe of what was going on at the show; it was a world that I didn't even realize existed. Once I walked into the grooming contest ring area I just sat in amazement. While watching the competition, I realized how little I knew about dog grooming. I watched the groomers scissoring dogs like I had never seen before. I knew that this was for me and boy, was I hooked.

I was very eager to learn as much as I could, so I started going to local dog shows to educate myself. I just couldn't help but to be drawn to the American Cocker Spaniels while I was there. They were sitting so beautifully with the most gorgeous long flowing coats. My jaw just dropped and at that point I knew I just had to have a puppy. The breeders who I met helped me with the grooming of my new show puppy and got me off to the right start. One year later I entered my first grooming competition and won Best in Show.

I was endlessly working with breeders and handlers of various breeds to educate myself. I began competing with several different breeds, and within three years of stepping into the contest ring I was ranked one of the top three groomers in the country — becoming a member of Groom Team USA. The second year on Groom Team I was ranked the #1 groomer in the country. I traveled with Groom Team USA to the World Tournament in Barcelona, Spain, in 2003, where I won Gold and Bronze medals for the United States. In 2007 I traveled again with Groom Team to Milan, Italy, where I won another Gold medal with my American Cocker Spaniel. Those are experiences that I will never forget. My hard work, dedication and perseverance had paid off.

In 2005 and 2006 I was awarded Best American Groomer at Intergroom in New Jersey. In 2005 I won the World Grand Champion title in the Oster Invitational Tournament of Champions. This competition was by invitation only where I competed against 42 top groomers from around the world!

Going back to 2003, I began to work with the Andis Clipper Company as a National Grooming Consultant. I was really enjoying meeting groomers from all over the United States and noticed how eager they were to learn. I looked back at how difficult it was for me to learn, as I only had basic training through an apprenticeship program. My more advanced training came from attending seminars, from working with breeders and from the competition ring. Educating groomers was becoming a passion of mine. I found it extremely rewarding and soon realized the next step for me was to produce an instructional DVD series to help educate our industry.

In 2007 my first few DVDs were released. I have now produced 44 titles to help groomers become the best that they can be. My DVDs have not only helped the newbie groomers get started but also have taught experienced groomers correct breed profiles and techniques. DVDs are a fabulous way to learn. You can take them to work, take them on airplanes, or just watch them in the privacy of your own home and create a library for many years to come.

I have written *Dog Grooming Simplified: Straight to the Point* to complement my DVD series. Having all this information completes the learning process.

Over the years I have achieved my Master certification title with two of our industry's organizations. I am a National Certified Master Groomer (NCMG) with the National Dog Groomers Association of America as well as a Master Pet Stylist, Meritus (MPS Meritus) with the International Society of Canine Cosmetology. Becoming a Certified groomer was a fabulous learning experience. I am now one of many certifiers with NDGAA testing groomers to their Master status.

I am very proud to say that my daughter, Mackensie, has followed in my footsteps. She has become a member of Groom Team USA ranking within the top 10 groomers in the country. I am looking forward to her continued success!

I hope you enjoy this book and that it helps you understand basic structure and correct pattern placement and simplifies learning about grooming dogs.

Best of luck to you!

Jodi

FOREWARD

I have been so excited collaborating with Jodi on this book, as I think it will raise the bar as far as new and innovative teaching methods. Her use of the AKC standards along with Miguel Betancourt's fabulous photography of current top winning show dogs is sure to make this book a highly sought after reference!

I have watched Jodi grow and excel in the grooming world for many years. I had the opportunity to judge the Oster Invitational Tournament of Champions the year she won and have to say that her work on her American Cocker Spaniel was outstanding. She went on to become a member of Groom Team USA for several years bringing home multiple gold and bronze medals from International tournaments. Jodi is now sharing her knowledge in many ways. She is an industry speaker and has produced an Instructional Grooming DVD Series. Jodi is also a Certifier for National Dog Groomers of America!

Using the structure of the dog and knowledge of the AKC breed standards together to correctly groom our pets on a daily basis is the purpose of this book. Jodi has made this very easy to comprehend within *Straight to the Point*.

Sally Hawks

Sarah ("Sally") Hawks, NCMG, NDGAA Certifier. Sarah, a Terrier specialist, is a multiple contest winner, earning many gold, silver and bronze medals at Intergroom, and was the "Intergroom International Groomer of the Year" in 2007. She qualified for Groom Team USA in 1995 and 1996, and was among the top 10 in 1997 and 2007. In 1995, she won Best Groomed Dog in Show in the Netherlands with her hand stripped Sealyham Terrier, Trigger. Because of her many achievements in the grooming contest ring Sarah was frequently invited to compete in the Oster International Tournament of Champions where, over the years, she won two bronze medals, two silver medals and, in both 2004 and 2009, won the title, Oster World Grand Champion. She is a mentor to up-and-coming groomers. Sarah is an owner, breeder and handler of top winning Sealyham Terriers. She has bred many Terrier champions.

Table of Contents

Acknowledgements iii
About the Author v
Introduction 1
How to Use This Book 3

Structure 5
    Points of Reference 11
    Measuring the Height and Length of a Dog 12

Techniques 15
    Double-Coated Breeds 17
        Shedding Techniques 17
        Shaving Double-Coats 19
    Thinning Shears: Theory & Techniques 21
    Snap-On Combs: Theory & Techniques 27
        Snap-On Combs vs. Blades 29
    Carding: Theory & Techniques 30
    Hand Stripping: Theory & Techniques 32
    Coat Preparation 35
    Point-to-Point Scissoring 37
        Shortcuts 41
        Leg Circumference 42

Setter-Like Pattern Lines 45
    Distinct in Nature 46
    Pattern Placement Diagrams 52
    Distinct in Nature: Common Breeds 55
        English Cocker Spaniel 56
        English Setter 60
        English Springer Spaniel 64
        Gordon Setter 68
        Irish Setter 72
        Welsh Springer Spaniel 76
    Subtle in Nature 80
    Subtle in Nature: Common Breeds 83
        American Water Spaniel 84
        Australian Terrier 88
        Boykin Spaniel 94
        Brittany 98
        Cavalier King Charles Spaniel 102

  Clumber Spaniel 106
  Field Spaniel 110
  German Wirehaired Pointer 114
  Longhaired Dachshund 118
  Sussex Spaniel 122
  Wirehaired Dachshund 126
 Breeds with a Ruff 130
  American Eskimo Dog 132
  Australian Shepherd 136
  Bernese Mountain Dog 140
  Border Collie 144
  Collie 148
  Flat-Coated Retriever 152
  Golden Retriever 156
  Great Pyrenees 160
  Japanese Chin 164
  Keeshond 168
  Longhaired Chihuahua 172
  Newfoundland 176
  Papillon 180
  Pomeranian 184
  Samoyed 188
  Shetland Sheepdog 192
  Tibetan Spaniel 196

Terrier-Like Pattern Lines 201
 Distinct in Nature 202
 Pattern Placement Diagrams 208
 Distinct in Nature: Common Breeds 209
  Affenpinscher 210
  Airedale Terrier 214
  Brussels Griffon 218
  Cesky Terrier 222
  Dandie Dinmont Terrier 228
  Giant Schnauzer 232
  Glen of Imaal Terrier 236
  Irish Terrier 240
  Lakeland Terrier 244
  Miniature Schnauzer 248
  Otterhound 252
  Petit Basset Griffon Vendeen 258
  Spinone Italiano 262
  Welsh Terrier 266
  Wirehaired Pointing Griffon 270
  Wire Fox Terrier 274
 Subtle in Nature 278
 Pattern Placement Diagrams 285
 Subtle in Nature: Common Breeds 287

    Cairn Terrier 288
    Norfolk Terrier 292
    Norwich Terrier 296
    Scottish Terrier 300
    Sealyham Terrier 304
    West Highland White Terrier 308

Sculpted Body Trims 313
    Bedlington Terrier 322
    Bichon Frise 328
    Black Russian Terrier 336
    Bouvier des Flandres 344
    Irish Water Spaniel 352
    Kerry Blue Terrier 358
    Lagotto Romagnolo 366
    Poodle 374
    Portuguese Water Dog 382
    Soft Coated Wheaten Terrier 392

American Cocker Spaniel 399
    Suburban Trim 410
    Field Trim 413

Show Trim Modified to Pet Trim 415
    West Highland White Terrier 416
    English Cocker Spaniel 422

Head Styles 425
    Rectangular Heads 427
    Round Heads 434
    Sporting Dog Heads 436

Ear Styles 441
    Short Natural Ears 443
    Long Natural Ears 444
    Clipped Ears 445

Tail Styles 447
    Flag Tail 449
    Lion Tail 450
    Rat Tail 451
    Carrot Tail 452
    Docked Tail 453
    Plumed Tail 454
    Poodle Tail 455

Mixing It Up 459

Using Sculpted Body Trims, Terrier-Like and Setter-Like Patterns on Various Breeds 460
Bichonpoo "Bichon Frise" 462
Cockapoo "Soft Coated Wheaten Terrier" 463
Maltese "Setter-Like Pattern" 464
Pompoo "Sculpted Body Trim" 465
Poodle "Bedlington Terrier" 466
Poodle "Kerry Blue Terrier" 467
Shih Tzu "Terrier-Like Pattern" 468
Yorkie "Terrier-Like Pattern" 469

Grooming Tips to Correct Faults 471

Closure 475
Glossary of Terms 476
Breed Index 479

Introduction

Educating groomers has been my passion for many years. My Instructional DVD Series has helped so many people learn to groom as well as improve their techniques. *Dog Grooming Simplified: Straight to the Point* was written to complement my DVD series. The information contained in this text along with my DVDs is a wealth of knowledge.

With over 190 breeds recognized by the American Kennel Club along with individual breed-specific grooming instructions, it can become very overwhelming for new groomers to retain the information. *Straight to the Point* is the solution to learning about pattern lines, which simplifies the learning process. Whether the patterns are set tight or left more natural . . . the patterns are set in the same fashion. Once a groomer understands basic patterns he or she will be able to groom any breed with ease.

The dogs pictured in this book are top winning show dogs presenting the correct profile according to their breed standards. I chose to illustrate this way for several reasons. First, a show dog presents an excellent representation of the breed and how it should be groomed per the breed standard. Second, the reader will be able to see the realistic depth and dimensions of the coat. Last, it will give the reader a vision of the pattern in a realistic view and will be a great reference source when grooming each breed.

Once the groomer understands correct pattern placement, it can easily be applied to pet trims. A pet dog does not have to be groomed using "show" techniques, i.e., hand stripping, to present the proper breed profile. With proper pattern placement and techniques described in this text, the groomer will be able to present a well-balanced, well-blended pet trim to the pet owner. The techniques recommended are based on pet trims and are not intended for show dogs. The content described is based on my opinion, my interpretation of the breed standard and the techniques that I have acquired and developed over the years.

It is important to read the following pages explaining techniques and structure terminology, which will be referred to throughout *Straight to the Point*.

How to Use This Book

The breeds discussed in *Straight to the Point* are categorized into three pattern groups. These groups are based on pattern similarities and not on the actual breed groups, i.e., Sporting, Terrier, Non-Sporting, Working, Toys, Hounds, and Herding. This approach was designed to simplify the learning process.

Two of the groups consist of "Terrier-Like" and "Setter-Like". These names were chosen due to the similar pattern "type". The breeds within these groups are not limited to Terriers or Setters by any means; however, the pattern carries that particular appearance.

Both groups are also broken down by "Subtle in Nature" and "Distinct in Nature". Pattern placement of each group is explained in detail. Once the pattern placements are described, photos and descriptions of common breeds that fall under that particular pattern group will follow.

The last group refers to breeds that are scissored following the dog's body contour and structure. This group is referred to as "Sculpted Body Trims". The pattern will be described comparing two different coat types, a drop coat and a curly coat. Photos and descriptions of common breeds that fall under this group will follow.

Diagrams of each breed will be shown along with a color scale. Recommended blades and snap-on combs as well as techniques will be included in the color scale for different parts of the dog. Coat lengths can be selected based on the pet owner's preference.

Important breed standard information is quoted in part with permission from participating breed clubs. The breed standard is a description of each breed that was written by each parent breed club. This information will help the groomer understand how each breed should look, which will facilitate in presenting a properly groomed dog. For complete breed standard information of each breed it is recommended to read *The Complete Dog Book*, the official publication of the American Kennel Club. In the event that the breed standard was not permitted for quotation, the author's interpretation of the standard is given.

While grooming each particular breed it is recommended to refer back to the pages that describe the appropriate pattern placement in detail. Slight deviations from the described pattern will be noted for each breed if necessary. Proper grooming techniques and recommended tools will also be noted for each breed.

While reading *Straight to the Point*, it will become evident how similar the patterns are for all breeds as they are set based on the same structure points.

STRUCTURE

STRUCTURE

Understanding basic canine structure is important in order to set patterns properly. The dog's structure is a map to setting pattern lines. It is important to be familiar with skeletal terminology while reading *Straight to the Point*. Feeling specific points of the dog's structure while trimming is the key to setting patterns correctly, i.e., the breastbone, the withers, the elbow and the pin bone.

Diagram A shows the canine anatomy identifying the bones.

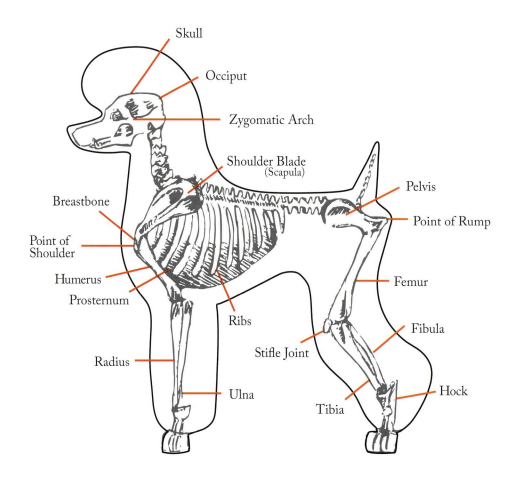

Diagram A

Diagram B shows the canine anatomy referencing body parts and areas of the dog that will be referred to often in *Straight to the Point*. This terminology is commonly used in the dog grooming industry.

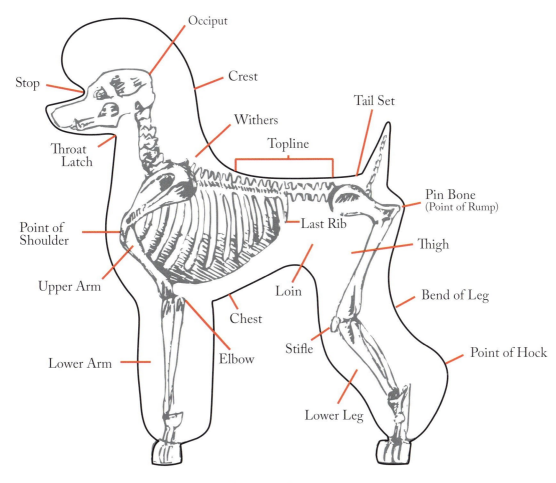

Diagram B

All dogs have the same bone structure. However, they differ in build and muscle tone. This is no different than the human skeleton. We all have the same bones and structure, yet we all have our own unique bodies and builds. Our length of bones vary, which makes us all different. Some people are short and petite while others are tall and have larger frames. The difference in muscle tone also creates individuality.

Even though dogs have the same bones, certain bones may vary in length and mass from one breed to the next. Some dogs have level toplines while others have a roach or a sloping topline; some dogs have short legs, some have long legs; some dogs are long in body while some are square. These are just some of the traits that change the appearance of each breed which makes them each unique. Comparing the human skeleton to the canine skeleton and the differences in traits is all synonymous.

For every purpose of a breed of dog there are specific builds that will enhance the breed's utility. For example, the correct placement and size of the bones of the Greyhound are crucial in producing the greatest speed. When comparing the Dachshund to the Poodle, the difference in length of bones is evident.

This creates their unique profiles. The Dachshund will rest its chest on the ground, which gives its front legs the freedom to dig through burrows. The front assembly is reduced in size in order for Dachshunds to be able to perform their job.

Front and rear angulation refers to the way the bones are slanted and meet at the joints. The shoulder and upper arm form the front angulation and the pelvis, upper and lower leg form the rear angulation. Structure can get complex and difficult to comprehend; however, the following information consists of basic knowledge that will help create a well-balanced trim.

Many Terriers give the impression of a straighter front than other breeds. When viewing the skeleton of a Terrier it is understandable why they present this type of front while other breeds appear to have more forechest.

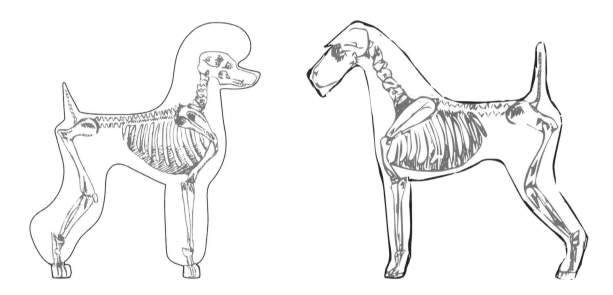

The upper arm of many Terriers, especially the short-legged Terriers, is shorter in length than in other breeds. In addition, the angle of the upper arm is set at a lesser degree. This bone slopes slightly towards the rear from the point of shoulder, instead of creating a 90-degree angle to the shoulder blade like the Poodle. This brings the front leg forward, which gives the illusion of a straight front. The structure of this front assembly has been developed for the particular job Terriers were bred to perform. Many Terriers "go to ground" and dig through burrows when they hunt fox and vermin. The short upper arm is beneficial for this job.

When viewing the structure of a Poodle, the shoulder blade and the upper arm are approximately the same length and form a 90-degree angle. This sets the front leg back under the dog, which will present a forechest. Many breeds are described to have this type of front assembly. In this case the withers should fall in line with the elbow.

Rear angulation is determined by the slope of the pelvis as well as the angle that the femur and tibia/fibula create when they meet at the stifle joint. If these bones are not of the proper length or are not angled properly, the angulation of the rear will be affected. The rear can then become straight or over-angulated.

The breed standards describe the proper angulation of the front and rear for each particular breed.

This is important for groomers to understand when grooming coated breeds. Oftentimes, pets are straighter in the front and rear than desired. In this case, a groomer can scissor these areas to create the illusion of correct structure.

Correct front and rear angulation are very important in order for a dog to move, or gait, correctly in the show ring. For pet grooming, angulation is important to understand in order to present a well-balanced groom.

Many dogs have structural faults. Some may not have the proper topline, depth of chest or rear angulation that they should have. As groomers, we can give the illusion of the proper structure when working with coated dogs by camouflage grooming. Leaving more coat under the chest to create the proper depth of chest, or scissoring a topline level when it has a dip, are ways to enhance the profile of the dog. This is a skill that comes with understanding basic structure as well as the breed standard of each particular breed.

When setting patterns it is important to show the proper topline, the shoulder layback, the muscle of the thigh and the angulation of the rear as well as the proper shape of the front assembly. Body patterns are all similar in this respect. The difference from breed to breed is the coat type, coat density, length of coat, bone structure and muscle tone which change the appearance of each breed.

The dogs pictured in this book are excellent specimens of their breed. That does not mean that they are all perfect. Many dogs have faults. However, they are groomed to the breed standard accentuating their attributes and hiding any fault that they may have. The dogs presented in *Straight to the Point* will give the reader a visual of what the breed should look like from the profile, the front and the rear. Using these dogs as a reference while grooming will help execute a perfect trim.

See "Grooming Tips to Correct Faults" on page 471.

STRUCTURE

Points of Reference

The following diagram describes reference points of the dog that will be referred to often throughout *Straight to the Point.* The back of the front leg (elbow) should fall in line with the withers (A).

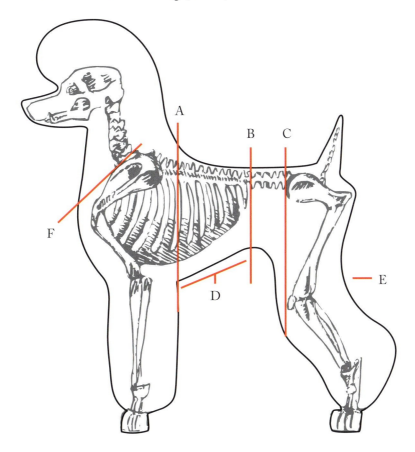

The tuck-up is set behind the last rib (B).

The stifle should fall approximately in line with the croup (C).

The underline should rise from the elbow to the loin (D).

The shortest point of the rear angulation is at the bend of the leg (E).

. . . . where the neck meets the shoulder blade (F).

These phrases will be used over and over again, among many others. View the anatomy of the dog and become familiar with these key points.

Measuring the Height and Length of a Dog

A dog's height is measured from the top of the withers to the ground (A). The length is measured from the breastbone to the point of rump (B).

If a dog is described in the breed standard to be square in body, then these measurements should be equal. If a dog should be slightly longer than it is tall, the length measurement will be greater than the height.

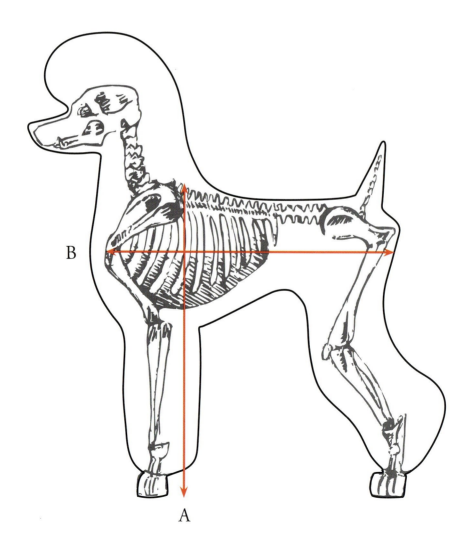

NOTES

TIP TO REMEMBER:

Developing proper techniques will come with practice, repetition and experience. Grooming is an art form that each individual develops at his/her own pace. Learning correct techniques is important in order to produce beautiful seamless pet trims.

Techniques

Double-Coated Breeds
    Shedding Coats
    Shaving Double-Coats

Thinning Shears: Theory & Techniques

Snap-On Combs: Theory & Techniques
    Snap-On Combs vs. Blades

Carding: Theory & Techniques

Hand Stripping: Theory & Techniques

Coat Preparation

Point-to-Point Scissoring
    Shortcuts
    Leg Circumference

TECHNIQUES

Techniques such as carding, thinning shear work, scissoring, shedding coats, and proper coat preparation will facilitate in presenting a well-groomed representation of any breed. The following pages will discuss these techniques in detail.

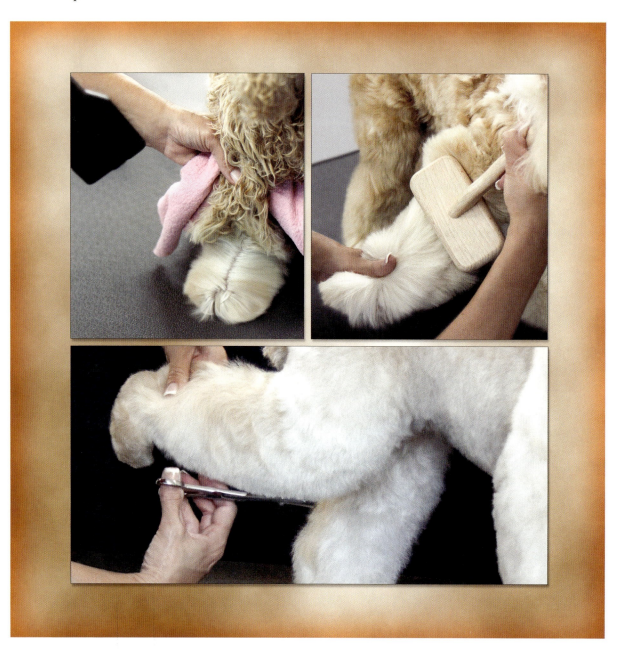

Double-Coated Breeds
Shedding Techniques

Wild animals develop a winter and summer coat based on daylight. As the days become shorter these animals will develop their heavy winter coats. As the days become longer they will start to shed their winter coats preparing for the warm weather. House pets, on the other hand, are exposed to artificial light and do not develop this exact cycle. Pets tend to shed all year round; however, the majority of the shedding does occur when the days become longer and pets are exposed to natural sunlight for longer periods of time.

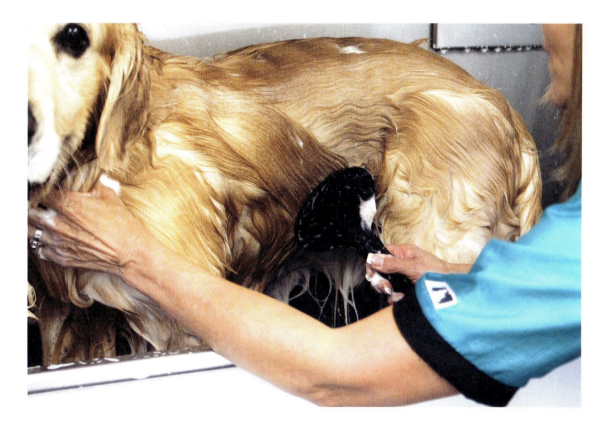

Shedding double-coated breeds, like the Golden Retriever for example, can be done easily and effectively during the bathing process. A warm bath can facilitate the release of undercoat by slightly dilating the hair follicles. This seems to be the prime time to remove undercoat. Brushing the coat while it is wet and soapy will remove a tremendous amount of coat. This can be done using a slicker brush. An undercoat rake can also be used if necessary. Brushing with the flow of water during the rinse process will also facilitate in the removal of excess undercoat. Once the coat is brushed thoroughly during the bath, applying a cool rinse is beneficial, as it will constrict the hair follicles.

Undercoat is a soft and downy type of hair. When dogs are washed with shampoo the undercoat becomes saturated and will take longer to dry than the guard hair. Once the excess undercoat is removed during the bath, the dog will dry very quickly.

This shedding procedure is not only extremely effective in the shedding process but is also healthier for the groomer. The common method of brushing out dirty, dry undercoat or force drying the coat with a high velocity dryer as a means of a shedding technique is very messy. The undercoat, dander and allergens are blown out and are easily inhaled. With the described shedding method, the undercoat is left wet in the bath tub and is easy to clean up.

Caution should be taken when brushing a wet coat, as the pins of a slicker brush can reach the skin more easily than when brushing a dry coat. Applying too much pressure to the brush could cause irritation to the skin.

The lifestyle of the pet should be given special consideration before using these shedding techniques. Pets who are exposed to cold temperatures for long periods of time or actively participate in the field work that they were bred for may need the excess undercoat to protect them from the elements.

Tip To Remember:

After bathing a thick double-coated breed, be sure to rinse the coat thoroughly. Leaving shampoo and/or conditioner residue in the coat can cause the dog to itch. The coat is rinsed thoroughly when the water runs clear. The thick-coated breeds can take much longer to rinse than other breeds.

Shaving Double-Coats

Most pet owners who own heavy double-coated breeds, like the Golden Retriever, are concerned that their dogs are very hot during the summer months. They do not understand the function of the double-coat. It is our job as pet care professionals to educate our clients before shaving a double-coated breed.

The undercoat serves as a type of insulation for dogs. It keeps them warm during the winter months by holding in body heat. They don't shed quite as much in the winter because they need the coat to keep them warm. When the warmer season approaches and the days become longer, these breeds will start to shed profusely. They are shedding their winter coat preparing for the summer heat. If they held onto their coat, they would be extremely hot during the summer months. Many of these breeds need assistance from groomers to remove the excess undercoat during the shedding season. Once the undercoat is removed and is maintained regularly, the dog will stay cooler. The pretty guard hair that these breeds have regulates their body temperature, keeping them cool and protecting their skin from the sun.

The double-coat serves to protect the dogs from weather conditions, cold water temperatures and rough terrain when performing the various jobs that they were bred for. Many of these coats have an oily protective coating that acts like the down of a duck and repels water. The undercoat insulates and prevents the water from reaching the skin. This is very important for water retrieving dogs. Of course, when these breeds are bathed with shampoo, the detergent will gradually break down the natural oils and the coat will become saturated. This is why it seems difficult to completely saturate these breeds when bathing them.

When these breeds are shaved, their natural cooling mechanism is destroyed. They do not have protection from the sun's harmful UV rays or the guard hair that serves to control their body temperature. Once shaved, the undercoat that was in the hair follicle still remains there. When the coat is clipped very short, the follicles can become clogged with undercoat. The dogs may lick the irritated skin and before long a hot spot or skin irritation can be triggered.

Dogs have numerous strands of hair in each follicle. It is believed that the follicle consists of only one guard hair and a multitude of undercoat hairs. When clippering a dog short, many of the guard hairs can be damaged and will be replaced with undercoat. In addition, undercoat grows at a much more rapid rate than guard hair. This is why after clippering these breeds it seems as though the coat grows back thicker with more undercoat.

Canine alopecia is a hair loss disorder that results from mange, infection, trauma, immune disease and endocrine system abnormalities as well as other underlying health conditions. Once double-coated breeds are shaved, "post-clippering alopecia" can be triggered. This disorder is most prevalent in the Pomeranian, Chow Chow, German Shepherd, Samoyed, Sheltie, Collie and Keeshond although it can happen in any heavy double-coated breed. This is often seen several weeks after the pet has been shaved as new growth is starting to appear. The coat will grow in leaving patchy areas of baldness. Canine alopecia has been linked to certain health issues including trauma to the skin, yet it is uncertain why some breeds that are shaved develop post-clippering alopecia and others do not. The dogs that do develop this disorder after being shaved may never grow their full coat back again.

These are the concerns and should be relayed to the pet owner. It is ultimately the pet owners' decision as to whether or not they want to have their pet shaved. However, it is the groomers' decision whether they want to perform the groom and be held responsible in the event that a skin and/or coat issue does arise after the groom. To alleviate any concern, a release form may be presented to the pet owner prior to the groom.

When shaving body patterns or performing complete shavedowns on any breed it is recommended to use blade lengths ranging from 7F, 5F, 4F or longer. Using blade lengths shorter than a 7F on body patterns can be detrimental to the skin. All dogs are different. Some may grow coat back perfectly fine with no irritation from clipping, while others may develop skin or coat issues.

In the event of a medical issue and/or old age, the pet's veterinarian may recommend to have the dog shaved. In this event, the health and comfort of the pet should be the deciding factor. If clipping is preferred, it is recommended to completely shed the coat using a slicker brush and/or shedding rake before shaving. Carding the coat after the shavedown will help to remove the remainder of the undercoat.

Snap-on combs of various lengths can also be used for a shorter trim as an alternative to blades.

Available on DVD: "Smooth Road to Shavedowns" and "Deshedding: Theory & Techniques"

Tip To Remember:

Drying the double-coated breeds thoroughly is very important. Leaving these breeds damp behind the ears, in the armpits and in the rear furnishings, for example, can cause skin issues and matting.

Thinning Shears: Theory & Techniques

Photo courtesy of Animalphotography - Ren Netherland

Thinning shears are available through many manufacturers. Some call them blenders, while others refer to them as thinning shears. The term "thinning shears" sometimes refers to a shear that has teeth on both blades, while "blenders" can refer to a shear with teeth on one side and a cutting edge on the other side. All manufacturers refer to them differently. A shear that has teeth on both blades can be a very aggressive shear and will not be discussed here. I prefer to use the term "thinning shears" as opposed to "blenders" to eliminate any confusion.

Thinning shears are one of the most valuable tools that a groomer can own. They can be used on almost every dog to finish the trim. Thinning shears act as an eraser and remove scissor lines and blade marks, but most importantly they blend pattern lines and soften scissor work. However, thinning shears are probably the most difficult tool to buy.

Every thinner will "blend" on a certain coat type. Unfortnately, there is not just one thinning shear that will handle every job. Unlike a straight or curved shear, the way a thinner feels in your hand is not as important as the teeth configuration. As a rule, the more teeth, the smoother blending capabilities the thinner will have. However, that also depends on the length of the shear. A 48-tooth shear that is 6″ in length will cut completely differently than 48 teeth on a 5″ shear. When purchasing a thinner, take a good look at the teeth. Are the teeth and the spaces between each tooth approximately the same width? If they are, this shear will most likely give a nice even blending effect. If the space between the teeth is wider than the width of the teeth, then more coat will fall between the spaces without being cut. This will leave a more natural finish.

At the top of each tooth is a V notch. The deeper the notch, the more coat will be trapped in the notch and cut. This is a very aggressive shear. Aggressive shears work very well on soft coats, as this gives a razor effect to the ends of the coat and will remove scissor marks very nicely. An aggressive shear also works well when trimming flag tails, Setter-like furnishings and long ears. This type of shear will cut off hair quickly but will leave a natural look.

There is also a thinning shear that has a scissor-like tooth. Each tooth is very wide. There is no V notch in this type of shear. The teeth resemble a straight edge, similar to a straight shear. It is fabulous for going over scissor work on Poodle-type coats to remove scissor marks. This shear also works very nicely on double-coated breeds to trim furnishings. Thinning shears will finish a trim, making it appear flawless, when used correctly.

After many years of participating in grooming competitions I have gained a tremendous amount of knowledge about using thinning shears merely on trial and error. I have purchased so many shears in the past and come home to find out that they were not doing the job that they were intended for. I finally took the time to figure it out and put together a line of my most favorite teeth configurations that I felt would tackle every job that I needed them for. I developed a line of four thinning shears, just for groomers, in order to take the confusion out of purchasing shears. This set of shears can handle any coat type and various techniques needed in dog grooming.

I named my shears based on the type of shear they are. The following illustrations show my line of thinning shears.

The Shaper

The Shaper is a 48-tooth shear that does a beautiful job with blending heads and pattern lines.

The Detailer

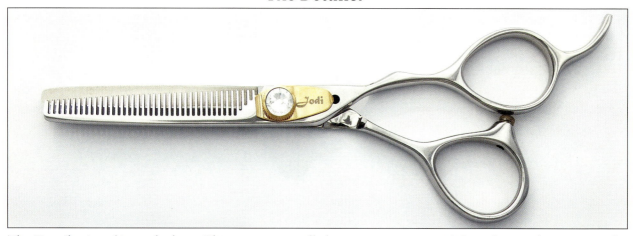

The Detailer is a 40-tooth shear. This is a very small shear, measuring 5 1/2″, and is used to trim under eyes and to blend short clipperwork into longer coat, e.g., eyebrows, beards, etc.

The Texturizer

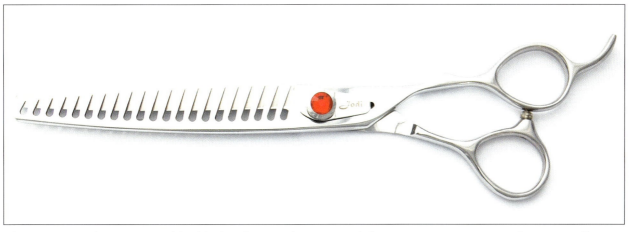

The Texturizer has a scissor-like blade of 21 teeth. It is used for going over scissor work on Poodle-type coats. It also can be used for furnishings of double-coated breeds and Terriers.

The Outliner

The Outliner is a 46-tooth shear and is very aggressive. It has a deep V notch on the top of each tooth, which captures a lot of hair and removes it quickly. These are wonderful for trimming furnishings for a natural look.

I have developed many techniques over the years using thinning shears. Coming from the beauty industry many years ago, the techniques that I had used with human hair have helped me understand coat and how to scissor it in a way that it falls flawlessly.

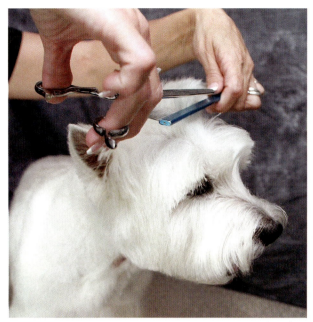 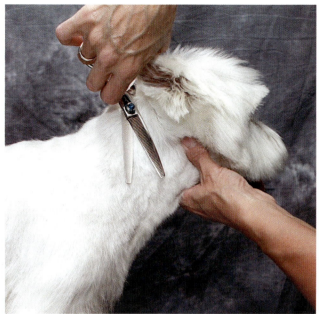

Photos by Renee Christensen

Lifting the coat with a comb and thinning the tips of the coat will remove scissor marks and blend beautifully. This can be done with the Shaper or Outliner depending on the coat type and density. This technique can be used as a finishing touch on round head styles to remove scissor marks and/or snap-on comb marks. Lifting an uneven area of coat with a comb will show the coat that needs to be trimmed for a well-blended look. This technique is similar to the way hairdressers hold human hair between their fingers and scissor it to achieve even layers.

Blend pattern lines on Sporting dogs, Terriers, etc., using the Shaper for a beautiful seamless outline. For finer coats, the Detailer blends lines well. Always use the blade edge against the skin when using thinning shears to blend short coat into longer coat.

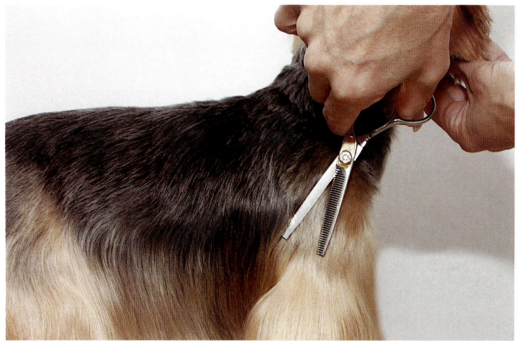

Photo by Renee Christensen

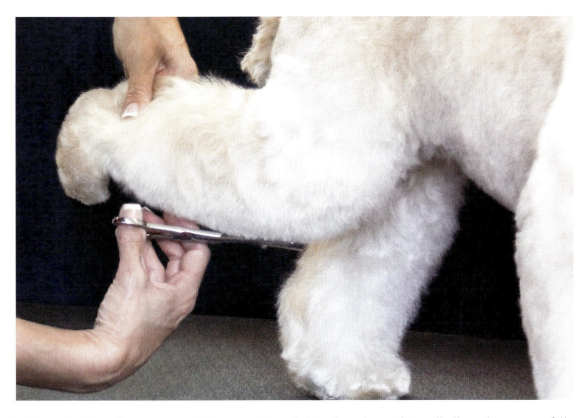

Lift the leg and allow drop-coats to fall naturally and thin the edges. This will allow the coat to fall without scissor marks.

Trim flag tails with a very aggressive shear. The Outliner will leave the tail looking very natural without scissor marks.

Photo by Renee Christensen

 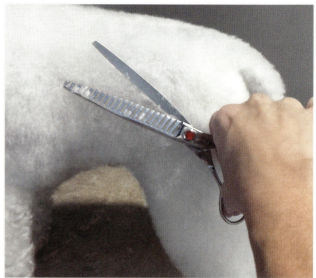

Neaten ears for a natural look using thinning shears. The shear used will be determined by the coat type. A more aggressive shear should be used on a thicker coat and a less aggressive shear can be used on a silky coat.

Use the Texturizer to scissor over difficult coats to remove scissor lines. This type of shear works beautifully on Poodle-type coats.

The Detailer will blend clipped areas into longer coat very nicely. This type of shear is for fine detail work.

Available on DVD: "Thinning Shears: Theory & Techniques"

Photo by Renee Christensen

Snap-On Combs: Theory & Techniques

Snap-on combs are a fabulous tool that no groomer should be without. These combs attach over the clipper blade allowing the groomer to leave more length on a dog than what a blade allows. They can be used to set lines quickly to prepare the trim for a scissor finish. These combs are available in lengths from 1/8″ to 1″. They are a great time saver. They can also be used to skim the drop-coated breeds to help the coat blend and fall nicely. The techniques that can be used with snap-on combs are endless.

A 10, 15, 30 or 40 blade can be used on the clipper, under the comb. All manufacturers are slightly different and some require a specific blade, so please read the packaging before selecting a blade. Blade selection can be based on the coat texture and density. For very thick coats a 10 or 15 blade could be used under the comb. For finer coats, a 30 blade is recommended. Selecting the proper blade is up to the groomer. Every coat type is different. A 15 blade works very well for almost all coat types.

Snap-on combs may also be used instead of blades. For example: When using a 4F or 5F blade and the coat does not feed into the blade properly, a snap-on comb equivalent to the same length may be used instead. Combs are available that are equivalent to 7F, 5F, 4F, 3 3/4, 5/8 and 3/4 blades. See the equivalency chart on page 29. This gives the groomer many options when having trouble with clipping thick, thin or difficult coats.

On Poodle-type coats, a snap-on comb will trim pretty accurately to the length of the comb. Using the comb with the lay of the coat on drop-coats, as in the Yorkshire Terrier, Maltese and Soft Coated Wheaten to name a few, will leave the coat a bit longer than the size of the comb. This is due to the fact that the coat is lying flat and has difficulty feeding into the comb attachment.

Each comb is identified by either a number or a letter. Some brands are color coded for quick identification. Manufacturers also mark the length of coat the comb will leave.

These markings can be difficult to see. For easy reference, the distance defined by the red line in the photo below, which is between the blade and the bottom of the comb, is the length the coat will be left after clipping. The picture shown below is a #1 comb which leaves the coat 1/2″. The length of the red line is also 1/2″. Knowing this will help to identify which comb to select without having to read the difficult markings on each comb.

Using a snap-on comb against the lay of the coat will take the coat much shorter than expected on drop-coated breeds. To avoid this, use a longer comb. This technique can come in handy while setting in patterns. For instance, the throats of many coated breeds are set tighter than the body. Using the same comb that was used to set the body in reverse, from the breastbone up under the throat latch, will take the throat shorter without having to change the comb to a different size.

Using combs in this manner will save time. When setting rear angulation, a comb may be used to set the angle from the pin bone down through the bend of leg. However, if the coat needs to be a bit shorter, taking the comb from the bend up to the pin bone will set the angulation tighter.

Many pet owners of double-coated breeds may request to have their dog neaten up all over without the extreme look and potential adverse reaction of a shavedown. Longer snap-on combs may be used in this case. Thinning shear techniques should be used to finish this type of trim for a well-blended appearance.

Available on DVD: "Snap-On Combs: Theory & Techniques"

Snap-On Combs vs. Blades

The following shows the various lengths of snap-on combs and the equivalent blade size. Snap-on combs may be substituted for blades depending on the density of the coat. One tool may clip more smoothly than the other. Having the option to use one or the other is always a benefit. Snap-on combs are available through many manufacturers, and the sizes may vary slightly.

Snap-On Comb	= Blade
#5 Comb (1/8")	7F
#4 Comb (1/4")	5F
#2 Comb (1/3")	4F
#1 Comb (1/2")	3 3/4 FC
#0 Comb (5/8")	5/8 HT
#A Comb (3/4")	3/4 HT

Carding: Theory & Techniques

Countless breeds require "carding" techniques. These are the breeds that have a double-coat that consists of guard hair and undercoat.

Undercoat is defined as the short, soft, dense hair that supports the outer coat or guard hair. The term "carding" describes the technique of removing undercoat from the follicles with the use of a stripping knife or shedding rake (Coat King). Undercoat has its purpose; however, when it becomes excessive it can cause skin and coat issues. Keeping undercoat at bay by using carding techniques is beneficial in many ways.

Shedding heavy double-coated breeds is a different technique than carding (see "Double-Coated Breeds" on page 17). Carding techniques are commonly used on the more flat-coated breeds like many of the Terriers and Sporting dogs. However, there are certain areas on heavy double-coated breeds where carding techniques can be used. These include the shorter areas of the dog, e.g., the front of the front legs, front of the hocks, top of the skull, etc.

This technique will promote healthy skin and coat by clearing the follicles of excessive undercoat. Undercoat is soft and dull in color and can prevent the skin from breathing if it becomes excessive, which in turn can cause hot spots and other skin issues in certain breeds. Once the excess undercoat is removed, the coat will shine and the skin will be able to breathe and will be healthier.

When using a stripping knife it is important to hold the skin taut with one hand while combing through the coat with the other. If the skin is not held taut it will move with every stroke, which can be uncomfortable for the pet. When the skin moves the tool will not be productive. The stripping knife should be held almost flat to the skin.

There are also other tools available to remove undercoat. A common tool called the Coat King will grab undercoat as well as some top coat (guard hair) and pull the coat from the root. This tool works very well on Terrier and Sporting dog coats as well as other breeds that should be hand stripped. This type of tool is not intended for show coats, as it is capable of cutting the guard hair, which is not appropriate for show dogs.

Many of these double-coated breeds, especially the Sporting breeds, may have a very natural flat back coat. It is recommended to start carding these coats when the dogs are puppies. If these techniques are done properly, clipping may never be necessary. Once a back coat is clipped it may never return to the same texture and color that it started with.

If clipping has previously been done or the pet owner prefers a clipped back, removing undercoat in conjunction with clipping will help the blades glide through the coat with ease.

Carding a coat can often stimulate new growth to come in with hard texture and vibrant color which would normally be lost by clipping alone.

When dogs are not carded, blades will often leave track marks in the coat. It is common to want to shave them with very short blades to ensure a smoother finish. However, the undercoat is what causes the blade to leave track marks, almost like the look of corduroy. Carding techniques will eliminate the corduroy issue so a longer blade can then be used.

Often when Terriers, Sporting dogs and other double-coated breeds are shaved with short blades without having the undercoat removed, the back coat will grow back very thick. Once it is carded on a regular basis the coat will lie nicely and a longer blade can be used. Using longer blades will give a more natural appearance that will be more true to the breed profile. The pattern lines will blend more easily into the longer furnishings when the undercoat is removed and a longer blade is used.

Undercoat can also be removed while the dog is being bathed. Brushing with a slicker brush or using a rubber curry brush while the dog is soapy will help remove excessive undercoat.

Carding techniques take very little time and will be beneficial in the end for the groomer and the pet.

Available on DVD: "Carding & Hand Stripping for Pets"

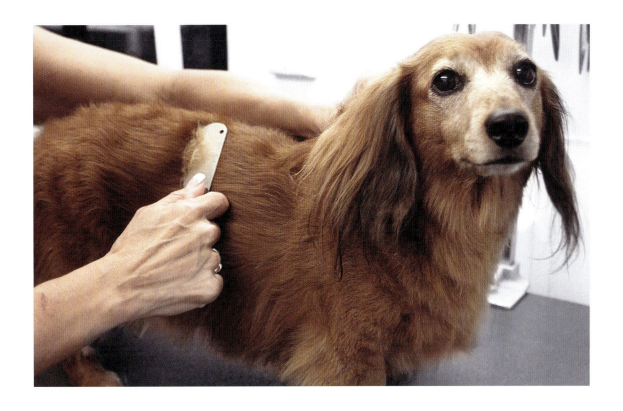

Hand Stripping: Theory & Techniques

In the pet grooming industry harsh-, wire- and broken-coated breeds as well as Spaniels and Setters are commonly clipped by groomers. These same breeds when being shown in the dog show ring are hand stripped, which is the proper grooming technique per their breed standard. This technique is now crossing over from the dog show world into the pet grooming world as groomers are now recognizing the benefits.

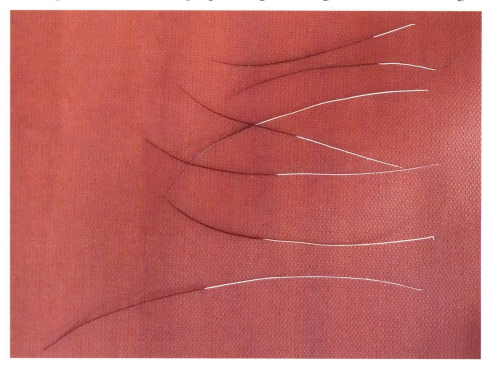

Hand stripping is extremely beneficial to the skin and coat of these breeds. It will maintain the proper coat texture as well as color. It is a technique that is done by plucking hairs from the hair follicle. The harsh-, wire- and broken-coat types, when hand stripped, have a vibrant color and harsh texture. This coat type grows to a certain length and then dies. The coat is harsh and colorful at the tips but then becomes soft, fine and faded at the root as it begins to die. Plucking these strands stimulates the follicle to produce another hair of the proper texture and color. Since the color is at the tip of the hair shaft, it is important to keep the coat at the desired length by plucking the longest hairs. As the tip of the new growth emerges from the skin, it will have the correct color and texture.

This photo shows several strands of hair that were plucked at different growth stages. Some strands were just starting to die while others were at the end of their life cycle. The color and texture is at the tip of each strand.

When this coat is clipped, the vibrant color is clipped off and the only coat that remains is the soft faded portion at the base of the skin. A clipped coat consists mostly of soft, fine and faded guard hair and undercoat. If clipping is preferred, carding techniques should always be done in addition to clipping. This technique will remove undercoat and will also pull some guard hair from the follicle which will give a clipped coat a slightly better texture and color.

The Spaniels and Setters keep their texture and color as long as they are not clipped. Their coat does not change in color and texture at the root when it is at the end of its growth cycle like the wire-coats; instead this coat will grow to a certain length and shed out on its own. Carding techniques should be done on this coat type to remove undercoat and to pull shedding guard hair. The longer guard hair can be plucked in order to achieve the proper length of the back coat or jacket. Clipping this coat type will change the color and texture of the coat. Carding techniques should be done, in addition to clipping, to encourage slightly better texture and color.

Numerous breeds that are hand stripped are shown in *Straight to the Point*. Take notice of the rich color and texture of these coats as opposed to the pets that groomers see on a daily basis that are clipped.

For groomers who are learning to hand strip it is best to use a latex glove, a stone, finger cots and/or chalk, which will help to grab the hair. A variety of stripping knives are available; however, the beginner will often cut the coat while using a knife, rather than pull the coat.

It is important to learn the proper technique when hand stripping. Keeping the wrist straight and using the arm from the shoulder to pull will avoid developing carpal tunnel issues. Bending or twisting the wrist while stripping will also result in breaking or cutting the coat while using a knife.

The key is to only pluck a few hairs at a time to avoid discomfort to the dog and to avoid removing too much hair at a time.

Always pull the ends of the coat in the direction that the hair grows, and support the skin above the area that is being stripped by pulling the skin taut.

The proper hand stripped harsh-coat consists of several layers of different lengths. The shortest layer is closest to the skin. This is the new growth of coat that is emerging from the skin from when the dog was last stripped. The next layer is longer and is the growth from when the dog was stripped two sessions before. The longest coat is the growth that was pulled three sessions prior. At each stripping session the groomer should pull the longest hairs. By doing this the groomer is constantly creating layers.

Each breed requires a different length of time between stripping sessions. Some breeds may need to be stripped more frequently than others. Different areas of the dog require various stripping schedules. This is based on the desired length of coat.

Most pet owners do not want to have their dogs completely hand stripped because of the time and money that it takes to perform and maintain this groom. However, as pet groomers it is possible to perform a "pet strip" which consists of partially hand stripping the pet to promote healthy skin and coat. Partially stripping the jacket (body), head and ears of breeds like the Wire Fox Terrier will preserve the proper texture and color. Thinning shears can then be used on the legs and sensitive areas to finish the trim.

Many tools are available for groomers that will pull the coat of these breeds, giving a result similar to the effect of hand stripping. Undercoat rakes, one of which is the Coat King, will grab undercoat as well as some top coat (guard hair) and pull the coat from the root. This can often stimulate new growth to come in with hard texture and vibrant color. This type of tool is not intended for show coats, as it can cut some of the guard hair instead of pulling it from the root.

If hand stripping is a technique that the pet owner and/or groomer desire, it is recommended to contact the particular breed club for specific hand stripping instructions for that particular breed. Working with experienced breeders/handlers is also recommended in order to develop the proper skills and techniques.

When dogs are spayed or neutered their coat can change. The undercoat tends to grow in thicker and the guard hair can become softer. Clipping may be the only alternative when dealing with a "spay coat". Carding techniques will help to keep the undercoat at bay after clipping.

Available on DVD: "Carding & Hand Stripping for Pets" and "The Border Terrier - Pet Strip"

Coat Preparation

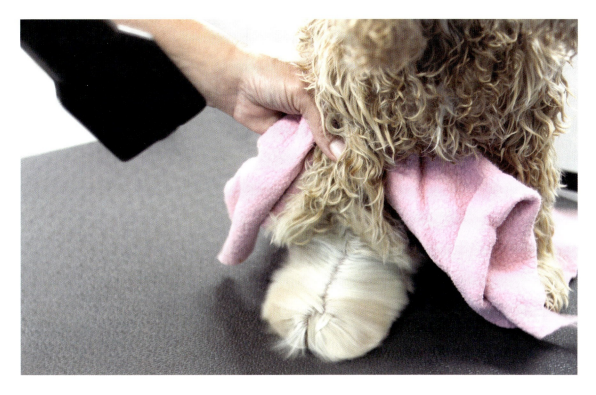

Proper coat preparation is the foundation of a good groom. It is extremely important to get the coat bathed and rinsed thoroughly. The drying process requires the proper techniques in order to get the coat as straight as possible, especially the curly-coated breeds. Once dry, the coat should be thoroughly brushed and combed leaving it tangle-free before grooming can be started.

After bathing, towel dry the dog thoroughly to remove excess water. Use a high-velocity dryer in a methodical manner to straighten the coat. Drying the coat layer by layer will help to prevent the possibility of missing sections.

If the coat is extremely curly it may be brushed with a slicker brush while it is wet. This will separate the strands of hair and help with the straightening process. Start drying from the toes and work up the legs. Do not move to a new section until the section being worked on is almost completely dry and straight. Holding a towel behind the leg while drying will prevent the excess water from being blown on the opposite leg. It will also help maximize the air flow to the focused area. Allow the dryer to do all the work. Steadily and slowly work the coat straight. Jumping to different sections of the dog with the dryer will cause the coat to partially dry and stay curly all over. This will make the coat hard to straighten in the end.

Once the coat is as straight as possible using the HV dryer, remove the dryer's nozzle. Use the HV dryer without the nozzle and "fluff" the entire coat. This allows more air flow through the coat, which will straighten the coat nicely. A stand dryer should now be used with a slicker brush to go over every inch of the dog. Brushing the coat in long slow strokes while using the warm stand dryer will finish straightening the coat to perfection.

While stand-drying Poodle-type coats and thick coats, brush the legs from the feet up towards the body. Brushing the coat up will lift the coat up off the skin and straighten it from the skin out. Drop-coats should be brushed and dried with the natural lay of the coat. If a stand dryer is not available a hand-held dryer may also be used. These dryers have heat settings that will straighten the coats more effectively than a high-velocity dryer alone. Most high-velocity dryers do not have a heating element and only project a minimal amount of heat, which is generated from the motor running.

In the end, if the coat is not straight it will be very hard to get a nice scissored finish. A groomer may have excellent scissoring skills; however, if a coat is not straight, the waves will turn and move every time the coat is combed, giving an uneven finish. Once the coat has been brushed through using a stand dryer, it must be combed thoroughly to ensure there are no tangles.

Caution should be taken when using heated dryers. The heat should be set to a comfortable temperature for the pet. A very low heat is all that is required to straighten a coat properly. If a heated dryer is not preferred, brushing the coat frequently while using the HV dryer will assist in getting the coat straight.

Available on DVD: "Before the Groom"

TECHNIQUES

Point-to-Point Scissoring

It is very important to have a system while grooming any breed. Always start in the same place and end in the same place on every dog. This will improve efficiency while grooming. Point-to-point scissoring is a methodical way of scissoring. It is similar to "connect the dots". This method will assist the groomer in scissoring body parts in an efficient manner.

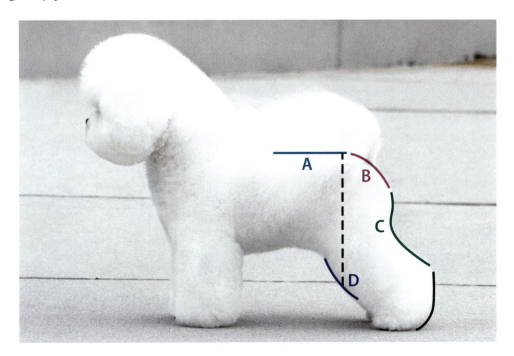

We will use the Bichon Frise as an example. Begin by scissoring the topline of the dog. Start the topline behind the withers, leaving the coat over the withers to be scissored in last (A). Once the topline is scissored, move to the rear of the dog. Scissor the hips to the pin bone (B). Scissor the tail-set, blending the tail-set into the hips.

Set the rear angulation from the pin bone to the bend of leg (C). The tightest point of the rear angulation is at the bend of the back leg. From the bend of leg to the hock the coat will become gradually longer (C). Leaving coat at the hock allows for a well angulated rear. If the hock hair is cut short, the angulation will drop and the angle will be lost.

Scissor the feet round at the base. Starting at the thigh, scissor a parallel line down to the outside of the foot. While scissoring the outside of the back leg, keep the muscle of the thigh in mind. Do not scissor this area flat. Remember to follow the contour of the leg, yet keep parallel lines in mind. Scissor the bend of the stifle (knee) into the scissored foot (D). The bend of stifle should line up approximately with the croup.

The rear angulation will be scissored considerably shorter than the outside and inside of the legs. Blend the tighter rear angulation scissor work into the longer coat on the outside and inside of the leg.

The inside of the leg can be scissored tight against the inside of the upper thigh with a straight contoured line down to the inside of the foot. The dotted lines reflect the actual legs of the dog. The leg is scissored tighter on the inside of the leg than the outside of the leg. When viewed from the rear, the Bichon should present an inverted U shape showing parallel lines.

Scissor the throat very tight from the throat latch to the breastbone (A). Scissor from the throat around to the shoulders (B) following the angle of the shoulder blade. The coat should become gradually longer on the shoulders from the throat area.

Using curved shears, scissor from the breastbone following the prosternum (lower chest) (C). When setting the chest into the lower arm, use curved shears in the reverse position. This will set the front legs under the dog. Once the shoulder and chest are set, the front legs can be scissored into columns (D).

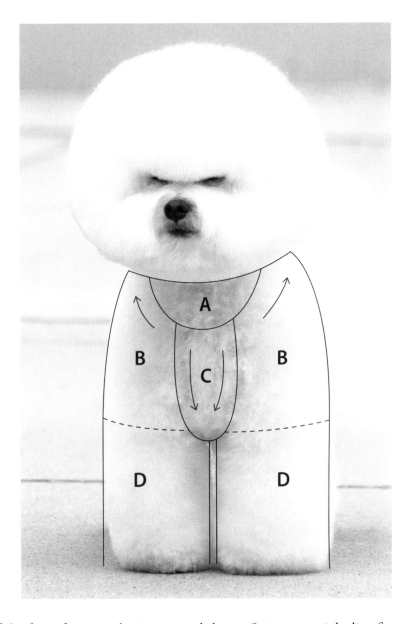

Scissor the base of the front feet round using curved shears. Scissor a straight line from the outside of the upper arm down to the outside of the front legs. Scissor around the entire leg to achieve a column-like appearance. Leaving more coat on the front of the front leg than on the back of the front leg will give this column-like appearance and will eliminate a visible foot. The back of the front leg should fall in line with the withers.

The body is now ready to be scissored. Once the rear and the front are set, the proper length of the dog can be determined. Refer to the breed standard of the particular breed that is being groomed and determine if the dog should be square in body, long in body, taller than the dog is long or whatever else the case may be.

This will determine where to set the tuck-up. The dog's natural tuck-up falls just below the last rib (A). However, if the dog is longer in body than what the breed standard calls for, then moving the tuck-up forward will help give the illusion of a shorter-backed dog. The same applies for a dog that is square when it should be longer in body. In this case, move the tuck-up back to give the illusion that the dog is longer in body. This is referred to as "camouflage grooming". Hiding the flaws in a dog's structure to give the illusion of correct structure is a technique that takes experience to master.

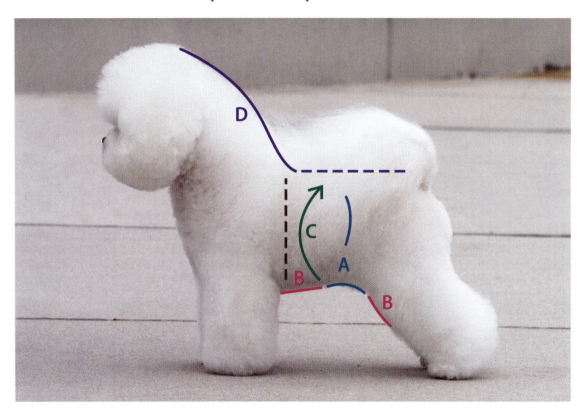

Once the tuck-up is set, the underline can be scissored in. The Bichon should have a moderate tuck-up with a straight sloping underline from the tuck-up to the elbow. Scissor the line from the tuck-up to the elbow. Blend the back leg into the loin area to meet the tuck-up (B).

Now that the topline and underline are set, use curved shears and scissor in the rib cage. Start at the underline and scissor up to meet the topline. Follow the contour of the rib cage (C). The widest part of the ribcage should be approximately midway between the topline and the underline.

Once the entire body and legs are scissored, the head and crest can then be done. Complete the grooming of the head before the crest. Once the head is complete, scissor in the crest to flow from the occiput to the topline; this will complete the continuity of the topline. The transition line for the crest into the topline should be over or just behind the withers (D). The withers should fall in line with the elbow. If the dog is longer in body than what the breed standard requires, the transition of the crest to the topline may be moved slightly back behind the withers to shorten the back of the dog.

Using a scissoring spray will help lift the coat while scissoring. Be sure to comb the coat frequently while scissoring to achieve a nice finish.

While scissoring it is important to set points to follow. You will notice that the feet were rounded before scissoring the legs. This gives the groomer a point to scissor to. Once the rear feet are scissored round, the parallel lines can be set from the thigh to the outside of the foot. Also, by setting the topline and underline it becomes easier to meet the two lines to scissor in the ribs.

This technique applies when grooming all parts of the dog. When scissoring a round head, for example, setting the chin first, then setting the top of the head makes it very easy to achieve a circle. The sides of the head can now be scissored in to meet those two lines.

Camouflage grooming may also be done when creating column-like front legs and setting rear angulation. If a dog does not have straight legs and tends to toe out or toe in, a groomer can give the illusion of straight legs by scissoring the legs in straight columns. Angulating a straight rear can be done by leaving more coat on the pin bone and point of hock, which will give the illusion of better angulation. See "Grooming Tips to Correct Faults" on page 471.

Available on DVD: "The Bichon Frise - Show Trim" and "Scissoring: Theory & Techniques"

Shortcuts

Snap-on combs are commonly used as a shortcut to roughly set the length of coat and the pattern lines on coated breeds, following the same sequence as described in "Point-to-Point Scissoring".

Various comb lengths can be used based on the preference of the pet owner as well as the dog's grooming schedule.

Snap-on combs can also be used on the legs of curly-coated dogs. Always use a longer comb on the legs than was used on the body. A well-balanced trim on coated breeds is one in which the body is tighter and the legs fuller.

The dog's body weight will also be a determining factor as to how long or short to trim the body. If the dog is overweight, leaving too much coat on the body will make the dog look even heavier. In this case, taking the body tight will give the trim balance. If the dog is underweight, leaving more coat on the body will be more flattering.

After setting the length with snap-on combs, the entire groom should be scissor finished as described in "Point-to-Point Scissoring" for a beautiful trim.

Leg Circumference

Parallel lines are referred to repeatedly throughout Straight to the Point. It is important to keep the circumference of the legs equal in addition to setting the parallel lines. The circumference of the front leg should be equal to the circumference of the back leg from the bend of knee to the stifle. This can be measured as seen below.

Tip To Remember:

Thinning shear and scissoring techniques take time to master. Proper coat preparation is the foundation to a well-groomed dog. A groomer may have excellent scissoring skills; however, if the dog is not prepared properly it will be very difficult to get a well-blended, well-scissored finish.

Tip To Remember:

When setting pattern lines the coat should appear as though it grew that way without distinct clipped lines. A well-blended seamless appearance should be the end result.

Setter-Like Pattern Lines

Distinct in Nature

Pattern Placement Diagrams
- English Cocker Spaniel
- English Setter
- English Springer Spaniel
- Gordon Setter
- Irish Setter
- Welsh Springer Spaniel

Subtle in Nature
- American Water Spaniel
- Australian Terrier
- Boykin Spaniel
- Brittany
- Cavalier King Charles Spaniel
- Clumber Spaniel
- Field Spaniel
- German Wirehaired Pointer
- Longhaired Dachshund
- Sussex Spaniel
- Wirehaired Dachshund

Breeds with a Ruff
- American Eskimo Dog
- Australian Shepherd
- Bernese Mountain Dog
- Border Collie
- Collie
- Flat-Coated Retriever
- Golden Retriever
- Great Pyrenees
- Japanese Chin
- Keeshond
- Longhaired Chihuahua
- Newfoundland
- Papillon
- Pomeranian
- Samoyed
- Shetland Sheepdog
- Tibetan Spaniel

SETTER-LIKE PATTERN LINES
Distinct in Nature

The pattern lines of the Irish Setter, as an example, are the same general pattern lines of many other breeds. For easy reference we will call this pattern "Setter-Like". This pattern can be of a distinct nature or a subtle nature. In this section we will discuss breeds that fall under "Setter-Like" patterns of a "Distinct" nature. Distinct patterns are those that are set fairly tight. The correct way to groom these breeds is to card out the undercoat and/or hand strip the back coat. However, on pet trims these patterns can be set with blades ranging from 4F, 5F to 7F or with snap-on combs. The longer the blade the more natural and true to the breed profile the trim will look.

This section describes setting patterns on pet trims with the use of various blade lengths. If a dog has a very natural flat back coat, clipping may not be necessary. The back coat may only require carding techniques for a more natural appearance.

You will see from this example that the body pattern on this show dog is hand stripped from the back of the skull (occiput) to the tail. The pattern falls from the topline over the lower part of the ribcage to the area just below the elbow. The pattern line rises from just below the elbow, slightly up to the loin. When clipping this pattern, the line should be well blended into the longer furnishings of the underline. To mimic this show trim, there should be no evident line between the clipped area and the furnishings.

Thinning shears should be used to blend the transition lines.

The shoulder and upper arm are tight following down the front of the front leg. The furnishings are left on the back of the front leg. The thigh muscle is tight to show the muscle tone, leaving furnishings on the front and rear of the back leg.

A stripping knife should be used after clipping these breeds to remove undercoat, which will help promote healthy skin and coat. Using a stripping knife will also allow the coat to lie down and look more natural even though the back coat is clipped. Clipping the back coat of these breeds shorter than a 7F blade is not recommended.

The furnishings should be trimmed keeping this outline in mind. The length of the furnishings may vary based on the preference of the client. The furnishings on the back of the front leg should angle up to the underline. The furnishings on the front of the back leg are trimmed to show the bend of the stifle (knee). Some breeds may carry more coat on the back legs than others.

The feet are trimmed tight without showing separation between the toes by using thinning shears for a natural appearance. The hocks are trimmed perpendicular to the ground. Do not trim the hock hair tight to the bone, as that will make the hock appear weak in bone.

Full furnishings may be left to present the correct outline for these breeds, or they may be trimmed as short as the pet owner prefers, using various lengths of snap-on combs, shears and/or thinning shears.

Tail styles will vary among the breeds that fall under Setter-Like patterns. Some will have a flag tail, like the Irish Setter, while other breeds like the English Springer Spaniel will have a docked tail. See "Tail Styles" on page 447 for instructions on grooming various tail styles.

The front pattern of this group is set from the underjaw down to approximately one to two finger widths above the breastbone. Blade lengths can vary from a 10 to 7F based on the coat density and sensitivity of the skin. These blades may also be used against the lay of coat (from the breastbone up towards the head) which will give a shorter appearance than clipping with the lay of coat. The line continues to the base of the ear creating a U-like pattern of the throat.

The throat is defined by a natural cowlick in the hair that runs from the base of the ear to the breastbone.

There is a cowlick in the chest area that separates the chest furnishings from the upper arm. The cowlick is a good rule of thumb to set the upper arm tight. The upper arm can be clipped with either a 5F or 7F blade. The transition point of the clipped throat and the clipped upper arm should be well blended with thinning shears.

The front of the front leg should be free of long coat. This area can be clipped, if necessary, with either a 4F or 5F blade or trimmed with thinning shears for a more natural look. A stripping knife can be used to card down the front of the front leg to remove fuzzy undercoat.

The furnishings of the front leg should only fall off the back of the leg. Furnishings that fall over the side of the leg should be removed with thinning shears. The inside and outside of the leg should be free of furnishings.

Using a 5F or 7F blade, clip from under the ear down the side of the neck, over the shoulder blade and upper arm. This will help blend the short throat work into the body work. For example, if a 4F or 5F is used to set the body pattern and a 10 blade is used to clip the throat, a 5F or 7F would then be used on the side of the neck, shoulder area and upper arm. This will blend the 7F or 10 blade work on the throat into the 4F or 5F blade work on the body very nicely. If the body pattern is left natural, a 5F or 7F can still be used to blend the side of the neck, shoulder and upper arm into the longer body coat.

Everything should look well blended and natural. Using various blade lengths will help achieve this. Thinning shears should be used to blend clipped lines into longer furnishings.

Trim the length of the chest furnishings at an angle and follow through between the front legs to the underline. Trimming at an angle will give the appearance of more chest. Leaving the chest furnishings long and bluntly trimmed will give the appearance of a straight front, which is not desirable.

The thigh should be well defined to show the muscle. This can be done by using a blade which is one blade length longer than what was used on the shoulder. This area can also be clipped with the same blade that was used on the body; however, thinning shears should then be used to define the muscle to the desired length and to blend into the furnishings.

The lower leg can vary in coat length. Some breeds like the Setters may not carry length of coat, while others like the English Cocker Spaniel may carry more furnishings on the lower leg.

The furnishings fall off the stifle and should be trimmed to show a well-bent stifle with proper angulation. Once trimmed, the bend of the stifle should fall approximately in line with the croup for proper balance.

The furnishings should fall at or below the point of hock in a position to reflect the proper length of the hock. If the hock is longer than desired, the furnishings can fall lower than the hock. This will give the illusion that the hock is of the appropriate length.

The hock should be trimmed perpendicular to the ground. Do not trim the coat too close to the hock bone, as it will make the hock appear weak in bone.

The area around the anus should be clipped tight. The coat directly below the anus will part naturally and fall to both sides, similar to a "mustache", as seen on this Irish Setter. This coat can be left natural and become part of the rear furnishings or it can be removed completely with thinning shears, as seen on the Brittany. Either way is correct. Removing this coat will accentuate the rear and rear angulation.

The coat that remains below this natural part is the coat that falls between the legs like a curtain.

The muscle of the thigh should be trimmed tight rolling around to the back of the leg. This can be done with the same blade that was used to set the body pattern. The coat that naturally falls toward the inside of the legs is referred to as the rear furnishings. Use thinning shears to blend the clipped lines into the rear furnishings.

The furnishings should be shaped in an inverted V and should not be longer than the point of hock.

Dog Grooming Simplified: Straight To The Point

Pattern Placement Diagrams

				Recommended Blade Lengths, Snap-On Comb Lengths and Techniques **Bold Print** = Preferred Choices for Pet Trims			
10 15	**10** 7F	**7F 5F carding**	7F **5F 4F carding**	thinning shears scissor			thinning shears carding

SETTER-LIKE PATTERN LINES

52

SETTER-LIKE PATTERN LINES

Recommended Blade Lengths, Snap-On Comb Lengths and Techniques **Bold Print** = Preferred Choices for Pet Trims							
10 15	**10** 7F	**7F** **5F** carding	7F **5F** **4F** carding	thinning shears scissor	hand strip leave natural thinning shears carding	define with thinning shears carding

53

Tip To Remember:

Several double-coated breeds as well as Sporting breeds, like the Golden Retriever, Pomeranian, Irish Setter and English Springer Spaniel, for example, have short natural tidy feet. To trim this type of foot, starting by the toe nails, brush the hair on the toes up away from the skin with a slicker brush. Brushing the hair up will pull the long hairs out from between the toes. Use thinning shears and scissor over the top of the foot for a neat, tidy appearance. Trim the longer hairs flush with the soft short natural hair of the foot. It is not desirable to see the separation between the toes. Thinning shears will give the foot a beautiful natural appearance.

Setter-Like Pattern Lines

Distinct in Nature

Common Breeds

The following are common breeds that have Distinct Setter-Like pattern lines. Minor deviations from the described pattern will be noted as well as recommended techniques and tools for each breed. Important breed standard information will be quoted in part from participating breed clubs. When grooming these breeds, refer back to the guidelines of setting this pattern on page 46.

English Cocker Spaniel

The English Cocker Spaniel is a Sporting dog that descends from the original Spaniels of Spain. The English Cocker Spaniel was separated from other Spaniels by the Kennel Club of England in 1892. It was bred to work in dense cover to flush and retrieve game.

This coat should be carded and hand stripped for show; however, if clipping is preferred, blades ranging from 4F, 5F to 7F are recommended. Carding and thinning shear techniques should be done in addition to clipping for a natural seamless appearance. The English Cocker Spaniel carries more furnishings on the back lower leg than the other breeds in this group; however, the thigh muscle is set tight.

The furnishings may be trimmed to present the proper profile of the breed. The length of furnishings may vary according to the preference of the pet owner.

See "Head Styles" on page 425 for instructions on grooming the heads of Sporting breeds.

See important information on "Carding" on page 30 and "Hand Stripping" on page 32.

Quoted in part with permission from the English Cocker Spaniel Club of America, Inc., Approved October 11, 1988:

Compactly built and short-coupled, with height at withers slightly greater than the distance from withers to set-on of tail.

Topline: The line of the neck blends into the shoulder and backline in a smooth curve. The backline slopes very slightly toward a gently rounded croup, and is free from sagging or rumpiness.

Neck: Graceful and muscular, arched toward the head and blending cleanly, without throatiness, into sloping shoulders; moderate in length and in balance with the length and height of the dog. The chest is deep; forechest well developed, prosternum projecting moderately beyond shoulder points. Brisket reaches to the elbow and slopes gradually to a moderate tuck-up.

The English Cocker is moderately angulated. Shoulders are sloping, the blade flat and smoothly fitting. Shoulder blade and upper arm are approximately equal in length.

Upper arm set well back, joining the shoulder with sufficient angulation to place the elbow beneath the highest point of the shoulder blade when the dog is standing naturally. Forelegs–Straight, with bone nearly uniform in size from elbow to heel. Feet–Proportionate in size to the legs, firm, round and catlike; toes arched and tight.

Hindquarters: Angulation moderate and, most importantly, in balance with that of the forequarters. Hips relatively broad and well rounded. Upper thighs broad, thick and muscular, providing plenty of propelling power. Second thighs well muscled and approximately equal in length to the upper. Stifle strong and well bent. Hock to pad short.

Skull: Arched and slightly flattened when seen both from the side and from the front. Viewed in profile, the brow appears not appreciably higher than the back-skull. Viewed from above, the sides of the skull are in planes roughly parallel to those of the muzzle. Stop definite, but moderate, and slightly grooved.

Muzzle: Equal in length to skull.

Coat: On head, short and fine; of medium length on body; flat or slightly wavy; silky in texture. The English Cocker is well-feathered, but not so profusely as to interfere with field work. Trimming is permitted to remove overabundant hair and to enhance the dog's true lines. It should be done so as to appear as natural as possible.

The English Cocker Spaniel

"is an active, merry sporting dog, standing well up at the withers and compactly built. He is alive with energy; his gait is powerful and frictionless, capable both of covering ground effortlessly and penetrating dense cover to flush and retrieve game."

SETTER-LIKE PATTERN LINES

10 15	**10** 7F	**7F** **5F** **carding**	7F **5F** **4F** **carding**	thinning shears scissor			thinning shears carding

Recommended Blade Lengths, Snap-On Comb Lengths and Techniques
Bold Print = Preferred Choices for Pet Trims

English Setter

The English Setter is a Sporting dog who hunts by pointing game. This Setter is an elegant, beautiful breed and is one of the oldest gun dogs developed in England. Before the use of firearms the English Setter would find the game and crouch down, or "set", on its front legs to allow the hunter to throw a net over the game. Once guns were introduced, a more upright pointing stance was bred into the Setter so hunters could easily see it.

This coat should be carded and hand stripped for show; however, if clipping is preferred, blades ranging from 4F, 5F to 7F are recommended. Carding and thinning shear techniques should be done in addition to clipping for a natural seamless appearance.

The furnishings may be trimmed to present the proper profile of the breed. The length of furnishings may vary based on the preference of the pet owner.

See "Head Styles" on page 425 for instructions on grooming the heads of Sporting breeds.

See important information on "Carding" on page 30 and "Hand Stripping" on page 32.

Quoted in part with permission from the English Setter Association of America, Inc., Approved November 11, 1986:

An elegant, substantial and symmetrical gun dog suggesting the ideal blend of strength, stamina, grace, and style. Flat-coated with feathering of good length.

Topline: In motion or standing appears level or sloping slightly downward without sway or drop from withers to tail forming a graceful outline of medium length.

Neck–long and graceful, muscular and lean. Arched at the crest and clean-cut where it joins the head at the base of the skull. Larger and more muscular toward the shoulders, with the base of the neck flowing smoothly into the shoulders. Forechest–well developed, point of sternum projecting slightly in front of point of shoulder/upper arm joint. Chest–deep, brisket deep enough to reach the level of the elbow. Ribs–long, springing gradually to the middle of the body, then tapering as they approach the end of the chest cavity. Loin–strong, moderate in length, slightly arched. Tuck-up moderate. Hip bones wide apart, hips rounded and blending smoothly into hind legs. Tail–a smooth continuation of the topline, tapering to a fine point with only sufficient length to reach the hock joint or slightly less.

Forequarters: Shoulder blade well laid back. Upper arm equal in length to and forming a nearly right angle with the shoulder blade. Shoulder blades lie flat and meld smoothly with contours of body. Forelegs straight and parallel. Pasterns–short, strong and nearly round with the slope deviating very slightly forward from the perpendicular. Feet–face directly forward. Toes closely set, strong and well arched.

Hindquarters: Wide, muscular thighs and well developed lower thighs. Stifle well bent and strong. Hock joint well bent and strong. Rear pastern short, strong, nearly round and perpendicular to the ground. Hind legs, when seen from the rear, straight and parallel to each other.

Skull: Oval when viewed from above, of medium width, without coarseness, and only slightly wider at the ear set than at the brow. Moderately defined occipital protuberance. Length of skull from occiput to stop equal in length of muzzle.

Muzzle: Long and square when viewed from the side.

Coat: Flat without curl or wooliness. Feathering on ears, chest, abdomen, underside of thighs, back of all legs and on the tail of good length but not so excessive as to hide true lines and movement or to affect the dog's appearance or function as a sporting dog.

The English Setter

"An elegant, substantial and symmetrical gun dog suggesting the ideal blend of strength, stamina, grace, and style."

SETTER-LIKE PATTERN LINES

				Recommended Blade Lengths, Snap-On Comb Lengths and Techniques			
				Bold Print = Preferred Choices for Pet Trims			
10 15	**10** 7F	**7F** **5F** **carding**	7F **5F** **4F** **carding**	thinning shears scissor		thinning shears carding	

English Springer Spaniel

The English Springer Spaniel is a Sporting dog that originated in England. The Cocker Spaniels and English Springer Spaniels were originally born in the same litters. The smaller dogs were used to hunt woodcock and were nicknamed "Cockers" while the larger dogs were used to flush and "spring" game. In 1902 the breeds were separated by size and type and the English Springer Spaniel was recognized by the AKC as a distinct breed.

This coat should be carded and hand stripped for show; however, if clipping is preferred, blades ranging from 4F, 5F to 7F are recommended. Carding and thinning shear techniques should be done in addition to clipping for a natural seamless appearance.

The furnishings may be trimmed to present the proper profile of the breed. The length of furnishings may vary according to the preference of the pet owner.

See "Head Styles" on page 425 for instructions on grooming the heads of Sporting breeds.

See important information on "Carding" on page 30 and "Hand Stripping" on page 32.

SETTER-LIKE PATTERN LINES

Quoted in part with permission from the English Springer Spaniel Club, Approved February 12, 1994:

The length of the body is slightly greater than the height at the withers. A Springer with correct substance appears well-knit and sturdy with good bone, however, his is never coarse or ponderous. The portion of the topline from withers to tail is firm and slopes very gently.

The neck is moderately long, muscular, clean and slightly arched at the crest. It blends gradually and smoothly into sloping shoulders. The body is short-coupled, strong and compact. The chest is deep, reaching the level of the elbows, with well-developed forechest. Ribs are fairly long, springing gradually to the middle of the body, then tapering as they approach the end of the ribbed section. The underline stays level with the elbows to a slight up-curve at the flank. Hips are nicely-rounded, blending smoothly into the hind legs. The croup slopes gently to the set of the tail, and tail-set follows the natural line of the croup.

Ideally, when measured from the top of the withers to the point of the shoulder to the elbow, the shoulder blade and upper arm are of apparent equal length, forming an angle of nearly 90 degrees; this sets the front legs well under the body and places the elbows directly beneath the tips of the shoulder blades. Forelegs are straight. Feet are round or slightly oval. They are compact and well-arched, of medium size with thick pads, and well-feathered between the toes.

The Springer should be worked and shown in hard, muscular condition with well-developed hips and thighs. His whole rear assembly suggests strength and driving power. Thighs are broad and muscular. Stifle joints are strong. For functional efficiency, the angulation of the hindquarter is never greater than that of the forequarter, and not appreciably less. The hock joints are somewhat rounded. Rear pasterns are short (about 1/3 the distance from the hip joint to the foot) and strong, with good bone. When viewed from behind, the rear pasterns are parallel.

The skull is medium-length and fairly broad, flat on top and slightly rounded at the sides and back. The occiput bone is inconspicuous. As the skull rises from the foreface, it makes a stop, divided by a groove, or fluting, between the eyes. The groove disappears as it reaches the middle of the forehead. The amount of stop is moderate. The muzzle is approximately the same length as the skull and one half the width of the skull. Viewed in profile, the toplines of the skull and muzzle lie in approximately parallel planes.

The Springer has an outer coat and undercoat. On the body, the outer coat is of medium length, flat or wavy, and is easily distinguishable from the undercoat, which is short, soft and dense. The quantity of undercoat is affected by climate and season. When in combination, outer coat and undercoat serve to make the dog substantially waterproof, weatherproof and thorn-proof. On ears, chest, legs and belly the Springer is nicely furnished with a fringe of feathering of moderate length and heaviness. On the head, front of the forelegs, and below the hock joints on the front of the hind legs, the hair is short and fine. The appearance should be natural.

The English Springer Spaniel

"The typical Springer is friendly, eager to please, quick to learn and willing to obey. Such traits are conducive to tractability, which is essential for appropriate handler control in the field."

SETTER-LIKE PATTERN LINES

				Recommended Blade Lengths, Snap-On Comb Lengths and Techniques **Bold Print** = Preferred Choices for Pet Trims			
10 15	**10** 7F	**7F** **5F** carding	7F **5F** **4F** carding	thinning shears scissor		thinning shears carding	

Gordon Setter

The Gordon Setter originated in Scotland. This black and tan beauty is heavier in bone than the Irish and English Setters. It is a Sporting dog who hunts by pointing game. It hunts with strength and stamina rather than speed.

This coat should be carded and hand stripped for show; however, if clipping is preferred, blades ranging from 4F, 5F to 7F are recommended. Carding and thinning shear techniques should be done in addition to clipping for a natural seamless appearance.

The furnishings may be trimmed to present the proper profile of the breed. The length of furnishings may vary according to the preference of the pet owner.

See "Head Styles" on page 425 for instructions on grooming the heads of Sporting breeds.

See important information on "Carding" on page 30 and "Hand Stripping" on page 32.

Key points to remember while grooming the Gordon Setter according to the breed standard:

The Gordon Setter is square in body, meaning that it is as tall from the withers to the ground as it is long. It has a moderately sloping topline. The topline slopes slightly to the tail-set. The tail should reach the point of hock and should present a flag shape.

The neck is long and is arched as it reaches the occiput. The chest is deep with well-sprung ribs and reaches to the level of the elbow. The Gordon has a pronounced forechest. The shoulders are well angulated and are the same length as the upper arm, forming a 90-degree angle. This sets the elbow in line with the withers. The front legs should appear straight with cat-like feet that are well arched. The feet should be neatly trimmed.

The rear legs are muscular with well-bent stifles. The hocks should be perpendicular to the ground.

The skull is rounded and is equal in length with the muzzle. The stop should be clearly defined.

The coat of the Gordon Setter should be soft and shining and should be either straight or have a slight wave.

Dog Grooming Simplified: Straight To The Point

10 15	**10** 7F	**7F** **5F** **carding**	7F **5F** **4F** **carding**	thinning shears scissor			thinning shears carding

Recommended Blade Lengths, Snap-On Comb Lengths and Techniques
Bold Print = Preferred Choices for Pet Trims

SETTER-LIKE PATTERN LINES

Tip To Remember:

When clipping ears with a short blade, a longer blade can be used against the lay of coat to transition the short blade work into the skull. For example, when clipping Setter ear leathers with a 10 blade, a 7F blade can then be used against the lay of coat from the 10 blade work up into the skull. This will blend the transition line.

Irish Setter

The Irish Setter is a Sporting dog who hunts by pointing game. It originated in Ireland and throughout the British Isles. The Irish Setter is an elegant, beautiful breed known for its mahogany red coat. Before the use of firearms the Irish Setter would find the game and crouch down, or "set", on its front legs to allow the hunter to throw a net over the game. Once guns were introduced, a more upright pointing stance was bred into the Setter so hunters could easily see it.

This coat should be carded and hand stripped for show. To keep the deep red color of the Irish Setter, carding is highly recommended without clipping. The Irish Setter carries a very flat natural back coat which should not require clipping. Clipping this coat will result in a color and texture change. Once the coat is clipped, it may never return to its deep red color and texture. However, if the pet owner prefers clipping, blades ranging from 4F, 5F to 7F are recommended. Carding and thinning shear techniques should be done in addition to clipping for a natural seamless appearance.

The furnishings may be trimmed to present the proper profile of the breed. The length of furnishings may vary based on the preference of the pet owner.

SETTER-LIKE PATTERN LINES

See "Head Styles" on page 425 for instructions on grooming the heads of Sporting breeds.

See important information on "Carding" on page 30 and "Hand Stripping" on page 32.

Quoted in part with permission from the Irish Setter Club of America, Inc., Approved August 14, 1990:

Proportion–Measuring from the breastbone to rear of thigh and from the top of the withers to the ground, the Irish Setter is slightly longer than it is tall.

Topline of body from withers to tail should be firm and incline slightly downward without sharp drop at the croup. The tail is set on nearly level with the croup as a natural extension of the topline, strong at root, tapering to a fine point, nearly long enough to reach the hock.

Neck is moderately long, strong but not thick, and slightly arched; free from throatiness and fitting smoothly into the shoulders. Chest is deep, reaching approximately to the elbows with moderate forechest, extending beyond the point where the shoulder joins the upper arm. Chest is of moderate width so that it does not interfere with forward motion and extends rearwards to well sprung ribs.

Forequarters: Shoulder blades long, wide, sloping well back, fairly close together at the withers. Upper arm and shoulder blades are approximately the same length, and are joined at sufficient angle to bring the elbows rearward along the brisket in line with the top of the withers. Forelegs straight and sinewy. Strong, nearly straight pastern. Feet rather small, very firm, toes arched and close.

Hindquarters: Hindquarters should be wide and powerful with broad, well developed thighs. Hind legs long and muscular from hip to hock; short and perpendicular from hock to ground; well angulated at stifle and hock joints.

Head: Long and lean, its length at least double the width between the ears. Beauty of head is emphasized by delicate chiseling along the muzzle, around and below the eyes, and along the cheeks.

The skull is oval when viewed from above or front; very slightly domed when viewed in profile. The brow is raised, showing a distinct stop midway between the tip of the nose and the well-defined occiput (rear point of skull). Thus the nearly level line from occiput to brow is set a little above, and parallel to, the straight and equal line from eye to nose.

Coat–Short and fine on head and forelegs. On all other parts of moderate length and flat. Feathering, long and silky on ears; on back of forelegs and thighs long and fine, with a pleasing fringe of hair on belly and brisket extending onto the chest. Fringe on tail, moderately long and tapering. All coat and feathering as straight and free as possible from curl or wave. The Irish Setter is trimmed for the show ring to emphasize the lean head and clean neck. The top third of the ears and the throat nearly to the breastbone are trimmed. Excess feathering is removed to show the natural outline of the foot. All trimming is done to preserve the natural appearance of the dog.

The Irish Setter

"has a rollicking personality. Shyness, hostility or timidity are uncharacteristic of the breed. An outgoing, stable temperament is the essence of the Irish Setter."

Available on DVD: "The Irish Setter - Show Trim"

SETTER-LIKE PATTERN LINES

Recommended Blade Lengths, Snap-On Comb Lengths and Techniques **Bold Print** = Preferred Choices for Pet Trims								
10 15	**10** 7F	**7F 5F** carding	7F **5F** 4F carding	thinning shears scissor		thinning shears carding	

Welsh Springer Spaniel

The Welsh Springer Spaniel is a Sporting dog originating in England. Its hunting style was to spring game toward the nets or in the air before the use of firearms. It is now a versatile hunter, flushing Spaniel, water dog and retriever.

This coat should be carded and hand stripped for show. The Welsh carries a natural flat back coat and can be easily maintained by using carding techniques. If clipping is preferred by the pet owner, blades ranging from 4F, 5F to 7F are recommended. Carding and thinning shear techniques should be done in addition to clipping for a natural seamless appearance.

The furnishings may be trimmed to present the proper profile of the breed. The length of furnishings may vary according to the preference of the pet owner.

The Welsh Springer Spaniel should have very lightly feathered ears. For a more natural appearance the ear may be blended with thinning shears. A 10 blade may be used on the inside of the ear.

See "Head Styles" on page 425 and "Ear Styles" on page 441 for instructions on grooming the heads of Sporting breeds.

See important information on "Carding" on page 30 and "Hand Stripping" on page 32.

Quoted in part with permission from the Welsh Springer Spaniel Club of America, Inc., Approved June 13, 1989:

Length of body from the withers to the base of the tail is very slightly greater than the distance from the withers to the ground. This body length may be the same as the height but never shorter, thus preserving the rectangular silhouette of the Welsh Springer Spaniel.

Topline is level. The loin is slightly arched, muscular, and close-coupled. The croup is very slightly rounded, never steep nor falling off.

The neck is long and slightly arched, clean in throat, and set into long, sloping shoulders. The chest is well developed and muscular with a prominent forechest, the ribs well sprung and the brisket reaching to the elbows. The tail is an extension of the topline.

The shoulder blade and upper arm are approximately equal in length. The upper arm is set well back, joining the shoulder blade with sufficient angulation to place the elbow beneath the highest point of the shoulder blade when standing. The forearms are of medium length, straight and moderately feathered.

The hindquarters must be strong, muscular, and well boned, but not coarse. When viewed in profile the thighs should be wide and the second thighs well developed. Bend of stifle is moderate. The bones from the hocks to the pads are short with a well angulated hock joint. When viewed from the side or rear they are perpendicular to the ground.

Skull: The Welsh Springer Spaniel head is unique and should in no way approximate that of other Spaniel breeds. Its overall balance is of primary importance. Head is in proportion to body, never so broad as to appear coarse nor so narrow as to appear racy. The skull is of medium length, slightly domed, with a clearly defined stop. It is well chiseled below the eyes. The top plane of the skull is very slightly divergent from that of the muzzle, but with no tendency toward a down-faced appearance.

Coat: The coat is naturally straight flat and soft to the touch, never wiry or wavy. It is sufficiently dense to be waterproof, thorn-proof and weatherproof. The back of the forelegs and hind legs above the hocks, chest and underside of the body are moderately feathered. The ears and tail are lightly feathered. Coat so excessive as to be a hindrance in the field is to be discouraged. Obvious barbering is to be avoided as well.

The Welsh Springer Spaniel

"is an active dog displaying a loyal and affectionate disposition. To this day he remains a devoted family member and hunting companion."

SETTER-LIKE PATTERN LINES

Recommended Blade Lengths, Snap-On Comb Lengths and Techniques							
Bold Print = Preferred Choices for Pet Trims							
10 15	**10** 7F	**7F** **5F** **carding**	7F **5F** **4F** **carding**	thinning shears scissor		thinning shears carding	

SETTER-LIKE PATTERN LINES

Subtle in Nature

Setter-Like pattern lines can also be of a Subtle nature. The breeds in this section are not Setters by any means; however, they fall under this pattern category. "Subtle" means that the pattern line is not set tight, yet the Setter-Like pattern is still visible. Some of the breeds here may not be clipped at all. They may just require carding with a stripping knife to remove undercoat, which will enhance the pattern lines. If the pet owner requests clipping, it is recommended that the dog be left more natural without a clipped look.

Many of the breeds in this group are also heavier double-coated breeds like the Golden Retriever, Newfoundland and Samoyed. They have a natural Setter-Like pattern. These breeds should be maintained using shedding and carding techniques. The furnishings are trimmed the same as the other breeds described. Before clipping a heavy double-coated breed, please see "Double-Coated Breeds" on page 17.

You will see from this example of the Longhaired Dachshund, the body has a natural pattern from the back of the skull (occiput), to the tail. The pattern falls from the topline over the lower part of the rib cage and rises at an angle to the loin. The natural pattern line transitions into the longer furnishings of the underline without a visible line.

The front, inside and outside of the front leg should be free from long furnishings with the longer furnishings falling off the back of the leg. The rear thigh muscle is free of long hair to show the muscle tone, leaving furnishings falling off the stifle as well as the rear of the back leg.

It is recommended that these breeds not be clipped unless the customer requests it. Using a stripping knife on the tighter-coated breeds and an undercoat rake on the heavier double-coated breeds will help the neck and body coat to lie nicely and look natural and will define the pattern lines.

Thinning shears may be used on the throat, neck and shoulders to tidy the appearance. A stripping knife will also remove fuzzy undercoat on the front of the front legs, shoulders, thighs and front of hocks.

If requested by the owner, these breeds may be clipped with a 7F, 5F, or 4F blade or various lengths of snap-on combs with the exception of the heavy double-coated breeds, which should not be clipped at all. The longer the coat is left, the more natural and true to the breed these dogs will look. Clipping these breeds could result in a color change, which can be lighter than the original color, as well as a change in texture.

The feet on most of these breeds are trimmed tight, without showing the separation between the toes, using thinning shears for a natural appearance. The furnishings are trimmed in the same manner as the Distinct Setter-Like patterns and may be trimmed to present the proper profile of the breed. The length of furnishings may vary based on the preference of the pet owner.

The tail styles will vary from breed to breed that fall under Setter-Like patterns. Some breeds, like the Longhaired Dachshund, will have a flag tail, where other breeds like the Sussex Spaniel will have a docked tail. See "Tail Styles" on page 447.

TIP TO REMEMBER:

When using a stripping knife it is important to hold the skin taut with one hand while combing through the coat with the other. If the skin is not held taut it will move with every stroke, which can be uncomfortable for the pet. When the skin moves the tool will not be productive. The stripping knife should be held almost flat to the skin.

Tip To Remember:

Many of the double-coated breeds, especially the Sporting breeds, may have a very natural flat back coat. It is recommended to start carding these coats when the dogs are puppies. If these techniques are done properly, clipping may never be necessary. Once a back coat is clipped it may never return to the same texture and color that it started with.

Setter-Like Pattern Lines

Subtle in Nature
Common Breeds

The following are common breeds that have Subtle Setter-Like pattern lines. Minor deviations from the described pattern will be noted as well as recommended techniques and tools for each breed. Important breed standard information will be quoted in part from participating breed clubs. When grooming these breeds, refer back to the guidelines of setting this pattern on page 46 keeping "Subtle in Nature" in mind.

Several of the following breeds require the throat to be clipped short even though the rest of the pattern is "Subtle". For example, the Longhaired Dachshund requires the throat to be clipped, while the throat of the Sussex Spaniel is left natural. These subtle differences will be noted for each breed.

American Water Spaniel

The American Water Spaniel is a Sporting dog that originated in the Great Lakes region of the United States. This is an all-purpose gun dog that retrieves from boats and is just as happy in the field.

The American Water Spaniel has a natural coat which does not require much trimming. The forehead should be smooth. This can be done by using carding techniques and/or thinning shears for a natural appearance.

The ears can be left natural or shaved.

The American Water Spaniel has a wavy-curly coat. Light trimming may be done to present a well-groomed appearance.

Quoted in part with permission from the American Water Spaniel Club, Approved March 13, 1990:

Proportion: Slightly longer than tall, not too square or compact.

Topline: level or slight, straight slope from withers.

Neck is round and of medium length, strong and muscular. Well-developed brisket extending to elbow neither too broad nor too narrow. The ribs well-sprung, but not so well-sprung that they interfere with the movement of the front assembly. The loins strong, but not having a tucked-up look. Tail is moderate in length, curved in a rocker fashion, can be carried either slightly below or above the level of the back. The tail is tapered, lively and covered with hair with moderate feathering.

Shoulders sloping, clean and muscular. Legs medium in length, straight and well-boned. Toes closely grouped, webbed and well-padded.

Well-developed hips and thighs with the whole rear assembly showing strength and drive. The hock joint slightly rounded, should not be small and sharp in contour, moderately angulated. Legs from hock joint to foot pad moderate in length, strong and straight with good bone structure. Hocks parallel.

Skull rather broad and full, stop moderately defined, but not too pronounced. Muzzle moderate in length, square with good depth. No inclination to snipiness. The lips are clean and tight without excess skin or flews. Ears set slightly above the eye line but not too high on the head, lobular, long and wide with leather extending to nose.

Coat can range from marcel (uniform waves) to closely curled. The amount of waves or curls can vary from one area to another on the dog. It is important to have undercoat to provide sufficient density to be of protection against weather, water or punishing cover, yet not too coarse or too soft. The throat, neck and rear of the dog are well-covered with hair. The ears are well-covered with hair on both sides. Forehead covered with short smooth hair and without topknot. Tail covered with hair to tip with moderate feathering. Legs have moderate feathering with waves or curls to harmonize with coat of dog. Coat may be trimmed to present a well-groomed appearance; the ears may be shaved; but neither is required.

The American Water Spaniel

"His demeanor indicates intelligence, eagerness to please and friendly. Great energy and eagerness for the hunt yet controllable in the field."

SETTER-LIKE PATTERN LINES

Recommended Blade Lengths, Snap-On Comb Lengths and Techniques **Bold Print** = Preferred Choices for Pet Trims							
10 15				scissor	leave natural	thinning shears carding	

87

Australian Terrier

The Australian Terrier is a Terrier breed originating in Australia. These Terriers were bred to control vermin and the snake population in the rugged Australian outback. They were also used as guard dogs and to help tend to livestock.

The Australian Terrier falls nicely under this group with the exception of the throat and neck. There is a natural "fan" of coat on the side of the neck which creates a ruff that is a characteristic of this breed. This area cowlicks naturally.

This coat should be carded and hand stripped for show. However, if clipping is preferred, a 4F blade or #2, #1 or various sizes of snap-on combs can be used. Carding and thinning shear techniques should be used in addition to clipping for a natural appearance.

A Coat King may also be used on the back coat to help remove undercoat and help preserve the color and texture of the coat. The ruff on the side of the neck should be tailored into the clipped trim with thinning shears to present the proper breed profile.

The muzzle and cheeks of the Australian Terrier can be neatened with thinning shears if the coat is not being hand stripped. An inverted V should be defined between the eyes and extend slightly over the bridge of the muzzle. The topskull and sideskull are covered with a distinct topknot that is characteristic of this breed. The ears can be shaved with a 10 or 15 blade.

The furnishings may be trimmed to present the proper profile of the breed. The length of furnishings may vary according to the preference of the pet owner.

See important information on "Carding" on page 30 and "Hand Stripping" on page 32.

Quoted in part with permission from the Australian Terrier Club of America, Inc., Approved August 9, 1988:

The body is long in proportion to the height of the dog. The length of back from withers to the front of the tail is approximately 1–1½ inches longer than from withers to the ground.

Topline: Level and firm. The body is of sturdy structure with ribs well-sprung but not rounded, forming a chest reaching slightly below the elbows with a distinct keel. The loin is strong and fairly short with slight tuck-up.

Neck: Long, slightly arched and strong, blending smoothly into well laid back shoulders.

Shoulders: Long blades, well laid back with only slight space between the shoulder blades at the withers. The length of the upper arm is comparable to the length of the shoulder blade. The angle between the shoulder and the upper arm is 90 degrees. Forelegs: Straight, parallel when viewed from the front; they should be set well under the body, with definite body overhang (keel) before them when viewed from the side. Feet: Small, clean, catlike; toes arched and compact.

Hindquarters: Strong; legs well angulated at the stifles and hocks, short and perpendicular from the hocks to the ground. Upper and lower thighs are well muscled. Viewed from behind the rear legs are straight from the hip joints to the ground and in the same plane as the forelegs. Tail: Set on high and carried erect at a twelve to one o'clock position, docked in balance with the overall dog leaving slightly less than one half, a good hand-hold when mature.

Outer Coat: Harsh and straight; 2½ inches all over the body except the tail, pasterns, rear legs from the hocks down, and the feet which are kept free of long hair. Hair on the ears is kept very short. Undercoat – Short and soft. Furnishings – Softer than body coat. The neck is well furnished with hair, which forms a protective ruff blending into the apron. The forelegs are slightly feathered to the pasterns. Topknot covering only the top of the skull; of finer and softer texture than the rest of the coat.

The Australian Terrier

"is spirited, alert, courageous, and self-confident, with the natural aggressiveness of a ratter and hedge hunter; as a companion, friendly and affectionate."

The head is long and strong. The length of the muzzle is equal to the length of the skull. Expression – Keen and intelligent. Ears – Small, erect and pointed; set high on the skull yet well apart, carried erect without any tendency to flare obliquely off the skull. Skull – Viewed from the front or side is long and flat, slightly longer than it is wide and full between the eyes, with slight but definite stop. Muzzle – Strong and powerful with slight fill under the eyes. The jaws are powerful. A desirable breed characteristic is an inverted V-shaped area free of hair extending from the nose up the bridge of the muzzle, varying in length in the mature dog.

DOG GROOMING SIMPLIFIED: STRAIGHT TO THE POINT

SETTER-LIKE PATTERN LINES

Recommended Blade Lengths, Snap-On Comb Lengths and Techniques **Bold Print** = Preferred Choices for Pet Trims							
10 15	10 **7F**	5F 4F **#2** **carding**	4F **#2** **#1** **carding**	thinning shears scissor			thinning shears carding

92

Tip To Remember:

When clipping with blades or snap-on combs, slightly feather off with the clipper when approaching the longer furnishings. Using the clipper in this fashion will help to blend the tighter body pattern work into the longer furnishings. Thinning shears can be used to blend the pattern lines together for a seamless appearance.

Boykin Spaniel

The Boykin Spaniel is a Sporting dog that was discovered in South Carolina in the early 1900s. It is an all-around hunting dog that will flush and retrieve birds from land or water. The Boykin has a beautiful rich, chocolate-brown coat that can be either straight or slightly wavy.

This coat should be maintained by carding and hand stripping for show. The Boykin has a very natural back coat and does not require clipping.

The ears should be flat and lie close to the cheek. They are set slightly higher than the eye. The top of the ear leather can be left natural or neatened with thinning shears. The throat can be clipped with a 7F or 10 blade or it can be left natural.

The furnishings may be trimmed to present the proper profile of the breed. The length of furnishings may vary based on the preference of the pet owner.

See "Head Styles" on page 425 for instructions on grooming the heads of Sporting breeds.

See important information on "Hand Stripping" on page 32 and "Carding" on page 30.

Key points to remember while grooming the Boykin Spaniel according to the breed standard:

The Boykin Spaniel appears slightly longer than it is tall. It has a level topline that slopes as it meets the tail-set. The tail is docked to 3 to 5 inches in length. There should be a slight tuck-up. The neck is described as moderately long and muscular. There is a slight arch as the crest of neck meets the occiput.

The shoulders are well angulated. The front legs should appear straight with round compact feet that have well-arched toes. The feet should be neatly trimmed.

The rear legs are muscular, which shows their strength and drive. The hocks are perpendicular to the ground.

The skull and muzzle of the Boykin Spaniel should be equal in length. The top skull should be flat; however, the sides and back of the skull should be slightly rounded. The muzzle is half the width of the skull. The stop should be moderate.

The Boykin Spaniel has a double-coat which consists of an undercoat and an outer coat. The coat can range from flat to slightly wavy. It is medium in length with a dense short undercoat. The furnishings of the Boykin are consistent with Setter-Like patterns. They have very light feathering. Trimming may be done to enhance the body lines.

Dog Grooming Simplified: Straight To The Point

Setter-Like Pattern Lines

				Recommended Blade Lengths, Snap-On Comb Lengths and Techniques **Bold Print** = Preferred Choices for Pet Trims		
10 15	**10** 7F			thinning shears scissor	hand strip leave natural thinning shears carding	define with thinning shears carding

Tip To Remember:

Many breeds have a natural flat back coat and do not require very much grooming. Carding techniques can be done to remove the dull undercoat. This will enhance the shine of the guard hair. Thinning shears can be used to tidy the appearance. The furnishings can be trimmed to the desired length. When working with this type of beautiful coat sometimes less is best.

Brittany

The Brittany was named after the French province from where the breed originated. This is a Sporting dog who hunts by pointing and retrieving game. The Brittany is an extremely popular dog in France and is one of the most common pointers owned by hunters in the United States.

The Brittany does not carry heavy furnishings. It carries a flat natural back coat which should be maintained by using carding and thinning shear techniques. The ear leathers are free of fringe and can be neatened with thinning shears or clipped with a 5F or 7F blade. The throat may be clipped with a 7F or 10 blade. The clipped area should be well blended into the side of the neck with thinning shears.

A stripping knife may be used on the topskull to remove fuzzy undercoat. The cheeks and muzzle may be lightly clipped with a 10 blade to neaten the appearance.

If body clipping is preferred, a 4F, 5F or 7F blade can be used. Carding and thinning shear techniques should be used in addition to clipping for a natural appearance.

The furnishings may be trimmed to present the proper profile of the breed. The length of furnishings may vary according to the preference of the pet owner.

See "Ear Styles" on page 441 and "Head Styles" on page 425 for instructions on grooming the heads of Sporting dogs.

See important information on "Carding" on page 30 and "Hand Stripping" on page 32.

Key points to remember when grooming the Brittany according to the breed standard:

The Brittany is a "leggy" breed, meaning that it is slightly taller than it is long or next to square.

The neck is of medium length with sloping shoulders. The topline has a slight slope from the withers to the tail. The Brittany has a deep chest that reaches the elbow with well-sprung ribs. The tuck-up is not extreme, with a short loin. The Brittany can either be tailless or have a tail that reaches four inches in length and can be natural or docked.

The shoulders are well laid back and are equal in length to the upper arm. This sets the elbow in line with the withers. The front legs are parallel to each other. The feet are small with well-arched toes and should be neatly trimmed.

The rear is strong and muscular with strong thighs and well-bent stifles. The hocks should be short and perpendicular to the ground.

The ears are short and triangular in shape, set high above the eye level. They should carry very little fringe. The skull is slightly wedge-shaped with a gently sloping stop. The muzzle should be two-thirds the length of the skull and should gradually taper to the nose.

The coat can be dense, flat or wavy. The legs carry very little furnishings.

The Brittany

"A compact, closely knit dog of medium size, a leggy dog having the appearance, as well as the agility, of a great ground coverer. Strong, vigorous, energetic and quick of movement. Ruggedness, without clumsiness, is a characteristic of the breed. He can be tailless or has a tail docked to approximately four inches."

SETTER-LIKE PATTERN LINES

Recommended Blade Lengths, Snap-On Comb Lengths and Techniques **Bold Print** = Preferred Choices for Pet Trims							
10 15	**10** 7F			thinning shears scissor	hand strip leave natural thinning shears carding	define with thinning shears carding

Cavalier King Charles Spaniel

The Cavalier King Charles Spaniel is a Toy breed that originated in England. These dogs have been commonly seen in paintings and tapestries for centuries together with the aristocratic families who enjoyed their loyal companionship. Most people of those times could only afford to have dogs that worked the land and farm. Cavaliers were obviously a luxury item, as they were kept as companion dogs. The Cavalier was a favorite of both Charles I and Charles II of Britain, which is how they took on the name "King Charles".

No trimming is permitted in the show ring for this breed including the feet.

The Cavalier has a natural flat back coat. For pet trims, this coat can be maintained by carding and light hand stripping. However, if clipping is preferred a 4F or 5F blade or various sizes of snap-on combs can be used. Carding and thinning shear techniques should be used in addition to clipping for a natural appearance. The furnishings and feet may be trimmed with thinning shears to tidy the appearance if requested by the pet owner.

The head and ears are left natural. If clipping is preferred, see "Ear Styles" on page 441 and "Head Styles" on page 425 for instructions on grooming the heads of Sporting breeds.

See important information on "Carding" on page 30 and "Hand Stripping" on page 32.

Quoted in part with permission from the American Cavalier King Charles Spaniel Club, Inc., Approved January 10, 1995:

The body approaches squareness, yet if measured from point of shoulder to point of buttock, is slightly longer than the height at the withers. The height from the withers to the elbow is approximately equal to the height from the elbow to the ground.

Topline: Level both when moving and standing.

Neck – Fairly long, without throatiness, well enough muscled to form a slight arch at the crest. Set smoothly into nicely sloping shoulders to give an elegant look. Body – Short-coupled with ribs well sprung but not barreled. Chest moderately deep, extending to elbows allowing ample heart room. Slightly less body at the flank than at the last rib, but with no tucked-up appearance. Tail – Well set on, carried happily but never much above the level of the back, and in constant characteristic motion when the dog is in action.

Shoulders well laid back. Forelegs straight and well under the dog with elbows close to the sides. Pasterns strong and feet compact with well-cushioned pads.

The hindquarters construction should come down from a good broad pelvis, moderately muscled; stifles well turned and hocks well let down. The hind legs when viewed from the rear should parallel each other from hock to heel.

The sweet, gentle, melting expression is an important breed characteristic. Eyes – Large, round, but not prominent and set well apart. There should be cushioning under the eyes which contributes to the soft expression. Ears – Set high, but not close, on top of the head. Leather long with plenty of feathering and wide enough so that when the dog is alert, the ears fan slightly forward to frame the face. Skull – Slightly rounded, but without dome or peak; it should appear flat because of the high placement of the ears. Stop is moderate, neither filled nor deep. Muzzle – Full muzzle slightly tapered. Length from base of stop to tip of nose about 1½ inches.

Coat: Of moderate length, silky, free from curl. Slight wave permissible. Feathering on ears, chest, legs and tail should be long, and the feathering on the feet is a feature of the breed. <u>No trimming of the dog is permitted. Specimens where the coat has been altered by trimming, clipping, or by artificial means shall be so severely penalized as to be effectively eliminated from competition.</u> Hair growing between the pads on the underside of the feet may be trimmed.

The Cavalier King Charles Spaniel

"is an active, graceful, well-balanced toy spaniel, very gay and free in action; fearless and sporting in character, yet at the same time gentle and affectionate."

SETTER-LIKE PATTERN LINES

Recommended Blade Lengths, Snap-On Comb Lengths and Techniques **Bold Print** = Preferred Choices for Pet Trims							
10 15					thinning shears scissor	hand strip leave natural thinning shears carding	define with thinning shears carding

Clumber Spaniel

The Clumber Spaniel is a Sporting dog that originated in France. It has a dense coat which allows the dog to hunt in heavy cover. The Clumber has a quiet hunting style, which allows the dog to get close up on game. This is a flushing Spaniel with a white coat, with minimal lemon or orange markings, which makes the dog easily seen by hunters.

This coat should be maintained by carding and hand stripping for show. Shedding techniques may be necessary for heavily coated dogs. The ears of the Clumber Spaniel are neatened with thinning shears for a natural appearance. The throat is left natural.

This coat should not be clipped and can be maintained by using carding techniques. If the pet owner prefers clipping, blades ranging from 4F to 5F or snap-on combs ranging from #0, #1 to #2 are recommended. Carding and thinning shear techniques should be done in addition to clipping for a natural appearance.

The furnishings may be trimmed to present the proper profile of the breed. The length of furnishings may vary according to the preference of the pet owner.

SETTER-LIKE PATTERN LINES

See "Ear Styles" on page 441 for instructions on grooming the heads of Sporting breeds.

See important information on "Carding" on page 30 and "Hand Stripping" on page 32.

Key points to remember while grooming the Clumber Spaniel according to the breed standard:

The Clumber Spaniel is slightly longer than it is tall. This is a very muscular breed with a heavy bone structure. The topline slopes slightly to the tail-set.

The shoulders are well laid back and are approximately the same length as the upper arm, which sets the elbow in line with the withers. The front legs should appear straight. The feet are large and round and should be neatly trimmed.

The rear legs are muscular with well-bent stifles. The hocks should appear perpendicular to the ground.

The Clumber Spaniel is known for its "massive" head with a heavy brow. The muzzle should appear square. The skull is slightly flat with a well-defined occiput. The ear set should be at the level of the eyes and should be slightly feathered showing a triangular shape with the tips rounded. The ears can be trimmed with thinning shears for a natural appearance.

The Clumber Spaniel has a dense straight double-coat. The furnishings are consistent with the Setter-Like patterns and should be trimmed accordingly. The tail is well feathered.

The Clumber Spaniel

"is a gentle, loyal and affectionate dog. He possesses an intrinsic desire to please. An intelligent and independent thinker, he displays determination and a strong sense of purpose while at work."

SETTER-LIKE PATTERN LINES

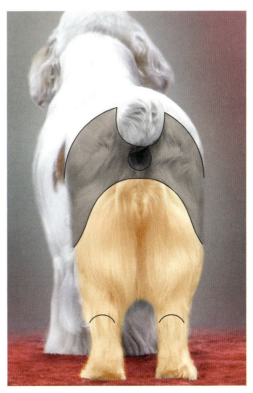

Recommended Blade Lengths, Snap-On Comb Lengths and Techniques						
Bold Print = Preferred Choices for Pet Trims						
10 15				thinning shears scissor	hand strip leave natural thinning shears carding	define with thinning shears carding

FIELD SPANIEL

The Field Spaniel is a Sporting dog that originated in England. It is a flushing Spaniel who is used to flush and retrieve birds from both land and water.

This coat should be hand stripped for show. The Field Spaniel has a very natural flat back coat and does not require clipping.

The furnishings may be trimmed to present the proper profile of the breed. The length of furnishings may vary according to the preference of the pet owner.

See "Head Styles" on page 425 for instructions on grooming the heads of Sporting breeds.

See important information on "Hand Stripping" on page 32 and "Carding" on page 30.

SETTER-LIKE PATTERN LINES

Quoted in part with permission from the Field Spaniel Society of America, Inc., Approved September 14, 1998:

A well balanced dog, somewhat longer than tall. The ratio of length to height is approximately 7:6. Solidly built, with moderate bone, and firm smooth muscles.

Topline: The neck slopes smoothly into the withers; the back is level, well muscled, firm and strong; the croup is short and gently rounded.

Neck–Long, strong, muscular, slightly arched, clean, and well set into shoulders. Body–The prosternum is prominent and well fleshed. The depth of chest is roughly equal to the length of the front leg from elbow to ground. The rib cage is long and extending into a short loin. Ribs are oval, well sprung and curve gently into a firm loin. Loin–Short, strong, and deep, with little or no tuck-up. Tail–Set on low, in line with the croup, just below the level of the back with a natural downward inclination. Docked tails preferred, natural tails are allowed.

Forequarters: Shoulder blades are oblique and sloping. The upper arm is closed-set; elbows are directly below the withers, and turn neither in nor out. Forelegs are straight and well boned to the feet. Feet face forward and are large, rounded, and webbed, with strong, well arched relatively tight toes and thick pads.

Hindquarters: Strong and driving; stifles and hocks only moderately bent. Hocks well let down; pasterns relatively short, strong and parallel when viewed from the rear. Hips moderately broad and muscular; upper thigh broad and powerful; second thigh well muscled.

Skull: The crown is slightly wider at the back than at the brow and lightly arched laterally; sides and cheeks are straight and clean. The occiput is distinct and rounded. Brows are slightly raised. The stop is moderate, but well defined by the brows. The face is chiseled beneath the eyes.

Muzzle: Strong, long and lean, neither snipy nor squarely cut. The nasal bone is straight and slightly divergent from parallel, sloping downward toward the nose from the plane of the top skull.

Coat: Single; moderately long; flat or slightly wavy; silky; and glossy; dense and water-repellent. Moderate setter-like feathering adorns the chest, underbody, backs of the legs, buttocks and may also be present on the second thigh and underside of the tail. Over-abundance of coat, or cottony texture, impractical for field work should be penalized. Trimming is limited to that which enhances the natural appearance of the dog.

The Field Spaniel

"is a combination of beauty and utility. It is a well balanced, substantial hunter-companion of medium size, built for activity and endurance in a heavy cover and water. It has a noble carriage; a proud but docile attitude; is sound and free moving. Symmetry, gait, attitude and purpose are more important than any one part."

SETTER-LIKE PATTERN LINES

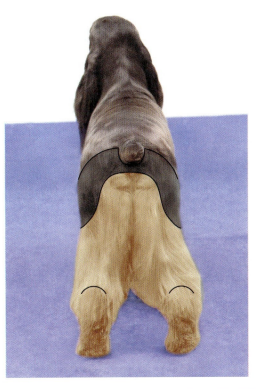

Recommended Blade Lengths, Snap-On Comb Lengths and Techniques **Bold Print** = Preferred Choices for Pet Trims							
10 15	**10** 7F			thinning shears scissor	hand strip leave natural thinning shears carding	define with thinning shears carding	

German Wirehaired Pointer

The German Wirehaired Pointer is a Sporting dog that originated in Germany. This is an all-purpose gun dog who is a true pointer by nature. It retrieves on land and water. The German Wirehaired Pointer has a weather-resistant and water-repellent coat which protects the dog from the brush as well as cold water temperatures.

This coat should be maintained by carding and hand stripping for show. Clipping this coat will change the texture and color and should be discouraged for pet trims. Carding and thinning shear techniques may be used to tidy the appearance for pet trimming. A Coat King may also be used on the back coat to help remove undercoat and help preserve the color and texture of the coat.

If the pet owner prefers clipping, blades ranging from 4F, 5F to 7F are recommended. Carding techniques should be done in addition to clipping to help preserve the color and texture of the coat.

The rear furnishings of the German Wirehaired Pointer slightly deviate from the Setter-Like pattern lines.

The rear and inside thigh muscles are set tight to the bend of knee.

The topskull and cheeks can be clipped for a smooth appearance, or thinning shears can be used for a more natural appearance.

See important information on "Carding" on page 30 and "Hand Stripping" on page 32.

Key points to remember when grooming the German Wirehaired Pointer according to the breed standard:

The German Wirehaired Pointer is slightly longer than it is tall. The topline slightly slopes to the croup. The shoulders are well laid back. The front legs are straight with webbed feet. The feet are arched with close toes.

The rear legs are muscular and well angulated. When viewed from the rear the legs should present parallel lines. The hocks are short and parallel to the ground.

The head is moderately long. The muzzle is broad with a medium stop. The eyebrows are triangular in shape. The cheeks and the top of skull should be stripped or clipped tight. The muzzle should have a beard of moderate length. The ears are rounded with minimal feathering and may be neatened with thinning shears.

The German Wirehaired Pointer has a true harsh wire coat that is characteristic of this breed. The coat is weather-resistant and almost water-repellent. The outer coat is approximately one to two inches in length lying flat against the body. The coat should never be long enough to hide the outline of the breed.

DOG GROOMING SIMPLIFIED: STRAIGHT TO THE POINT

SETTER-LIKE PATTERN LINES

				Recommended Blade Lengths, Snap-On Comb Lengths and Techniques **Bold Print** = Preferred Choices for Pet Trims		
10 15	10 **7F**			thinning shears scissor	hand strip leave natural thinning shears carding	define with thinning shears carding

Tip To Remember:

Many wire-coated breeds should be hand stripped for the show ring. If hand stripping is not desired by the pet owner there are tools available, as well as techniques that can be used, which will slightly preserve the harsh texture of the coat. If the coat is being clipped, using a Coat King prior to clipping will help remove undercoat as well as pull some guard hair from the follicle. After clipping the coat, carding techniques should then be used to remove the remainder of the excess undercoat. This will allow the coat to lie nicely and appear natural. An alternative to clipping would be to use thinning shears to tidy the appearance and to tighten the pattern lines.

Longhaired Dachshund

The Dachshund is a Hound that was bred in Germany to go underground to hunt badgers in burrows. This explains the long and low body build and deep chest. The Dachshund will rest its chest on the ground while digging through tight burrows. In fact, the name Dachshund means "badger dog" in German. The Dachshund is shown in two sizes: standard and miniature. There are three coat varieties: smooth, longhaired and wirehaired.

The longhaired coat should be maintained by using carding techniques for show; however, if clipping is preferred, blades ranging from 4F, 5F, to 7F or a #2 snap-on comb may be used. Carding and thinning shear techniques should be used in addition to clipping for a natural seamless appearance.

The throat can be clipped with a 7F or 10 blade. The clipped area should be well blended into the side of the neck with thinning shears. A stripping knife can be used on the top of the skull to remove fuzzy undercoat. The ears are left natural.

The furnishings may be trimmed to present the proper profile of the breed. The length of furnishings may vary based on the preference of the pet owner.

See important information on "Carding" on page 30 and "Hand Stripping" on page 32.

Quoted in part with permission from the Dachshund Club of America, Inc., Approved January 9, 2007:

Low to ground, long in body and short of leg, with robust muscular development. Bred and shown in two sizes, standard and miniature.

When viewed in profile, the back lies in the straightest possible line between the withers and the short, very slightly arched loin.

Forequarters: For effective underground work, the front must be strong, deep, long and cleanly muscled. The breast-bone is strongly prominent in front so that on either side a depression or dimple appears. Shoulder blades–long, broad, well-laid back and firmly placed upon the fully developed thorax, closely fitted at the withers. Upper Arm–Ideally the same length as the shoulder. Forearm–Short. The inclined shoulder blades, upper arms and curved forearms form parentheses that enclose the ribcage, creating the correct "wraparound front." Front paws are full, tight, compact, with well-arched toes and tough, thick pads.

Hindquarters: Strong and cleanly muscled. The pelvis, the thigh, the second thigh, and the rear pastern are ideally the same length and give the appearance of a series of right angles. From the rear, the thighs are strong and powerful. Rear pasterns–Short and strong, perpendicular to the second thigh bone. When viewed from behind, they are upright and parallel. Hind Paws–Smaller than the front paws with four compactly closed and arched toes with tough, thick pads. Croup–Long, rounded and full, sinking slightly toward the tail. Tail–Set in continuation of the spine, extending without kinks, twists, or pronounced curvature, and not carried too gaily.

Viewed from above or from the side, the head tapers uniformly to the tip of the nose. The bridge bones over the eyes are strongly prominent. The ears are set near the top of the head, not too far forward, of moderate length, rounded, not narrow, pointed, or folded. Their carriage, when animated, is with the forward edge just touching the cheek so that the ears frame the face. The skull is slightly arched, neither too broad nor too narrow, and slopes gradually with little perceptible stop into the finely-formed, slightly arched muzzle, giving a Roman appearance.

Coat: The sleek, glistening, often slightly wavy hair is longer under the neck and on forechest, the underside of the body, the ears and behind the legs. The coat gives the dog an elegant appearance. Short hair on the ear is not desirable. Too profuse a coat which masks type, equally long hair over the whole body, a curly coat, or a pronounced parting on the back are faults. Tail–Carried gracefully in prolongation of the spine; the hair attains its greatest length here and forms a veritable flag.

The Dachshund

"is clever, lively and courageous to the point of rashness, persevering in above- and below-ground work, with all the senses well-developed."

SETTER-LIKE PATTERN LINES

10 15	**10** 7F			thinning shears scissor	hand strip leave natural thinning shears carding	define with thinning shears carding	

Recommended Blade Lengths, Snap-On Comb Lengths and Techniques
Bold Print = Preferred Choices for Pet Trims

121

Sussex Spaniel

The Sussex Spaniel is a Sporting dog that originated in Sussex, England. It is a field dog who hunts by flushing and retrieving. The Sussex is known for its beautiful rich golden liver coat.

This coat should be carded and hand stripped for show. The Sussex Spaniel has a natural flat back coat and does not require clipping. Carding techniques may be done to maintain the back coat. Thinning shears may be used to tidy the appearance. The ears and throat of the Sussex Spaniel are left natural.

The furnishings may be trimmed to present the proper profile of the breed. The length of furnishings may vary according to the preference of the pet owner.

See "Ear Styles" on page 441 for instructions on grooming the heads of Sporting breeds.

See important information on "Carding" on page 30 and "Hand Stripping" on page 32.

Key points to remember when grooming the Sussex Spaniel according to the breed standard:

The Sussex Spaniel has a rectangular outline, meaning that it is slightly longer than it is tall. It appears "low and long" and very muscular with a heavy bone structure. The topline is level and drops slightly down to a low-set tail.

The Sussex Spaniel has a short, strong neck with a slightly arched crest. The chest is deep. The shoulders are well laid back. The upper arm and shoulder blade are approximately the same length, which sets the elbow in line with the withers. The front legs are short and are heavily boned. They should be straight but can have a slight bow. The feet are large and round and should be neatly trimmed.

The rear legs are muscular and have a well-angulated stifle. The hocks should be perpendicular to the ground.

The Sussex Spaniel is known for its serious expression. It carries a heavy brow that creates a frowning expression. The ears are set moderately low and are heavily furnished. The skull is longer than the muzzle, the muzzle measuring approximately three inches in length. The muzzle should appear square and broad when viewed from the profile.

The coat of the Sussex Spaniel is flat or slightly wavy. The furnishings are well-feathered. The hocks should be trimmed. The neck has a frill. The tail is covered with moderately long feathering. The Sussex should not be trimmed for the show ring with the exception of neatening the feet and hocks. However, for pet trims the furnishings may be trimmed to the length desired by the pet owner.

DOG GROOMING SIMPLIFIED: STRAIGHT TO THE POINT

SETTER-LIKE PATTERN LINES

				Recommended Blade Lengths, Snap-On Comb Lengths and Techniques **Bold Print** = Preferred Choices for Pet Trims		
10 15				thinning shears scissor	hand strip leave natural thinning shears carding	define with thinning shears carding

124

Tip To Remember:

The feet on most of the breeds in this section are trimmed tight, without showing the separation between the toes, using thinning shears for a natural appearance. The furnishings are trimmed in the same manner as the Distinct Setter-Like patterns and may be trimmed to present the proper profile of the breed. The length of furnishings may vary based on the preference of the pet owner.

Wirehaired Dachshund

The Dachshund is a Hound that was bred in Germany to go underground to hunt badgers in burrows. This explains the long and low body build and deep chest. The Dachshund will rest its chest on the ground while digging through tight burrows. In fact, the name Dachshund means "badger dog" in German. The Dachshund is shown in two sizes: standard and miniature. There are three coat varieties: smooth, longhaired and wirehaired.

The wirehaired coat should be maintained by carding and hand stripping for show. Using carding techniques on pet trims will help keep the wire texture of the coat. Clipping should be discouraged, as it will alter the texture of the coat. However, if the pet owner prefers clipping, blades ranging from 4F, 5F to 7F are recommended. Carding and thinning shear techniques should be done in addition to clipping for a natural appearance. The throat may be clipped with a 7F or 10 blade. The clipped area should be well blended into the side of the neck with thinning shears.

The rear furnishings of the Wirehaired Dachshund slightly deviate from the Setter-Like pattern lines. The rear and inside thigh muscles are set tight to the bend of knee.

The Wirehaired Dachshund has a beard and small triangular eyebrows. The ears should be smooth and can be clipped with a 7F or 10 blade if not being hand stripped. The top of the skull may be neatened with thinning shears. The cheeks can be either tightened with thinning shears or clipped with a 7F or 10 blade. The furnishings may be trimmed to present the proper profile of the breed.

See important information on "Carding" on page 30 and "Hand Stripping" on page 32.

Quoted in part with permission from the Dachshund Club of America, Inc., Approved January 9, 2007:

Low to ground, long in body and short of leg, with robust muscular development. Bred and shown in two sizes, standard and miniature.

When viewed in profile, the back lies in the straightest possible line between the withers and the short, very slightly arched loin.

Forequarters: For effective underground work, the front must be strong, deep, long and cleanly muscled. The breast-bone is strongly prominent in front so that on either side a depression or dimple appears. Shoulder blades–long, broad, well-laid back and firmly placed upon the fully developed thorax, closely fitted at the withers. Upper Arm–Ideally the same length as the shoulder. Forearm–Short. The inclined shoulder blades, upper arms and curved forearms form parentheses that enclose the ribcage, creating the correct "wraparound front." Front paws are full, tight, compact, with well-arched toes and tough, thick pads.

Hindquarters: Strong and cleanly muscled. The pelvis, the thigh, the second thigh, and the rear pastern are ideally the same length and give the appearance of a series of right angles. From the rear, the thighs are strong and powerful. Rear pasterns–Short and strong, perpendicular to the second thigh bone. When viewed from behind, they are upright and parallel. Hind Paws–Smaller than the front paws with four compactly closed and arched toes with tough, thick pads. Croup–Long, rounded and full, sinking slightly toward the tail. Tail–Set in continuation of the spine, extending without kinks, twists, or pronounced curvature, and not carried too gaily.

Viewed from above or from the side, the head tapers uniformly to the tip of the nose. The bridge bones over the eyes are strongly prominent. The ears are set near the top of the head, not too far forward, of moderate length, rounded, not narrow, pointed, or folded. Their carriage, when animated, is with the forward edge just touching the cheek so that the ears frame the face. The skull is slightly arched, neither too broad nor too narrow, and slopes gradually with little perceptible stop into the finely-formed, slightly arched muzzle, giving a Roman appearance.

Coat: With the exception of jaw, eyebrows, and ears, the whole body is covered with a uniform tight, short, thick, rough, hard, outer coat but with finer, somewhat softer, shorter hairs (undercoat) everywhere distributed between the coarser hairs. The distinctive facial furnishings include a beard and eyebrows. On the ears the hair is shorter than on the body, almost smooth. The general arrangement of the hair is such that the wirehaired Dachshund, when viewed from a distance, resembles the smooth. Any sort of soft hair in the outer-coat, wherever found on the body, especially on the top of the head, is a fault. The same is true of long, curly, or wavy hair, or hair that sticks out irregularly in all directions. Tail–Robust, thickly haired, gradually tapering to a point.

The Wirehaired Dachshund

"His hunting spirit, good nose, loud tongue and distinctive build make him well-suited for below-ground work and for beating the bush."

SETTER-LIKE PATTERN LINES

Recommended Blade Lengths, Snap-On Comb Lengths and Techniques **Bold Print** = Preferred Choices for Pet Trims							
10 15	10 **7F**			thinning shears scissor	hand strip leave natural thinning shears carding	define with thinning shears carding	

SETTER-LIKE PATTERN LINES

129

SETTER-LIKE PATTERN LINES
Breeds with a Ruff

The following breeds include several heavy double-coated breeds that carry the same natural Subtle Setter-Like pattern lines. However, unlike the others, they carry a ruff around their neck. Some breeds carry a heavier ruff than others. These breeds should not be clipped. They require shedding and carding techniques as well as neatening with thinning shears to tidy the appearance.

Using the Golden Retriever as an example, you will see that when the undercoat is properly brushed out, the coat will lie beautifully and will be vibrant in color.

The front of the front legs and front of the hocks (ankle) can be carded to remove fuzzy undercoat. The thigh and stifle area may also require carding techniques. It is best to card out this short fuzzy undercoat rather than cut it with shears or thinning shears. The coat will shine once the dull undercoat is removed.

Thinning shears and/or straight/curved shears may be used to trim the furnishings to create the correct profile.

The shoulder and upper arm can be lightly trimmed with thinning shears to remove long fly-away hairs. On breeds that carry a heavier ruff, the ruff may be neatened to remove fly-aways.

Carding techniques can be used on the front of the front legs to remove fuzzy undercoat. The feet are neatened with thinning shears for a tight appearance.

The underside of the base of the tail can be set tight using thinning shears for a natural appearance. The area around the anus can either be clipped with a 10 blade or tightened with thinning shears for sanitary purposes.

The rear furnishings, often referred to as "pants", can be shaped with thinning shears or curved shears and should not fall past the point of hock.

American Eskimo Dog

The American Eskimo Dog is registered as a Non-Sporting breed that originated in the United States. The "Eskie" was used as a traveling circus dog due to its trainability, intelligence and quick agility skills

This coat should be maintained using shedding techniques. No trimming is allowed in the show ring for this breed with the exception of trimming the feet and the hocks.

Carding techniques may be used on the front of the front legs and front of hocks to remove fuzzy undercoat.

The feet may be trimmed neatly with thinning shears. The furnishings may be trimmed to present the proper profile of the breed. The length of furnishings may vary according to the preference of the pet owner.

See important information on "Double-Coated Breeds" on page 17.

Key points to remember when grooming the American Eskimo Dog according to the breed standard:

There are three different sizes of the American Eskimo Dog: Toy, Miniature and Standard. The body of the American Eskimo is strong and compact with a level topline. They have a deep chest with well sprung ribs which reaches to the level of the elbow. The tail is set moderately high and should reach the point of hock. The tail is heavily covered with longer hair. This breed has a slight tuck-up.

The shoulder blades are well angulated and are the same length as the upper arm. The front legs are straight with oval, compact feet. The rear legs are well angulated with well bent stifles. The skull is wedge-shaped with triangular ears that are held erect. The ears are covered with short hair with longer tufts of hair in front of the ear canal.

The American Eskimo has a double-coat. The undercoat is dense with longer guard hair. They should carry a ruff around the neck. They carry furnishings on the back of the front legs and back of the rear legs to the hocks.

The American Eskimo Dog

"is a loving companion dog, presents a picture of strength and agility, alertness and beauty. It is a small to medium-size Nordic type dog, always white, or white with biscuit cream. The American Eskimo Dog is compactly built and well balanced, with good substance, and an alert, smooth gait."

Dog Grooming Simplified: Straight To The Point

SETTER-LIKE PATTERN LINES

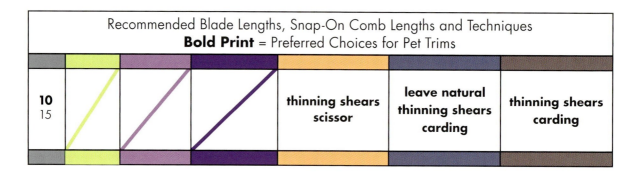

10 15				thinning shears scissor	leave natural thinning shears carding	thinning shears carding

Recommended Blade Lengths, Snap-On Comb Lengths and Techniques
Bold Print = Preferred Choices for Pet Trims

Tip To Remember:

Removing the fine fuzzy undercoat from the top of short natural heads, like the Cavalier King Charles Spaniel for example, or the front of the front legs of the Golden Retriever can be difficult. Thread a rubber-band through the teeth of a comb and comb through the coat. The rubber-band will pull the fine hairs out with ease.

Australian Shepherd

The Australian Shepherd is a herding breed that originated in the United States, despite its name. The "Aussie" was developed by ranchers in the western regions of the United States. It has a strong herding and guarding instinct and was used as an all-purpose farm dog. The Aussie is very eager to please and has a high energy level. It is extremely intelligent and is often used in search and rescue and also used as a guide and therapy dog.

Photo courtesy of Heidi Mobley, 2MC Design

This coat should be maintained using shedding techniques. Carding techniques may be used on the front of the front legs and front of hocks to remove fuzzy undercoat.

The feet may be trimmed neatly with thinning shears. The furnishings may be trimmed to present the proper profile of the breed. The length of furnishings may vary according to the preference of the pet owner.

See important information on "Double-Coated Breeds" on page 17.

Key points to remember when grooming the Australian Shepherd according to the breed standard:

The Australian Shepherd is slightly longer than it is tall. It has a level topline with a moderately sloped croup. The ribs are well sprung with a moderate tuck-up. The tail can be docked or will be naturally bobbed.

The shoulders are well laid back and are equal in length to the upper arm. The front legs are straight. The feet are oval, compact with well arched toes.

The rear is well angulated. The hocks are short and perpendicular to the ground.

The muzzle is the same length as the skull or can be slightly shorter. The ears are triangular and are set high on the head. The skull is flat to slightly domed.

The Australian Shepherd has a double-coat which is weather resistant and is of medium length. They carry a moderate mane of coat around the neck. The hair is short and smooth on the head, ears, front of front legs and front of hocks. The back of the front legs, underline and rear carry moderate furnishings.

The Australian Shepherd

"is an intelligent working dog of strong herding and guarding instincts. He is a loyal companion and has the stamina to work all day. He is well balanced, slightly longer than tall, of medium size and bone, with coloring that offers variety and individuality."

Dog Grooming Simplified: Straight To The Point

SETTER-LIKE PATTERN LINES

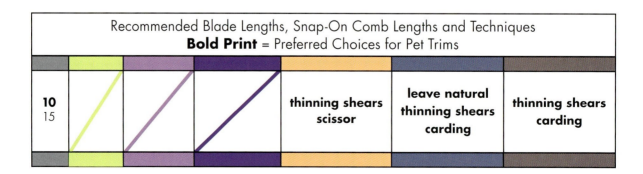

| 10 15 | | | | thinning shears scissor | leave natural thinning shears carding | thinning shears carding |

Tip To Remember:

Educating clients is our job as pet care professionals. Double-coated breeds should be groomed on a regular basis to keep the undercoat at bay. This is especially important during the warmer months. Brushing double-coated breeds in the bath tub while they are soapy will facilitate in removing excessive undercoat. Using quality shampoos and conditioners will promote healthy skin and coat.

Bernese Mountain Dog

The Bernese Mountain Dog is a Working breed that originated in Switzerland. They were used as all-purpose farm dogs. Their strength and calm demeanor made them ideal for pulling carts to market. The Bernese Mountain Dogs made great companions for farmers. They thrive in cold weather and today they excel in carting, agility, tracking, herding and therapy work.

This coat should be maintained using shedding and thinning shear techniques.

The feet and ears may be trimmed neatly with thinning shears. The furnishings may be trimmed to present the proper profile of the breed. The length of furnishings may vary according to the preference of the pet owner. Carding techniques may be used on the front of the front legs and front of hocks to remove fuzzy undercoat.

See important information on "Carding" on page 30 and "Double-Coated Breeds" on page 17.

Quoted in part with permission from the Bernese Mountain Dog Club of America, Inc., Approved February 10, 1990:

The neck is strong, muscular and of medium length. The topline is level from the withers to the croup. The chest is deep and capacious with well-sprung, but not barrel-shaped, ribs and brisket reaching at least to the elbows. The back is broad and firm. The tail is bushy. The bones in the tail should feel straight and should reach to the hock joint or below.

The shoulders are moderately laid back, flat-lying, well-muscled and never loose. The legs are straight and strong and the elbows are well under the shoulder when the dog is standing. The feet are round and compact with well-arched toes.

The thighs are broad, strong and muscular. The stifles are moderately bent and taper smoothly into the hocks. The hocks are well let down and straight as viewed from the rear.

The ears are medium sized, set high, triangular in shape, gently rounded at the tip, and hang close to the head when in repose. The skull is flat on top and broad, with a slight furrow and a well-defined, but not exaggerated stop. The muzzle is strong and straight.

The coat is thick, moderately long and slightly wavy or straight. It has a bright natural sheen. The Bernese Mountain Dog is shown in natural coat and undue trimming is to be discouraged.

The Bernese Mountain Dog

"is a striking, tri-colored, large dog. He is sturdy and balanced. He is intelligent, strong and agile enough to do the draft and droving work for which he was used in the mountainous regions of his origin."

DOG GROOMING SIMPLIFIED: STRAIGHT TO THE POINT

SETTER-LIKE PATTERN LINES

				Recommended Blade Lengths, Snap-On Comb Lengths and Techniques **Bold Print** = Preferred Choices for Pet Trims		
10 15				thinning shears scissor	leave natural thinning shears carding	thinning shears carding

142

TIP TO REMEMBER:

After clipping the pads of double-coated breeds as well as other breeds with a tight natural foot, lightly skim up the side of the pads with the clipper. This will edge in the base of the foot to ensure a nice tight foot. Use thinning shears to tidy the top of the foot for a natural appearance. A 40 blade is preferred for this technique.

BORDER COLLIE

The Border Collie is a Herding breed that originated in Scotland. They are known for their exquisite sheep herding abilities. They are a breed of extreme intelligence with a natural herding instinct. They have an intense look about them while at work, which is referred to as the "eye".

This coat should be maintained using shedding and thinning shear techniques.

The feet may be trimmed neatly with thinning shears. The furnishings may be trimmed to present the proper profile of the breed. The length of furnishings may vary according to the preference of the pet owner.

Carding techniques may be used on the front of the front legs and front of hocks to remove fuzzy undercoat.

See important information on "Carding" on page 30 and "Double-Coated Breeds" on page 17.

Key points to remember when grooming the Border Collie according to the breed standard:

The Border Collie is slightly longer than it is tall. It has a level topline gently sloping to the tail-set. The neck is muscular and slightly arched.

The chest is deep and broad, reaching the elbow. The Border Collie should show a slight tuck-up. The tail is set low and reaches the hock.

The shoulders are well laid back and are approximately the same length as the upper arm, which sets the elbow in line with the withers. The front legs are straight with compact feet that are oval in shape. The feet should be neatly trimmed showing moderately arched toes.

The rear legs are muscular with well-bent stifles. The hocks are perpendicular to the ground and may be slightly turned in.

The skull is slightly flat and is the same length as the muzzle. The ears are of medium size and are carried either erect or semi-erect.

The Border Collie is a double-coated breed and can have either a rough coat or a smooth coat. The rough coat falls under this pattern group and is well feathered but not excessive. The smooth coat is short all over but may have minimal feathering.

The Border Collie

"is a well balanced, medium-sized dog of athletic appearance, displaying style and agility in equal measure with soundness and strength. Its hard, muscular body conveys the impression of effortless movement and endless endurance. The Border Collie is extremely intelligent, with its keen, alert expression being a very important characteristic of the breed."

DOG GROOMING SIMPLIFIED: STRAIGHT TO THE POINT

SETTER-LIKE PATTERN LINES

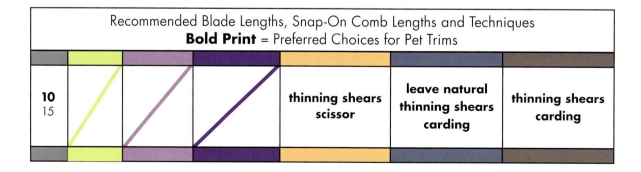

Recommended Blade Lengths, Snap-On Comb Lengths and Techniques **Bold Print** = Preferred Choices for Pet Trims						
10 15				thinning shears scissor	leave natural thinning shears carding	thinning shears carding

Tip To Remember:

Sanitary trims (belly) are not necessary on heavy double-coated breeds unless requested by the pet owners. Clipping the belly of these breeds will remove the longer furnishings that could possibly take away from the volume of the underline. Unless the pet has had the belly shaved in the past there could be irritation after shaving.

COLLIE

The Collie is a Herding breed that originated in Scotland. They were bred to guide cows and sheep to market. The Collie is known to be loyal and affectionate. It has a natural instinct of being a self-appointed guardian to everything it sees and hears, especially small children. It is very hard not to associate the Collie with the longtime TV show star "Lassie".

This coat should be maintained using shedding and thinning shear techniques.

The feet may be trimmed neatly with thinning shears. The furnishings may be trimmed to present the proper profile of the breed. The length of furnishings may vary according to the preference of the pet owner.

Carding techniques may be used on the front of the front legs and front of hocks to remove fuzzy undercoat.

See important information on "Carding" on page 30 and "Double-Coated Breeds" on page 17.

Quoted in part with permission from the Collie Club of America, Inc., Approved May 10, 1977:

The neck is firm, clean, muscular, sinewy and heavily frilled. It is fairly long, carried upright with a slight arch at the nape and imparts a proud, upstanding appearance showing off the frill.

The body is firm, hard and muscular, a trifle long in proportion to the height. The ribs are well-rounded behind the well-sloped shoulders and the chest is deep, extending to the elbows. The back is strong and level, supported by powerful hips and thighs and the croup is sloped to give a well-rounded finish. The loin is powerful and slightly arched.

The forelegs are straight and muscular, with a fair amount of bone considering the size of the dog. The hind legs are less fleshy, muscular at the thighs, very sinewy and the hocks and stifles are well bent. The comparatively small feet are approximately oval in shape, the toes are well arched and close together.

Both in front and profile view the head bears a general resemblance to a well-blunted lean wedge, being smooth and clean in outline and nicely balanced in proportion. On the sides it tapers gradually and smoothly from the ears to the end of the black nose, without being flared out in backskull (cheeky) or pinched in muzzle (snipy). In profile view the top of the backskull and the top of the muzzle lie in two approximately parallel, straight planes of equal length, divided by a very slight but perceptible stop or break. A mid-point between the inside corners of the eyes (which is the center of a correctly placed stop) is the center of balance in length of head.

The well-fitting, proper-textured coat is the crowning glory of the rough variety of Collie. It is abundant except on the head and legs. The outer coat is straight and harsh to the touch. The undercoat, however, is soft, furry and so close together that it is difficult to see the skin when the hair is parted. The coat is very abundant on the mane and frill. The face or mask is smooth. The forelegs are smooth and well feathered to the back of the pasterns. The hind legs are smooth below the hock joints. Any feathering below the hocks is removed for the show ring. The hair on the tail is very profuse and on the hips it is long and bushy.

The Collie

"is a lithe, strong, responsive, active dog, carrying no useless timber, standing naturally straight and firm. The deep, moderately wide chest shows strength, the sloping shoulders and well-bent hocks indicate speed and grace, and the face shows high intelligence."

DOG GROOMING SIMPLIFIED: STRAIGHT TO THE POINT

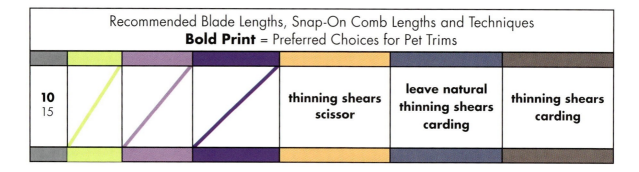

Recommended Blade Lengths, Snap-On Comb Lengths and Techniques
Bold Print = Preferred Choices for Pet Trims

10 15				thinning shears scissor	leave natural thinning shears carding	thinning shears carding

SETTER-LIKE PATTERN LINES

Tip To Remember:

When shaping the underline of double-coated breeds this quick trick can save time: Clip with a 40 blade, and a very steady hand, by skimming the desired shape of the underline removing the long stray hairs. This trick also works well on many other breeds to neaten the underline and tuck-up. A 40 blade will remove hair very quickly. This trick is for the more experienced groomer.

Flat-Coated Retriever

The Flat-Coated Retriever is a Sporting dog that originated in England. It was bred to flush and retrieve both upland game and waterfowl. The Flat-Coated Retriever is slightly racier and lighter in bone than the other retrievers. It has a beautiful flat, straight, solid black or liver-colored coat.

This coat should be maintained by using carding, shedding and thinning shear techniques. The Flat-Coated Retriever carries a beautiful flat back coat that is true to this breed's name.

The furnishings may be trimmed to present the proper profile of the breed. The length of furnishings may vary according to the preference of the pet owner.

See important information on "Carding" on page 30 and "Double-Coated Breeds" on page 17.

Quoted in part with permission from the Flat-Coated Retriever Society of America, Inc., Approved September 11, 1990:

This utilitarian retriever is well balanced, strong, but elegant; never cobby, short legged or rangy. The length of the body from the point of the shoulder to the rearmost projection of the upper thigh is slightly more than the height at the withers.

A level topline combined with a deep, long rib cage tapering to a moderate tuck-up create the impression of a blunted triangle.

Neck strong and slightly arched for retrieving strength. Coat on neck is untrimmed. Chest is deep, reaching to the elbow and only moderately broad. Forechest–Prow prominent and well developed. Deep chest tapering to a moderate tuck-up. Tail fairly straight, well set on, with bone reaching approximately to the hock joint.

Shoulders long, well laid back shoulder blade with upper arm of approximately equal length to allow for efficient reach. Forelegs straight and strong with medium bone of good quality. Feet oval or round. Medium sized and tight with well arched toes and thick pads.

Hindquarters: Powerful with angulation in balance with the front assembly. Upper thighs powerful and well muscled. Good turn of stifle with sound, strong joint. Hock joint strong, well let down.

The long, clean, well molded head is adequate in size and strength to retrieve a large pheasant, duck or hare with ease. The impression of the skull and muzzle being "cast in one piece" is created by the fairly flat skull of moderate breadth and flat, clean cheeks, combined with the long, strong, deep muzzle which is well filled in before, between and beneath the eyes. Viewed from above, the muzzle is nearly equal in length and breadth to the skull. Stop–There is a gradual, slight, barely perceptible stop, avoiding a down or dish-faced appearance. Brows are slightly raised and mobile, giving life to the expression. Stop must be evaluated in profile so that it will not be confused with the raised brow. Occiput not accentuated, the skull forming a gentle curve where it fits well into the neck. Ears relatively small, well set on, lying close to the side of the head and thickly feathered. Not low set (houndlike or setterish).

Coat: The Flat-Coat is a working retriever and the coat must provide protection from all types of weather, water and ground cover. This requires a coat of sufficient texture, length and fullness to allow for adequate insulation. When the dog is in full coat the ears, front, chest, back of forelegs, thighs and underside of tail are thickly feathered without being bushy, stringy or silky. Since the Flat-Coat is a hunting retriever, the feathering is not excessively long.

Trimming: The Flat-Coat is shown with as natural a coat as possible and must not be penalized for lack of trimming, as long as the coat is clean and well brushed. Tidying of ears, feet, underline and tip of tail is acceptable. Whiskers serve a specific function and it is preferred that they not be trimmed. Shaving or barbering of the head, neck or body coat must be severely penalized.

The Flat-Coated Retriever

"is a versatile family companion hunting retriever with a happy and active demeanor, intelligent expression, and clean lines."

DOG GROOMING SIMPLIFIED: STRAIGHT TO THE POINT

SETTER-LIKE PATTERN LINES

Recommended Blade Lengths, Snap-On Comb Lengths and Techniques **Bold Print** = Preferred Choices for Pet Trims							
10 15					thinning shears scissor	leave natural thinning shears carding	thinning shears carding

Tip To Remember:

After grooming the flat-coated breeds, apply mink oil to a horse-hair glove or hound glove. Run the glove over the dog from the head to tail and continue over the rib cage. This will put a beautiful sheen on the dog, giving the coat a mirror finish.

Golden Retriever

The Golden Retriever is a Sporting dog that originated in Scotland. The breed was developed over the years into the Golden that we know today and was registered in England in the early 1900s. It was bred to retrieve game on land and in the water. The golden-colored coat is the hallmark of the Golden Retriever.

This coat should be maintained using carding, shedding and thinning shear techniques. The ears and feet should be free of fringe and should be neatened with thinning shears.

Carding techniques may be used on the front of the front legs, top of skull and front of hocks to remove fuzzy undercoat.

The furnishings may be trimmed to present the proper profile of the breed. The length of furnishings may vary according to the preference of the pet owner.

See important information on "Double-Coated Breeds" on page 17.

Key points to remember when grooming the Golden Retriever according to the breed standard:

The Golden Retriever is slightly longer than it is tall. The topline is level from the withers to a slightly sloping croup.

The neck is of medium length transitioning into well-laid-back shoulder blades. The tail is thick at the base, and the tip should not reach below the level of the hock.

The shoulder blade and upper arm are of equal length forming a 90-degree angle that sets the elbow under the withers. The front legs are straight. The feet are round and compact and should be neatly trimmed.

The stifles are well bent with strong thighs. The hocks are short and perpendicular to the ground.

The Golden Retriever is a double-coated breed. It should have a dense water-repellent undercoat. The ruff, chest, back of front legs, underbelly, back of thighs and underside of tail should have moderate furnishings. The natural appearance of this breed should be kept in mind, as a Golden should not appear over-groomed.

The Golden Retriever

"is a symmetrical, powerful, active dog, sound and well put together, not clumsy nor long in the leg, displaying a kindly expression and possessing a personality that is eager, alert and self-confident."

Available on DVD: "The Golden Retriever"

Dog Grooming Simplified: Straight To The Point

SETTER-LIKE PATTERN LINES

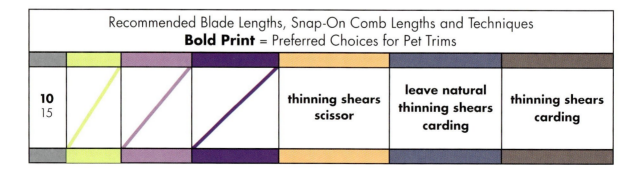

				Recommended Blade Lengths, Snap-On Comb Lengths and Techniques **Bold Print** = Preferred Choices for Pet Trims		
10 15				thinning shears scissor	leave natural thinning shears carding	thinning shears carding

Tip To Remember:

When shedding double-coated breeds, be sure to brush the tail thoroughly, as most breeds have an abundant amount of undercoat throughout the tail. The rear furnishings also tend to have excess undercoat. When brushing the rear, be careful not to brush and scrape the skin, as this area is extremely sensitive.

GREAT PYRENEES

The Great Pyrenees is a Working breed that originated in Asia or Siberia and followed the migration to Europe. Its keen sight and ability to scent were invaluable for the shepherd guarding the farm from wolves and bears. It was a true guardian and devoted pet and companion.

This coat should be maintained using shedding and thinning shear techniques.

The furnishings may be trimmed to present the proper profile of the breed. The length of furnishings may vary according to the preference of the pet owner.

Carding techniques may be used on the front of the front legs and front of hocks to remove fuzzy undercoat.

See important information on "Double-Coated Breeds" on page 17.

Key points to remember when grooming the Great Pyrenees according to the breed standard:

The topline is level, slightly sloping to a low-set tail. The tail is well feathered and is carried over the back. The ribs are well sprung. The neck is strong and muscular. The shoulders are well laid back and are approximately the same length as the upper arm, which allows the elbows to fall in line with the withers.

The front legs are straight. The feet are round with well-arched toes. The rear legs are muscular with well-bent stifles.

The head is wedge-shaped with a slightly rounded skull. The ears are small to medium in size and are V-shaped with rounded tips. The ears are set at the level of the eyes. The muzzle and the skull are of equal lengths.

The Great Pyrenees has a weather-resistant double-coat. It consists of a longer flat outer coat that is coarse in texture with a dense fine undercoat. This breed carries a heavier coat around the neck and shoulders forming a ruff or mane.

The Great Pyrenees

"conveys the distinct impression of elegance and unsurpassed beauty combined with great overall size and majesty. He possesses a keen intelligence and a kindly, while regal, expression."

DOG GROOMING SIMPLIFIED: STRAIGHT TO THE POINT

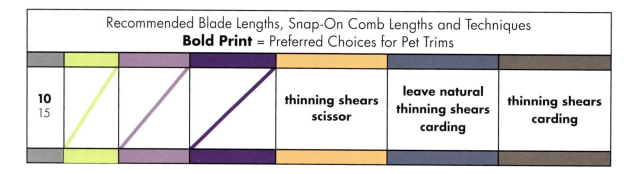

TIP TO REMEMBER:

Always bathe a dog in lukewarm to cool water. The normal body temperature for dogs is 101-102.5° whereas the normal body temperature for humans is 98.6°. Dogs will heat up very quickly if bathed in water that is too warm. Caution should also be taken when using cage dryers and/or heated dryers. Dogs can heat up very quickly under dryers and should never be left unattended.

Japanese Chin

The Japanese Chin is a Toy breed that originated in China. They were bred primarily as companions for the Chinese aristocracy. The Japanese Chins were kept by the noble people and were often given as gifts to diplomats on special occasions.

This coat should be maintained using carding, shedding and thinning shear techniques.

The feet may be trimmed neatly with thinning shears. The furnishings may be trimmed to present the proper profile of the breed. The length of furnishings may vary according to the preference of the pet owner.

Carding techniques may be used on the front of the front legs and front of hocks to remove fuzzy undercoat.

See important information on "Carding" on page 30 and "Double-Coated Breeds" on page 17.

Quoted in part with permission from the Japanese Chin Club of America, Approved October 11, 2011:

Length between the sternum and the buttock is equal to the height at the withers. Topline – level.

Neck – moderate in length and thickness. Well set on the shoulders enabling the dog to carry its head up proudly. Body – square, moderately wide in the chest with rounded ribs. Depth of rib extends to the elbow. Tail – set on high, carried arched up over the back and flowing to either side of the body.

Forequarters: Legs – straight, and fine boned, with the elbows set close to the body. Feet – hare-shaped with feathering on the ends of the toes in the mature dog.

Hindquarters: Legs – straight as viewed from the rear and fine boned. Moderate bend of stifle.

The distinctive Oriental expression is characterized by the large broad head, large wide-set eyes, short broad muzzle, ear feathering, and the evenly patterned facial markings. A small amount of white showing in the inner corners of the eyes is a breed characteristic that gives the dog a look of astonishment. Ears – hanging, small, V-shaped, wide apart, set slightly below the crown of the skull. The ears are well feathered and fit into the rounded contour of the head. Skull – large, broad, slightly rounded between the ears but not domed. Forehead is prominent, rounding toward the nose. Stop – deep. Muzzle – short and broad with well-cushioned cheeks and rounded upper lips that cover the teeth. Nose – very short with wide, open nostrils. Set on a level with the middle of the eyes and upturned.

Coat: Abundant, straight, single, and silky. Has a resilient texture and a tendency to stand out from the body, especially on neck, shoulders, and chest areas where the hair forms a thick mane or ruff. The tail is profusely coated and forms a plume. The rump area is heavily coated and forms culottes or pants. The head and muzzle are covered with short hair except for the heavily feathered ears. The forelegs have short hair blending into profuse feathering on the backs of the legs. The rear legs have the previously described culottes, and in mature dogs, light feathering from hock joint to the foot.

The Japanese Chin

"is a small, well balanced, lively, aristocratic toy dog with a distinctive Oriental expression. It is light and stylish in action."

Dog Grooming Simplified: Straight To The Point

SETTER-LIKE PATTERN LINES

Recommended Blade Lengths, Snap-On Comb Lengths and Techniques **Bold Print** = Preferred Choices for Pet Trims							
10 15				thinning shears scissor	leave natural thinning shears carding	thinning shears carding	

166

Tip To Remember:

Many natural breeds just require shedding and carding techniques to neaten their appearance. Thinning shears can be used to neaten the longer stray hairs. Trim around the anus for cleanliness using thinning shears or a 10 blade. While clipping around the anus, never clip over the sensitive opening.

Keeshond

The Keeshond is a Non-Sporting breed that originated in Holland. It was used as a watchdog on riverboats, barges and farms and was often referred to as the "barge dog". The Keeshond is known for the unique markings around the eyes resembling "spectacles".

This coat should be maintained using shedding and thinning shear techniques.

The furnishings may be trimmed to present the proper profile of the breed. The length of furnishings may vary according to the preference of the pet owner.

Carding techniques may be used on the front of the front legs and front of hocks to remove fuzzy undercoat.

See important information on "Double-Coated Breeds" on page 17.

Key points to remember when grooming the Keeshond according to the breed standard:

The Keeshond carries a level topline. The body is compact with a slight tuck-up.

The shoulders are well laid back and are approximately the same length as the upper arm, which sets the elbows in line with the withers. The front legs are straight with round tight feet that appear cat-like.

The rear legs are well angulated and muscular with moderately bent stifles. The rear legs are parallel when viewed from the rear. The hocks are perpendicular to the ground.

The head is wedge-shaped with a definite stop. The ears are small and triangular in shape. They are set high on the head and carried erect.

The Keeshond has a double-coat. The body carries a heavy, long, straight harsh coat with a thick undercoat. The head, muzzle, skull and ears are covered with short, smooth soft hair. The neck and shoulders carry a mane, which is heavier in males.

The Keeshond should be shown as natural as possible with only minimal trimming of the feet and hocks.

The Keeshond

"(pronounced kayz-hawnd) is a natural, handsome dog of well-balanced, short-coupled body, attracting attention not only by his coloration, alert carriage, and intelligent expression, but also by his stand-off coat, his richly plumed tail well curled over his back, his foxlike expression, and his small pointed ears."

Dog Grooming Simplified: Straight To The Point

SETTER-LIKE PATTERN LINES

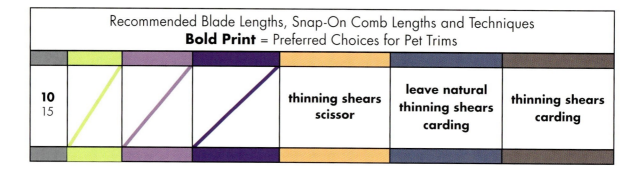

| | | | | thinning shears scissor | leave natural thinning shears carding | thinning shears carding |

10
15

Tip To Remember:

Toenails should be trimmed as short as possible on a regular basis. While trimming nails, angle the nail trimmer up so the nail is cut at a slight angle from the base of the nail to the top of the nail. This will stretch the life of the nail trim.

Longhaired Chihuahua

The Chihuahua is a Toy breed that originated in Mexico. It was described as a popular pet and a religious necessity. It was believed that the Chihuahua could guide the human soul to its ultimate destination, fighting off evil spirits.

This coat should be maintained using carding, shedding and thinning shear techniques.

The feet may be trimmed neatly with thinning shears. The furnishings may be trimmed to present the proper profile of the breed. The length of furnishings may vary according to the preference of the pet owner.

See important information on "Double-Coated Breeds" on page 17 and "Carding" on page 30.

Quoted in part with permission from the Chihuahua Club of America, Inc., Approved August 12, 2008:

Proportion: The body is off-square; hence, slightly longer when measured from point of shoulder to point of buttocks, than height at the withers.

Topline: Level. Tail – Moderately long, carried sickle either up or out, or in a loop over the back with tip just touching the back.

Neck: Slightly arched, gracefully sloping into lean shoulders. Ribs rounded and well sprung (but not too much "barrel-shaped").

Shoulders: Lean, sloping into a slightly broadening support above straight forelegs that set well under, giving free movement at the elbows. Shoulders should be well up, giving balance and soundness, sloping into a level back (never down or low). Feet – A small, dainty foot with toes well split up but not spread, pads cushioned.

Hindquarters: Muscular, with hocks well apart, neither out nor in, well let down, firm and sturdy.

A well rounded "apple dome" skull, with or without molera. Ears – Large, erect type ears, held more upright when alert, but flaring to the sides at a 45 degree angle when in repose, giving breadth between the ears. Stop – Well defined. When viewed in profile, it forms a near 90 degree angle where muzzle joins skull. Muzzle – Moderately short, slightly pointed. Cheeks and jaws lean.

Coat: In Long Coats, the coat should be of a soft texture, either flat or slightly wavy, with undercoat preferred. Ears – Fringed. Tail – Full and long (as a plume). Feathering on feet and legs, pants on hind legs and large ruff on the neck desired and preferred.

The Chihuahua

"A graceful, alert, swift-moving compact little dog with saucy expression, and with terrier-like qualities of temperament."

Dog Grooming Simplified: Straight To The Point

SETTER-LIKE PATTERN LINES

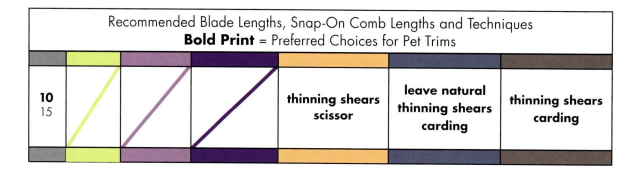

10 15				thinning shears scissor	leave natural thinning shears carding	thinning shears carding	

Recommended Blade Lengths, Snap-On Comb Lengths and Techniques
Bold Print = Preferred Choices for Pet Trims

TIP TO REMEMBER:

The whiskers of the more natural breeds, like the Longhaired Chihuahua and Golden Retriever for example, should not be removed unless requested by the pet owner. To remove the whiskers a 10 blade can be used by lightly skimming over the muzzle being careful not to clip the actual coat.

Newfoundland

The Newfoundland is a Working breed that originated in Newfoundland. They were used to pull nets for the fisherman and to haul wood from the forest. They are known for their heavy coats that protect them from the icy waters. The Newfoundland excels at long-distance swimming and has a natural lifesaving instinct. For generations the Newfoundland has taken on the role of being the children's protector and playmate.

This coat should be maintained using shedding and thinning shear techniques.

The furnishings may be trimmed to present the proper profile of the breed. The length of furnishings may vary according to the preference of the pet owner.

The ears should be trimmed with thinning shears following the shape of the ear leather.

The feet should be trimmed with thinning shears so they appear cat-like. Carding techniques may be used on the front of the front legs and front of hocks to remove fuzzy undercoat.

See important information on "Carding" on page 30 and "Double-Coated Breeds" on page 17.

Quoted in part with permission from the Newfoundland Club of America, Inc., Approved May 8, 1990:

The neck is strong and well set on the shoulders and is long enough for proud head carriage. The back is strong, broad, and muscular and is level from just behind the withers to the croup. The chest is full and deep with the brisket reaching at least down to the elbows. Ribs are well sprung. The flank is deep. The croup is broad and slopes slightly. Tail-set follows the natural line of the croup. The tail is broad at the base and strong. It has no kinks, and the distal bone reaches to the hock.

Shoulders are muscular and well laid back. Elbows lie directly below the highest point of the withers. Forelegs are muscular, heavily boned, straight, and parallel to each other, and the elbows point directly to the rear. The distance from elbow to ground equals about half the dog's height. Feet are proportionate to the body in size, webbed, and cat foot in type.

The rear assembly is powerful, muscular, and heavily boned. Viewed from the rear, the legs are straight and parallel. Viewed from the side, the thighs are broad and fairly long. Stifles and hocks are well bent and the line from hock to ground is perpendicular. Hocks are well let down.

The head is massive, with a broad skull, slightly arched crown, and strongly developed occipital bone. Cheeks are well developed. Ears are relatively small and triangular with rounded tips. They are set on the skull level with, or slightly above, the brow and lie close to the head.

The adult Newfoundland has a flat, water-resistant, double coat that tends to fall back into place when rubbed against the nap. The outer coat is coarse, moderately long, and full, either straight or with a wave. The undercoat is soft and dense, although it is often less dense during the summer months or in warmer climates. Hair on the face and muzzle is short and fine. The backs of the legs are feathered all the way down. The tail is covered with long dense hair. Excess hair may be trimmed for neatness.

The Newfoundland

"is a sweet-dispositioned dog that acts neither dull nor ill-tempered. He is a devoted companion. A multipurpose dog, at home on land and in water, the Newfoundland is capable of draft work and possesses natural lifesaving abilities."

DOG GROOMING SIMPLIFIED: STRAIGHT TO THE POINT

SETTER-LIKE PATTERN LINES

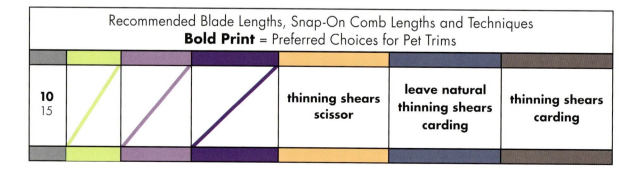

10 15				thinning shears scissor	leave natural thinning shears carding	thinning shears carding

Tip To Remember:

Double-coated breeds can be very dense and thick with undercoat. A high quality slicker brush is recommended to handle this coat type. Thick coats can take a toll on slicker brushes. Check brushes regularly to make sure the teeth are not bending. Bent teeth will scratch the skin and could cause brush burn.

Papillon

The Papillon is a Toy breed that originated in Italy. It was known as the Dwarf Spaniel back in the sixteenth century. The Dwarf Spaniel had drop ears; however, over time came the more erect ears which are fringed, resembling the wings of a butterfly. The Dwarf Spaniel was then given the name Papillon, meaning "butterfly" in French. The drop-eared dogs are referred to as Phalenes and are born in the same litter as the Papillon. Both ear types are acceptable in the AKC show ring.

This coat should be maintained using carding, shedding and thinning shear techniques. The ears should never be trimmed unless the pet owner desires this. The feet may be trimmed neatly with thinning shears. Carding techniques may be used on the front of the front legs and front of hocks to remove fuzzy undercoat.

The furnishings may be trimmed shorter if requested by the pet owner.

See important information on "Double-Coated Breeds" on page 17 and "Carding" on page 30.

Quoted in part with permission from the Papillon Club of America, Inc., Approved June 10, 1991:

Proportion: Body must be slightly longer than the height at withers.

Ears of the erect type are carried obliquely and move like the spread wings of a butterfly. When alert, each ear forms an angle of approximately 45 degrees to the head.

Neck of medium length. Topline – The backline is straight and level. Body – The chest is of medium depth with ribs well sprung. The belly is tucked up. Tail long, set high and carried well arched over the body. The tail is covered with a long, flowing plume. The plume may hang to either side of the body.

Forequarters: Shoulders well developed and laid back to allow freedom of movement. Forelegs slender, fine-boned and must be straight. Feet thin and elongated (hare-like), pointing neither in nor out.

Hindquarters: Well developed and well angulated. The hind legs are slender, fine-boned, and parallel when viewed from behind. Hocks inclined neither in nor out.

Skull – The head is small. The skull is of medium width and slightly rounded between the ears. A well-defined stop is formed where the muzzle joins the skull. Muzzle – The muzzle is fine, abruptly thinner than the head, tapering to the nose. The length of the muzzle from the tip of the nose to stop is approximately one-third the length of the head from tip of nose to occiput. Nose – black, small, rounded and slightly flat on top.

Coat: Abundant, long, fine, silky, flowing, straight with resilient quality, flat on back and sides of body. A profuse frill on chest. Hair short and close on skull, muzzle, front of forelegs, and from hind feet to hocks. Ears well fringed. Backs of the forelegs are covered with feathers diminishing to the pasterns. Hind legs are covered to the hocks with abundant breeches (culottes). Tail is covered with a long, flowing plume. Hair on feet is short, but fine tufts may appear over toes and grow beyond them, forming a point.

The Papillon

"is a small, friendly, elegant toy dog of fine-boned structure, light, dainty and of lively action; distinguished from other breeds by its beautiful butterfly-like ears."

Dog Grooming Simplified: Straight To The Point

SETTER-LIKE PATTERN LINES

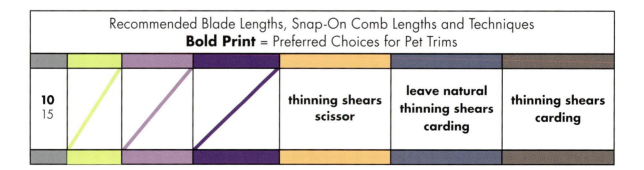

Tip To Remember:

Undercoat is defined as the short, soft, dense hair that supports the outer coat or guard hair. The term "carding" describes the technique of removing undercoat from the follicles with the use of a stripping knife or shedding rake (Coat King). Undercoat has its purpose; however, when it becomes excessive it can cause skin and coat issues. Keeping undercoat at bay by using carding and shedding techniques is beneficial to the skin and coat. Carding techniques work best on flat coats. Shedding techniques are recommended for dense double-coated breeds.

Pomeranian

The Pomeranian is a Toy breed that originated in Germany. Originally weighing close to thirty pounds, the Pomeranian was used for herding sheep. Today's Pomeranian can weigh anywhere from three to seven pounds. This is a big dog in a little body with a natural instinct to protect.

This coat should be maintained using shedding and thinning shear techniques.

The feet may be trimmed with thinning shears for a neat appearance. The furnishings may be trimmed to present the proper profile of the breed. The length of furnishings may vary according to the preference of the pet owner. Carding techniques may be used on the front of the front legs and front of hocks to remove fuzzy undercoat.

See important information on "Carding" on page 30 and "Double-Coated Breeds" on page 17.

Quoted in part with permission from the American Pomeranian Club, Inc., Approved July 12, 2011:

Neck – set well into the shoulders with sufficient length to allow the head to be carried proud and high. Topline – level from withers to croup. Body – compact and well-ribbed. Chest – oval tapered extending to the point of elbows with a pronounced prosternum. Back – short-coupled, straight and strong. Loin – short with slight tuck-up. Tail – heavily plumed, set high and lies flat and straight on the back.

Shoulders well laid back. Shoulder blade and upper arm length are equal. Legs when viewed from the front are moderately spaced, straight and parallel to each other, set well behind the forechest. Height from withers to elbows approximately equals height from ground to elbow. Shoulders and legs are moderately muscled. Feet – round, tight, appearing cat-like, well-arched, compact.

Hindquarters – angulation balances that of the forequarters. Buttocks are well behind the set of the tail. Thighs – moderately muscled. Upper thigh and lower leg length are equal. Stifles – strong, moderately bent and clearly defined. Legs when viewed from the rear straight and parallel to each other. Hocks when viewed from the side are perpendicular to the ground and strong.

Head – in balance with the body, when viewed from above, broad at the back tapering to the nose to form a wedge. Ears – small, mounted high and carried erect. Skull – closed, slightly round but not domed. Stop – well pronounced. Muzzle rather short, straight, free of lippiness, neither coarse nor snipey. Ratio of length of muzzle to skull is 1/3 to 2/3.

The Pomeranian is a double-coated breed. The body should be well covered with a short, dense undercoat with long harsh-textured guard hair growing through, forming the longer abundant outer coat which stands off from the body. The coat should form a ruff around the neck, framing the head, extending over the shoulders and chest. Head and leg coat is tightly packed and shorter in length than that of the body. Forelegs are well-feathered. Thighs and hind legs are heavily coated to the hock forming a skirt. Tail is profusely covered with long, harsh spreading straight hair forming a plume.

The Pomeranian

"is alert in character, exhibits intelligence in expression, is buoyant in deportment, and is inquisitive by nature. The Pomeranian is cocky, commanding, and animated as he gaits. He is sound in composition and action."

Dog Grooming Simplified: Straight To The Point

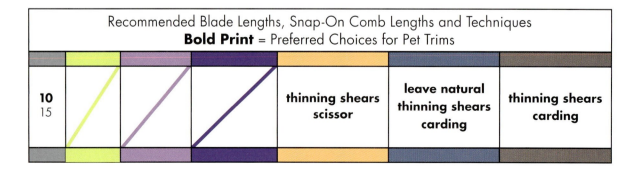

Tip To Remember:

Many pet owners love the look of those cute Pomeranians that have been shaved leaving just a little round head. It is important to know that once double-coated breeds are shaved, "post-clippering alopecia" can be triggered. This disorder is most prevalent in the Pomeranian, Chow Chow, German Shepherd Dog, Samoyed, Sheltie, Collie and Keeshond although it can happen in any heavy double-coated breed. This is often seen several weeks after the pet has been shaved as new growth is starting to appear. The coat will grow in leaving patchy areas of baldness. Canine alopecia has been linked to certain health issues including trauma to the skin, yet it is uncertain why some breeds that are shaved develop post-clippering alopecia and others do not. The dogs that do develop this disorder after being shaved may never grow their full coat back again.

Samoyed

The Samoyed is a Working breed that originated in Siberia. They were bred for herding and hunting and to haul sleds. They were also great guard dogs and were cherished by the Samoyed people. They are known for their black lips and the famous "Samoyed smile".

This coat should be maintained using shedding and thinning shear techniques.

The feet may be trimmed neatly with thinning shears. The furnishings may be trimmed shorter if requested by the pet owner. Carding techniques may be used on the front of the front legs and front of hocks to remove fuzzy undercoat.

See important information on "Double-Coated Breeds" on page 17 and "Carding" on page 30.

Key points to remember when grooming the Samoyed according to the breed standard:

The Samoyed is slightly longer than it is tall and is considered "just off square". The front legs are straight with large, long hare feet. The shoulders are well laid back with the elbows falling in line with the withers. The topline is level.

The rear legs show a well-developed thigh and a well-bent stifle. The legs should appear parallel when viewed from the rear. The hocks should appear perpendicular to the ground.

The skull has a wedge-shaped appearance. The muzzle should taper as it reaches the nose. The whiskers should not be removed. The ears are erect and triangular in shape with rounded tips.

The Samoyed has a double-coat that consists of a soft, thick undercoat and a longer, harsh outer coat. This coat is weather resistant and has a silver sheen. Samoyeds have a ruff of coat around the neck and shoulders.

The Samoyed

"being essentially a working dog, should present a picture of beauty, alertness and strength, with agility, dignity and grace. As his work lies in cold climates, his coat should be heavy and weather-resistant, well groomed, and of good quality rather than quantity. The male carries more of a "ruff" than the female."

Dog Grooming Simplified: Straight To The Point

SETTER-LIKE PATTERN LINES

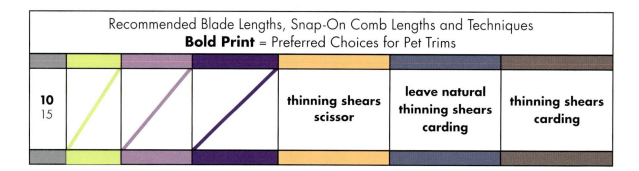

				thinning shears scissor	leave natural thinning shears carding	thinning shears carding
10 15						

Tip To Remember:

Oftentimes the heavy double-coated breeds will develop matted hair behind their ears. These mats are often very tight to the skin. It is always best to shave this area out using a 10 blade as opposed to using scissors or other dematting tools. The skin behind the ears is very thin and can be easily cut or torn when using the wrong tools. Clipping is the safest technique to remove these mats.

Shetland Sheepdog

The Shetland Sheepdog, commonly referred to as the "Sheltie", originated in the Shetland Islands. This is a Herding breed who worked the farm and acted as a guard dog. It is the nature of the breed to be extremely obedient, which makes them great agility and obedience competition dogs.

This coat should be maintained using shedding and thinning shear techniques.

The feet should be trimmed neatly with thinning shears.

The furnishings may be trimmed to present the proper profile of the breed. The length of furnishings may vary according to the preference of the pet owner.

Carding techniques may be used on the front of the front legs and front of hocks to remove fuzzy undercoat.

See important information on "Double-Coated Breeds" on page 17.

Quoted in part with permission from the American Shetland Sheepdog Association, Approved May 12, 1959, Reformatted July 18, 1990:

The Shetland Sheepdog is a small, alert, rough-coated, longhaired working dog. In overall appearance, the body should appear moderately long as measured from shoulder joint to ischium (rearmost extremity of the pelvic bone). Back should be level and strongly muscled.

The upper arm should join the shoulder blade at as nearly as possible a right angle. Elbow joint should be equidistant from the ground and from the withers. Forelegs straight viewed from all angles, muscular and clean, and of strong bone. Feet should be oval and compact with the toes well arched and fitting tightly together.

The thigh should be broad and muscular. Stifle bones join the thighbone and should be distinctly angled at the stifle joint. The hock (metatarsus) should be short and straight viewed from all angles.

The head should be refined and its shape, when viewed from top or side, should be a long, blunt wedge tapering slightly from ears to nose. Top of skull should be flat, showing no prominence at nuchal crest (the top of the occiput). Cheeks should be flat and should merge smoothly into a well-rounded muzzle. Skull and muzzle should be of equal length, balance point being inner corner of eye. In profile the top line of skull should parallel the top line of muzzle, but on a higher plane due to the presence of a slight but definite stop.

Coat: The coat should be double, the outer coat consisting of long, straight, harsh hair; the undercoat short, furry, and so dense as to give the entire coat its "standoff" quality. The hair on face, tips of ears and feet should be smooth. Mane and frill should be abundant, and particularly impressive in males. The forelegs well feathered, the hind legs heavily so, but smooth below the hock joint. Hair on tail profuse.

The Shetland Sheepdog

"is a small, alert, rough-coated, longhaired working dog. The Shetland Sheepdog is intensely loyal, affectionate, and responsive to his owner."

DOG GROOMING SIMPLIFIED: STRAIGHT TO THE POINT

SETTER-LIKE PATTERN LINES

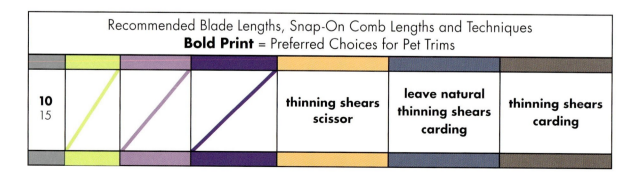

10 15				thinning shears scissor	leave natural thinning shears carding	thinning shears carding

Recommended Blade Lengths, Snap-On Comb Lengths and Techniques
Bold Print = Preferred Choices for Pet Trims

Tip To Remember:

Many double-coated breeds have a very thick mane around their neck. This area can become packed with undercoat. Line brush this area to ensure the entire mane has been brushed out. Use a wide-tooth comb and comb the area thoroughly from the skin out. The entire dog should be combed after the shedding process has been completed. If the comb glides through the coat with ease the undercoat has been successfully removed.

Tibetan Spaniel

The Tibetan Spaniel is registered in the Non-Sporting group and originated in Tibet. They were companion dogs and were commonly referred to as "little lions" by their owners. They would sit on monastery walls and act as guard dogs.

The Tibetan Spaniel is shown in a very natural state.

This coat should be maintained using carding and shedding techniques. Light thinning shear techniques may be done on pet trims.

The furnishings may be trimmed to present the proper profile of the breed. The length of furnishings may vary according to the preference of the pet owner.

See important information on "Carding" on page 30.

Key points to remember when grooming the Tibetan Spaniel according to the breed standard:

The Tibetan Spaniel is slightly longer than it is tall with a level topline with a high tail-set. The tail is plumed and carried over the back when moving.

The shoulders are well laid back. The front legs are slightly bowed and fall beneath the withers. The feet are small and hare-like. The rear legs are moderately angulated. The hocks are perpendicular to the ground.

The ears are well feathered and are set high. The skull is domed.

The Tibetan Spaniel has a double-coat with a silky texture. It is smooth on the face and the front of the legs. The furnishings are well feathered. The neck has a "mane" or "shawl" of longer hair. The feet should be feathered. However, for pet trims they may be neatened with thinning shears for a natural appearance.

The Tibetan Spaniel

"Should be small, active and alert. The outline should give a well balanced appearance, slightly longer in body than the height at withers."

DOG GROOMING SIMPLIFIED: STRAIGHT TO THE POINT

SETTER-LIKE PATTERN LINES

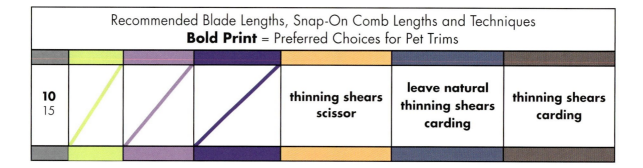

10 15				thinning shears scissor	leave natural thinning shears carding	thinning shears carding

Recommended Blade Lengths, Snap-On Comb Lengths and Techniques
Bold Print = Preferred Choices for Pet Trims

Tip To Remember:

Many breeds have short natural ears like the Tibetan Spaniel. A fine detail thinning shear may be used to neaten the edge of the ear leathers for a neat appearance. This type of shear will leave the ear looking very natural.

Tip To Remember:

Distinct patterns are those that are set fairly tight. However, several breeds that fall under this pattern group are left more natural, yet the pattern is set in the same manner. Recommended tools and techniques for these more natural breeds will be noted.

Terrier-Like Pattern Lines

Distinct in Nature
Pattern Placement Diagrams

- Affenpinscher
- Airedale Terrier
- Brussels Griffon
- Cesky Terrier
- Dandie Dinmont Terrier
- Giant Schnauzer
- Glen of Imaal Terrier
- Irish Terrier
- Lakeland Terrier
- Miniature Schnauzer
- Otterhound
- Petit Basset Griffon Vendeen
- Spinone Italiano
- Welsh Terrier
- Wirehaired Pointing Griffon
- Wire Fox Terrier

Subtle in Nature
Pattern Placement Diagrams

- Cairn Terrier
- Norfolk Terrier
- Norwich Terrier
- Scottish Terrier
- Sealyham Terrier
- West Highland White Terrier

TERRIER-LIKE PATTERN LINES
Distinct in Nature

The pattern lines of the Wire Fox Terrier, as an example, are the same general pattern lines of many other breeds. For easy reference we will call this pattern "Terrier-Like". This pattern can be of a distinct nature or a subtle nature. In this section we will discuss breeds that fall under Terrier-Like patterns of a Distinct nature.

Distinct patterns are those that are set fairly tight. However, several breeds that fall under this pattern group are left more natural, yet the pattern is set in the same manner. Recommended tools and techniques for these more natural breeds will be noted.

Many of these breeds should be hand stripped and carded for show. However, on pet trims these patterns can be set with blades ranging from 4F, 5F to 7F. The longer the blade the more natural and true to the breed profile the trim will look. This section describes setting patterns on pet trims with the use of various blade lengths. A Coat King may also be used on the back coat to help remove undercoat and help preserve the color and texture of the coat.

You will see from this example that the body on this show dog is hand stripped tight from the back of the skull (occiput) to the tail. The pattern is set from the topline and falls over the lower part of the ribcage just below the elbow line. The line slightly rises from below the elbow to the loin. The pattern line should be well blended into the slightly longer furnishings of the underline showing no evident transition.

When clipping pet trims, skim off with the clipper to lightly blend the clipped area into the furnishings. Use thinning shears to blend the transition lines on pet trims to mimic the show look.

The length of coat of the underline will vary depending on the breed. Some breeds will only have enough length to create the proper outline as seen on the Wire Fox Terrier pictured, while others may have more of a skirt. However, the body patterns are still the same.

The shoulder and upper arm are set tighter than the body. The pattern should be set to where the upper arm and lower arm meet (at the elbow line).

The rear thigh muscle is set tight to show the muscle tone, leaving furnishings on the front of the back leg. The inner thigh area will have the same pattern as the outside thigh.

It is recommended to use a stripping knife after clipping these breeds to remove excess undercoat, which will help promote healthy skin and coat. Using a stripping knife to card the coat will also allow the coat to lie down and look more natural even though the back coat is clipped.

Clipping Terrier coats causes the coat to lighten in color and soften in texture. Depending on the breed, using carding techniques after clipping will help to keep some texture and color of certain coats that would normally be lost by clipping alone.

The length of the furnishings should not be profuse, and should be scissored to create the Terrier-Like outline as above. The front legs are scissored into columns. When achieving a column look, the coat on the back of the front leg is set shorter, while the coat on the front of the front leg is left longer to create the column.

Many of the breeds in this pattern group may not carry heavy furnishings on the front legs; however, a column-like appearance should be strived for. The furnishings should be trimmed keeping this outline in mind. The length of the furnishings may vary based on the preference of the pet owner.

The tail styles will vary from breed to breed that fall under Terrier-Like patterns. Some breeds, like the Lakeland, have a docked tail, where other breeds, like the Westie, have a carrot tail. See "Tail Styles" on page 447 for instructions on grooming various tail styles.

The entire throat is clipped. The front pattern starts with the underjaw. The line is set from behind the canine tooth (in breeds with goatees) or at the back of the lower lip or whisker nodule (in breeds with beards) and is set to the breastbone. The throat line continues to the base of the ear creating a U-like pattern to the breastbone. This can be done using a 7F or 10 blade based on the coat density and sensitivity of the skin. These blades may also be used against the lay of coat (from the breastbone up towards the head), which will give a shorter appearance than using them with the lay of coat.

The throat is defined by a natural cowlick in the hair that runs from the base of the ear to the breastbone.

When setting the front of these breeds imagine a W pattern (see diagram on page 208). The upper arm should be set tight to where it joins the lower arm, using a 7F or 5F blade.

Use thinning shears to blend the clipper work into the chest furnishings that fall below the breastbone. The chest furnishings cover the prosternum (lower chest).

The sides of the neck, shoulder and upper arm are set tight using one to two blade lengths longer than what was used on the throat, preferably a 5F or 7F. Clip under the ear, clipping down the side of the neck to where the upper arm and lower arm join at the elbow line.

When using different blade lengths, i.e., 7F or 10 on the throat, 7F or 5F on the shoulders and 4F or 5F on body pattern, the coat should blend nicely together. Use thinning shears to enhance a well-blended trim.

The thigh should be well defined to show the muscle. This can be done by using a blade which is one blade length longer than what was used on the shoulder. This area can also be clipped with the same blade that was used on the body; however, thinning shears should then be used to define the muscle to the desired length and to blend into the furnishings. When clipping the thigh, skim off with the clipper to lightly blend the clipped thigh into the furnishings of the stifle.

The bend of the stifle should be trimmed to fall approximately in line with the croup for proper balance. The furnishings should not be profuse, having just enough coat to create the proper bend of the stifle.

The hocks should be set perpendicular to the ground.

The feet should be trimmed tight around the base.

Clip around the anus and just slightly up the back of the base of the tail with a 10 blade.

The entire rear should be set very tight using 7F or 5F blades. There is a natural part directly under the anus where the coat cowlicks, similar to a "mustache". Clip or use thinning shears to set this area tight.

A 10 or 7F blade may be used on the inside of the thigh. Use thinning shears, a 4F or a 5F blade to accentuate the rear angulation, setting the back of the leg tight to the bend. The entire rear should be set tight as pictured on this hand stripped show dog.

The furnishings on the inside of the back legs should create parallel lines.

When setting the inside parallel lines of the back legs, use the inside stifle coat to help create the parallel line.

TERRIER-LIKE PATTERN LINES

Pattern Placement Diagrams

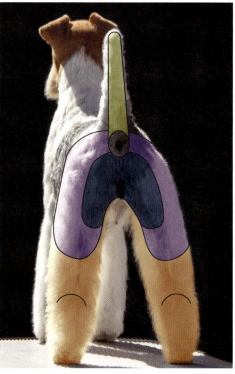

Recommended Blade Lengths, Snap-On Comb Lengths and Techniques **Bold Print** = Preferred Choices for Pet Trims							
10 15	**10** 7F	**7F** 5F carding	7F **5F** 4F carding	thinning shears scissor	**7F**		

208

TERRIER-LIKE PATTERN LINES
Distinct in Nature
Common Breeds

The following are common breeds that have Distinct Terrier-Like pattern lines. Minor deviations from the described pattern as well as recommended tools and techniques will be noted for each breed. Important breed standard information will be quoted in part from participating breed clubs. When grooming these breeds, refer back to the guidelines of setting this pattern on page 202.

Affenpinscher

The Affenpinscher is a Toy breed that originated in Central Europe. It was nicknamed the "little devil with a moustache" and was used on farms to hunt and kill vermin. Affenpinschers soon became companions in the home, where their "ratter" skills were used to keep the mice out. The monkey-like appearance is the hallmark of the breed.

This coat should be carded and hand stripped for show. If hand stripping is not desired by the pet owner, it is recommended to use a Coat King to remove the undercoat and dead coat following the pattern lines as described. This pattern is not as tight as with the other breeds in this group.

This breed should present a "shaggy" appearance. If clipping is preferred, various lengths of snap-on combs are recommended, preferably a #2, #1, or #0. Carding and thinning shear techniques should be done in addition to clipping for a natural appearance and to enhance the body lines.

The head of the Affenpinscher can be shaped by finger plucking (hand stripping) or by the use of thinning shears for pet trims. There is a natural cape on the back of the neck that should blend into the topline over the withers.

See important information on "Carding" on page 30 and "Hand Stripping" on page 32.

Quoted in part with permission from the Affenpinscher Club of America, Approved June 12, 2000:

The Affenpinscher is a balanced, wiry-haired Terrier-like toy dog whose intelligence and demeanor make it a good house pet. Originating in Germany, the name Affenpinscher means, "monkey-like Terrier."

Withers height is approximately the same as the length of the body from the point of the shoulder to point of the buttocks, giving a square appearance.

Topline straight and level. Tuck-up is slight. The back is short and level with a strong loin. The croup has just a perceptible curve. Tail may be docked or natural.

Front angulation is moderate. Shoulders–with moderate layback. The length of the shoulder blade and the upper arm are about equal. Elbows–close to the body. Front legs straight when viewed from any direction. Feet small, round, and compact.

Rear angulation is moderate to match the front. Hind legs straight when viewed from behind. From the side, hind legs are set under the body to maintain a square appearance. The length of the upper thigh and the second thigh are about equal with moderate bend to the stifle. Hocks–Moderately angulated.

The head is in proportion to the body, carried confidently with monkey-like facial expression. Ears–Cropped to a point, set high and standing erect; or natural, standing erect, semi-erect or dropped. All of the above types of ears, if symmetrical, are acceptable as long as the monkey-like expression is maintained. Skull–Round and domed, but not coarse. Stop–Well-defined. Muzzle–Short and narrowing slightly to a blunt nose. The length of the muzzle is approximately the same as the distance between the eyes.

Dense hair, rough, harsh, and about 1″ in length on the shoulders and body. May be shorter on the rear and tail. Head, neck, chest, stomach and legs have longer, less harsh coat. The mature Affenpinscher has a mane or cape of strong hair which blends into the back coat at the withers area. The longer hair on the head, eyebrows and beard stands off and frames the face to emphasize the monkey-like expression. Hair on the ears is cut very short.

A correct coat needs little grooming to blend the various lengths of hair to maintain a neat but shaggy appearance.

Recommended Blade Lengths, Snap-On Comb Lengths and Techniques **Bold Print** = Preferred Choices for Pet Trims							
10 15	4F **#2** #1	4F #2 **#1** carding	#2 #1 **#0** carding	thinning shears scissor			

Airedale Terrier

The Airedale Terrier is the largest of the Terrier breeds. They originated in the Valley of Aire in England. They have been called the "King of Terriers", being the hardiest of the Terrier breeds. They were used as messengers, rodent controllers and all-around hunters of bird and game. They were considered "the dog that could do it all".

This coat should be carded and hand stripped for show. If clipping is preferred, blades ranging from 4F, 5F to 7F are recommended. Carding and thinning shear techniques should be done in addition to clipping for a natural appearance. A Coat King may also be used on the back coat to help remove undercoat and help preserve the color and texture of the coat.

The Airedale Terrier has a rectangular-shaped head with small triangular eyebrows, beard and goatee. See "Rectangular Heads" on page 427 for instructions on grooming this head type.

See important information on "Carding" on page 30 and "Hand Stripping" on page 32.

Available on DVD: "The Airedale Terrier - Pet Trim"

Quoted in part with permission from the Airedale Terrier Club of America, Approved July 14, 1959:

Back should be short, strong and level. Ribs well sprung.

Shoulders long and sloping well into the back. Shoulder blades flat. From the front, chest deep but not broad. The depth of the chest should be approximately on a level with the elbows.

Forelegs should be perfectly straight, with plenty of muscle and bone. Elbows should be perpendicular to the body, working free of sides. Thighs should be long and powerful with muscular second thigh, stifles well bent, not turned either in or out, hocks well let down parallel with each other when viewed from behind. Feet should be small, round and compact.

Head should be well balanced with little apparent difference between the length of skull and foreface. Skull should be long and flat, not too broad between the ears and narrowing very slightly to the eyes. Stop hardly visible and cheeks level and free from fullness. Ears should be V-shaped with carriage rather to the side of the head, not pointing to the eyes, small but not out of proportion to the size of the dog. The topline of the folded ear should be above the level of the skull.

Coat: Should be hard, dense and wiry, lying straight and close, covering the dog well over the body and legs. Some of the hardest are crinkling or just slightly waved. At the base of the hard very stiff hair should be a shorter growth of softer hair termed the undercoat.

10 15	**10** 7F	**7F** 5F carding	7F **5F** **4F** carding	thinning shears scissor	**7F**		

Tip To Remember:

When clipping harsh-, wire- and broken-coat types, an undercoat rake or Coat King can be used prior to clipping to help improve coat texture and color which would otherwise be lost by clipping alone. Carding techniques can also be done after clipping.

Brussels Griffon

The Brussels Griffon is a Toy breed with a Terrier-like disposition. They originated in Belgium, where they were bred to catch rats in the stables. During the 1800s they were referred to as Griffons d'Ecurier (wire-coated stable dogs).

This coat is wiry and should be carded and hand stripped for show. This pattern is not as tight as the other breeds in this group. Due to the rough nature of the coat it carries sufficient length to determine the appropriate texture; however, the coat should not appear shaggy.

If clipping is preferred, blades ranging from 4F to 5F or various lengths of snap-on combs are recommended. Carding and thinning shear techniques should be done in addition to clipping for a natural appearance.

There are two coat varieties for the Brussels Griffon, a smooth coat and a rough coat.

See important information on "Carding" on page 30 and "Hand Stripping" on page 32.

Key points to remember when grooming the Brussels Griffon according to the breed standard:

The Brussels Griffon is a square dog, which means that it is as long as it is tall. It has a level topline transitioning into the high-set tail. The neck is of medium length with a short thick-set body. The ribs are well sprung.

The front legs are straight and parallel. The rear legs are muscular with well-bent stifles. The hocks are well let down and perpendicular to the ground.

The rough coat is wiry and dense. The smooth coat is tight, short and straight and should not have a wire texture.

TERRIER-LIKE PATTERN LINES

The Brussels is said to have an "almost human expression". The ears are set high and carried semi-erect. The ears are small and smooth and can be clipped with a 10 blade for pet trims. The skull is large and round. The forehead is domed with a deep stop. The top of the head is covered with short smooth coat and can be clipped with a 4F, 5F or 7F for pet trims. The coat should be slightly longer around the eyes, beard and cheeks.

TERRIER-LIKE PATTERN LINES

10 15	7F **5F** 4F	5F **4F** #2 carding	5F 4F **#2** carding	thinning shears scissor			

Recommended Blade Lengths, Snap-On Comb Lengths and Techniques
Bold Print = Preferred Choices for Pet Trims

Cesky Terrier

The Cesky Terrier (pronounced "chess – key") is a hunting Terrier that originated in the Czech Republic. It was developed to hunt in packs, for pheasant, ducks, rabbits, fox and wild boar. Unlike other short-legged Terriers, the Cesky has natural drop ears, a natural tail and a soft, silky long coat.

Photos courtesy of Devin Murphy

The Cesky Terrier pattern is clipped very tight using a variety of blades for the show ring.

The topline is clipped with a 5F blade creating a longer "saddle", which helps to create the proper topline. The saddle begins at the back of the occiput and ends in a V shape on the tail, creating a "rat" tail. See "Tail Styles" on page 451 for instructions on grooming this tail type.

The area of the rib cage, between the saddle and long furnishings of the underline, can be clipped with a 7F. This area should be well blended with the 5F work of the topline. The transition line into the long furnishings should be well blended with thinning shears. For pet trims the saddle and the rib cage can be clipped with the same blade if preferred.

The feet should be trimmed around the base without giving a beveled appearance.

A 10 or 7F blade can be used to set the front depending upon the sensitivity of the skin and density of the coat. This pattern is set lower than for the other breeds in this group. The front pattern is set to the lower part of the chest, where the upper and lower arm meet. The side of the neck is clipped over the shoulder and upper arm to meet this line with the same blade. Once the sides of the neck and front are clipped, the pattern will consist of a straight horizontal line across the lower chest. This line should be blended into the longer furnishings. A subtle U shape is clipped on the upper third portion of the outside of the front leg to accentuate the muscle of the upper leg.

The thigh is clipped with the same blade that was used to clip the shoulder, preferably a 10 or 7F blade.

The rear angulation is clipped tight using a 7F or 10 blade over the point of rump to just above the hock. The inner thigh is also clipped tight using a 10 blade. The inside of the rear legs should form a horsehoe shape. The hocks are parallel and perpendicular to the ground. The furnishings should be well blended into the clipped areas.

The Cesky has a full beard and a partial fall with small triangular eyebrows. The fall and brows start behind the supraorbital ridge. The fall covers a small portion of the inside corner of the eyes and stop area. The ears, topskull and cheeks are clipped close with a 7F or 10 blade. The cheeks are clipped from the cowlick at the front of the ear canal to the outside corner of the eye. The clipped line continues to the corner of the mouth and around the underjaw.

Quoted in part with permission from the American Cesky Terrier Fanciers Association, Inc., Approved October 18, 2010:

The length of body, measured from sternum to buttocks, ideally between 15 and 17 inches. To be in a ratio of approximately 1½ (Length) to 1 (Height).

Photo courtesy of Jumpstart Imagery

Topline: Not straight but with a slight rise over the loin and rump.

Body: Fully muscled, longer than high. Withers not very pronounced with the neck set rather high. Rump is strongly developed, muscular; pelvis moderately slanting with the hip bones often slightly higher than the withers.

Forequarters: Shoulder: Muscular, well laid back and powerful. Elbows should fit closely to the sides and be neither loose or tight. Forelegs are short, straight, well boned and parallel.

Hindquarters: Strong, well-muscled and longer than the forelegs. Thigh – Longer in proportion to the lower leg with stifle well bent. Hock Joint – Strong and well developed. Well let down and parallel to each other. Lower leg is straight from hock to heel.

Skull is shaped like a blunt wedge with the broadest part between the ears which tapers moderately towards the supraorbital ridges. Ears – Medium size, dropping in such a way to well cover the orifice. Ears are set rather high with forward edge lying close to the cheek. Shaped like a triangle, with the shorter side of the triangle at the fold of the ear.

The transition between clipped and unclipped areas should be pleasing to the eye and never abrupt. The final haircut should show off the strong, muscled Cesky Terrier.

Coat: Long, fine but slight texture. Furnishings slightly wavy with a silky gloss. Shorter hair can have more curl. Not overdone with too much furnishings.

TERRIER-LIKE PATTERN LINES

Recommended Blade Lengths, Snap-On Comb Lengths and Techniques Bold Print = Preferred Choices for Pet Trims							
10 15	**10**	**10** 7F	**7F** 5F	scissor	7F **5F**		

Tip To Remember:

When using a variety of blades on different parts of the body, blending the transition lines will give a seamless appearance. "Stepping" the blades will help achieve a well blended appearance with very little thinning shear work required. Stepping blades refers to using various blade lengths to blend transition areas. For example: When clipping the throat with a 10 blade and the shoulder with a 5F blade, blending is required to transition the two areas together. This is commonly done with thinning shears. However, a 7F blade can be used over the transition line to blend the 10 blade work in with the 5F blade work.

Dandie Dinmont Terrier

The Dandie Dinmont Terrier is a Terrier breed that originated in Scotland. It was bred to "go to ground" to hunt otter and badger. Today the Dandie Dinmont makes an excellent house dog who is fond of children and is an excellent guard dog.

The Dandie Dinmont is low at the withers with an arch over the loin. The underline should mimic the topline. The pattern line is the same as with the other breeds; the body structure is the only difference.

This coat should be carded and hand stripped for show. If clipping is preferred, blades ranging from 4F, 5F to 7F or various snap-on combs are recommended. Carding and thinning shear techniques should be done in addition to clipping for a natural appearance. The Dandie carries longer furnishings than other breeds in this group; however, the pattern lines are the same.

See important information on "Carding" on page 30 and "Hand Stripping" on page 32.

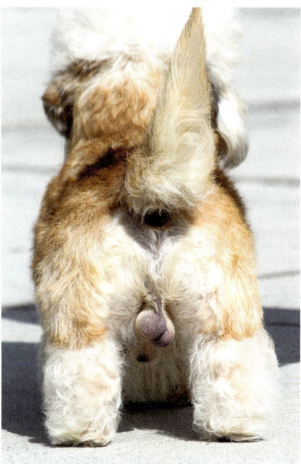

Key points to remember when grooming the Dandie Dinmont Terrier according to the breed standard:

The Dandie Dinmont is longer than it is tall. The topline is lowest at the shoulders with an arch over the loins. The topline drops from the top of the loins to the base of the tail. The underline should mimic the topline, both having gentle curves.

The body of the DDT is very strong with well-sprung ribs and a well-developed forechest. The front legs are straight. The rear legs are longer than the front legs and are set wider apart. The thighs are muscular with well-bent stifles. The hocks are perpendicular to the ground.

The tail is shaped like a scimitar with about two inches of feathering on the underside tapering to a point.

The head of the Dandie Dinmont is the hallmark of the breed. It is large and round and is covered with soft silky hair. This topknot covers the upper portion of the tasseled ears and frames the eyes. The topknot extends slightly beyond the occiput for a well-rounded appearance. The ears can be clipped with a 10 or 15 blade leaving about 1/3 to 1/4 of the ear tip, which will create the tassel. The clipped line at the bottom of the ear should appear as an inverted V. The lower part of the cheek, below the eye level, can be tightened lightly with thinning shears so the ears fall nicely and frame the face.

The coat should be approximately two inches on the body and should consist of 2/3 coarse hair and about 1/3 soft hair when hand stripped for the show ring.

TERRIER-LIKE PATTERN LINES

Recommended Blade Lengths, Snap-On Comb Lengths and Techniques **Bold Print** = Preferred Choices for Pet Trims							
10 15	7F **5F** 4F	5F **4F** #2 carding	5F 4F **#2** carding	thinning shears scissor			

Giant Schnauzer

The Giant Schnauzer is a Working breed that originated in Germany. It was bred to work the farms and to help drive sheep and livestock to market. The Giant Schnauzer displays strength and power and is extremely intelligent. In World War I this breed was trained and used to assist the German police.

This coat should be carded and hand stripped for show. If clipping is preferred, blades ranging from 4F, 5F to 7F are recommended. Carding and thinning shear techniques should be done in addition to clipping for a natural appearance. The Giant Schnauzer displays a strong forechest and carries longer furnishings on the underline than the Miniature and Standard Schnauzers.

The Giant Schnauzer has a rectangular-shaped head with long, triangular arched eyebrows and a full beard. See "Rectangular Heads" on page 427 for instructions on grooming this head type.

See important information on "Carding" on page 30 and "Hand Stripping" on page 32.

Quoted in part with permission from the Giant Schnauzer Club of America, Inc., Approved October 11, 1983:

The Giant Schnauzer is compact, substantial, short-coupled, and strong, with great power and agility. The height at the highest point of the withers equals the body length from breastbone to point of rump. Back: Short, straight, strong, and firm. The breastbone is plainly discernible, with strong forechest.

The forequarters have flat, somewhat sloping shoulders and high withers. Forelegs are straight and vertical when viewed from all sides with strong pasterns and good bone. Chest– Medium in width, ribs well sprung. The brisket descends at least to the elbows, and ascends gradually toward the rear with the belly moderately drawn up. The sloping shoulder blades (scapulae) are strongly muscled, yet flat. They are well laid back so that from the side the rounded upper ends are in a nearly vertical line above the elbows. They slope well forward to the point where they join the upper arm (humerus), forming as nearly as possible a right angle. Such an angulation permits the maximum forward extension of the forelegs without binding or effort. Both shoulder blades and upper arm are long, permitting depth of chest at the brisket.

The hindquarters are strongly muscled, in balance with the forequarters; upper thighs are slanting and well bent at the stifles. The legs from the hock joint to the feet are short, perpendicular to the ground while the dog is standing naturally, and from the rear parallel to each other. The hindquarters do not appear over-built or higher than the shoulders.

Head: Strong, rectangular in appearance, and elongated; narrowing slightly from the ears to the eyes, and again from the eyes to the tip of the nose. The total length of the head is about one-half the length of the back (withers to set-on of tail). The top line of the muzzle is parallel to the top line of the skull; there is a slight stop which is accentuated by the eyebrows. Skull–(Occiput to Stop). Moderately broad between the ears: occiput not too prominent. Top of skull flat; skin unwrinkled. Cheeks–Flat, but with well-developed chewing muscles; there is no "cheekiness" to disturb the rectangular head appearance (with beard).

Coat: Hard, wiry, very dense; composed of a soft undercoat and a harsh outer coat which, when seen against the grain, stands slightly up off the back, lying neither smooth nor flat. Coarse hair on top of head; harsh beard and eyebrows, the Schnauzer hallmark.

The Giant Schnauzer

"Temperament which combines spirit and alertness with intelligence and reliability. Composed, watchful, courageous, easily trained, deeply loyal to family, playful, amiable in repose, and a commanding figure when aroused."

TERRIER-LIKE PATTERN LINES

	Recommended Blade Lengths, Snap-On Comb Lengths and Techniques **Bold Print** = Preferred Choices for Pet Trims						
10 15	**10** 7F	**7F** 5F carding	7F **5F 4F** carding	thinning shears scissor	**7F**		

Glen of Imaal Terrier

The Glen of Imaal Terrier is a Terrier breed that originated in Ireland. They were bred to hunt vermin, badger and fox on the farms. They were also commonly used as turnspit dogs. A turnspit is a large wheel with a pulley that was propelled by the dogs walking the wheel, similar to a hamster wheel. It was used to rotate the rotisserie to cook over the hearth.

This coat should be carded and hand stripped for show.

If hand stripping is not desired by the pet owner, it is recommended to use a Coat King to remove the undercoat and dead coat following the pattern lines as described. The pattern falls under this pattern group; however, it should appear very subtle and natural. Thinning shears may be used to tidy the appearance.

If clipping is preferred, various lengths of snap-on combs are recommended following the breed profile. Carding and thinning shear techniques should be done in addition to clipping for a natural appearance.

The head is broad and round with the muzzle to skull ratio being 3:5. This breed should not appear overly trimmed. The "rough and ready" working Terrier appearance should be kept in mind when grooming this breed. See important information on "Carding" on page 30 and "Hand Stripping" on page 32.

Quoted in part with permission from the Glen of Imaal Terrier Club of America, Approved June 11, 2001:

Longer than tall and sporting a double coat of medium length.

Topline – Straight, slightly rising to a very strong well-muscled loin with no drop-off at the croup.

Body – Deep, long and fully muscled. Longer than high with the ideal ratio of body length to shoulder height approximately five (length) to three (height). Chest – Wide, strong and deep, extending below the elbows. Ribs – Well sprung with neither a flat nor a barrel appearance. Loin – Strong and well muscled. Tail – Docked to approximately half-length, in balance with the overall dog and long enough to allow a good handhold. Strong at root, well set on and carried gaily.

Shoulder – Well laid back, broad and muscular. Forelegs – Short, bowed and well boned. Forearm should curve slightly around the chest. Upper arm (humerus) nearly equal in length to the shoulder blades (scapula). Feet to turn out slightly but perceptibly from pasterns. Feet – Compact and strong with rounded pads.

Hindquarters – Strong and well muscled, with ample bone and in balance with forequarters. Good bend of stifle and a well-defined second thigh. Hocks turn neither in nor out, are short, well let down and perpendicular from hock to ground. Feet – As front, except they should point forward.

The head must be powerful and strong with no suggestion of coarseness. Impressive in size yet in balance with, and in proportion to, the overall size and symmetry of the dog. Skull – Broad and slightly domed; tapering slightly towards the brow. Of fair length, distance from stop to occiput being approximately equal to distance between ears. Muzzle – Foreface of power, strong and well filled below the eyes, tapering toward the nose. Ratio of length of muzzle to length of skull is approximately three (muzzle) to five (skull.) Stop – Pronounced.

Its distinctive head with rose or half-prick ears, its bowed forequarters with turned out feet, its unique outline and topline are hallmarks of the breed and essential to the breed type.

Coat – Medium length, of harsh texture with a soft undercoat. The coat may be tidied to present a neat outline characteristic of a rough-and-ready working Terrier. Over trimming of dogs is undesirable.

TERRIER-LIKE PATTERN LINES

Recommended Blade Lengths, Snap-On Comb Lengths and Techniques **Bold Print** = Preferred Choices for Pet Trims						
10 15				thinning shears scissor	leave natural thinning shears carding	define with thinning shears carding

239

Irish Terrier

The Irish Terrier is a Terrier breed that originated in Ireland. It was bred to control vermin and was an excellent guard of the farm and the family. The Irish Terrier is a natural water dog and was trained to retrieve in water and on land. It possesses many of the Sporting dog traits but is a true Terrier at heart.

The Irish Terrier carries very little furnishings, but the pattern is still slightly visible.

This coat should be carded and hand stripped for show. If clipping is preferred, blades ranging from 4F, 5F to 7F are recommended. Carding and thinning shear techniques should be done in addition to clipping for a natural appearance. A Coat King may also be used on the back coat, if necessary, to help remove undercoat and help preserve the color and texture of the coat.

The Irish Terrier has a rectangular-shaped head with small triangular eyebrows, beard and goatee. See "Rectangular Heads" on page 427 for instructions on grooming this head type.

See important information on "Carding" on page 30 and "Hand Stripping" on page 32.

Quoted in part with permission from the Irish Terrier Club of America, Approved December 10, 1968:

Neck should be of fair length and gradually widening toward the shoulders; well and proudly carried, and free from throatiness. Generally there is a slight frill in the hair at each side of the neck, extending almost to the corner of the ear.

Shoulders must be fine, long, and sloping well into the back. The chest should be deep and muscular, but neither full nor wide.

The body should be moderately long. The short back is not characteristic of the Irish Terrier, and is extremely objectionable. The back must be strong and straight, and free from an appearance of slackness or "dip" behind the shoulders. The loin should be strong and muscular, and slightly arched, the ribs fairly sprung, deep rather than round, reaching to the level of the elbow.

Hindquarters should be strong and muscular; thighs powerful; hocks near the ground; stifles moderately bent.

Head: Long, but in nice proportion to the rest of the body; the skull flat, rather narrow between the ears, and narrowing slightly toward the eyes; free from wrinkle, with the stop hardly noticeable except in profile. The jaws must be strong and muscular, but not too full in the cheek, and of good punishing length. The foreface and the skull from occiput to stop should be approximately equal in length. The hair on the upper and lower jaws should be similar in quality and texture to that on the body, and of sufficient length to present an appearance of additional strength and finish to the foreface.

Coat: Should be dense and wiry in texture, rich in quality, having a broken appearance, but still lying fairly close to the body, the hairs growing so closely and strongly together that when parted with the fingers the skin is hardly visible; free of softness or silkiness, and not so long as to alter the outline of the body, particularly in the hindquarters. On the sides of the body the coat is never as harsh as on the back and quarters, but it should be plentiful and of good texture. At the base of the stiff outer coat there should be a growth of finer and softer hair, lighter in color, termed the undercoat.

The Irish Terrier

"He is of good temper, most affectionate, and absolutely loyal to mankind. Tender and forbearing with those he loves, this rugged, stout-hearted terrier will guard his master, his mistress and children with utter contempt for danger or hurt."

TERRIER-LIKE PATTERN LINES

Recommended Blade Lengths, Snap-On Comb Lengths and Techniques **Bold Print** = Preferred Choices for Pet Trims							
🟫	🟨	🟪	🟣	🟧	🟦	🟫	
10 15	**10** 7F	**7F** 5F carding	7F **5F 4F** carding	thinning shears scissor	**7F**		

LAKELAND TERRIER

The Lakeland Terrier is a Terrier breed that originated in England. They were used by farmers to prevent fox and vermin from destroying sheep herds. They have been known to follow vermin so far underground that farmers have had to blast through rock to retrieve the dog.

This coat should be carded and hand stripped for show. If clipping is preferred, blades ranging from 4F, 5F to 7F are recommended. Carding and thinning shear techniques should be done in addition to clipping for a natural appearance. A Coat King may also be used on the back coat to help remove undercoat and help preserve the color and texture of the coat.

The Lakeland Terrier has a rectangular-shaped head with a fall, beard and goatee. See "Rectangular Heads" on page 427 for instructions on grooming this head type.

See important information on "Carding" on page 30 and "Hand Stripping" on page 32.

Quoted in part with permission from the United States Lakeland Terrier Club, Approved January 15, 1991:

The dog is squarely built, and bitches may be slightly longer than dogs. Balance and proportion are of primary importance. The withers, that point at the back of the neck where neck and body meet, are noticeably higher than the level of the back. The topline, measured from the withers to the tail, is short and level.

The body is strong and supple. The moderately narrow oval chest is deep, extending to the elbows. The ribs are well sprung and moderately rounded off the vertebrae. There is moderate tuck-up. The tail is set high on the back.

The shoulders are well angulated. An imaginary line drawn from the top of the shoulder blade should pass through the elbow. The shoulder blade is long in proportion to the upper arm, which allows for reasonable angulation while maintaining the more upright "Terrier front." The musculature of the shoulders is flat and smooth. The elbows are held close to the body, standing or moving. The forelegs are strong, clean and straight when viewed from the front or side. There is no appreciable bend at the pasterns. The feet are round and point forward, the toes compact and strong.

The thighs are powerful and well muscled. The hind legs are well angulated.

The skull is flat on top and moderately broad, the cheeks flat and smooth as possible. The stop is barely perceptible. The muzzle is strong with straight nose bridge and good fill-in beneath the eyes. The head is well balanced, rectangular, the length of skull equaling the length of the muzzle when measured from occiput to stop, and from stop to nose tip. The proportions of the head are critical to correct type. The ears are small, V-shaped, their fold just above the top of the skull, the inner edge close to the side of the head, and the flap pointed toward the outside corner of the eye.

Coat: Two-ply or double, the outer coat is hard and wiry in texture, the undercoat is close to the skin and soft and should never overpower the wiry outer coat. The Lakeland is hand stripped to show his outline. (Clipping is inappropriate for the show ring.) The appearance should be neat and workmanlike. The coat on the skull, ears, forechest, shoulders and behind the tail is trimmed short and smooth. The coat on the body is longer (about one-half to one inch) and may be slightly wavy or straight. The furnishings on the legs and foreface are plentiful as opposed to profuse and should be tidy. They are crisp in texture. The legs should appear cylindrical. The face is traditionally trimmed, with the hair left longer over the eyes to give the head a rectangular appearance from all angles, with the eyes covered from above. From the front, the eyes are quite apparent, giving the Lakeland his own unique mischievous expression.

The Lakeland Terrier

"The typical Lakeland Terrier is bold, gay and friendly, with a confident, cock-of-the-walk attitude."

TERRIER-LIKE PATTERN LINES

Recommended Blade Lengths, Snap-On Comb Lengths and Techniques
Bold Print = Preferred Choices for Pet Trims

10 15	**10** 7F	**7F** 5F carding	7F **5F** **4F** carding	thinning shears scissor	**7F**		

Miniature Schnauzer

The Miniature Schnauzer is a Terrier breed that originated in Germany. It was bred to be a small farm dog and was used to "go to ground" to attack vermin.

This coat should be carded and hand stripped for show. If clipping is preferred, blades ranging from 4F, 5F to 7F are recommended. Carding and thinning shear techniques should be done in addition to clipping for a natural appearance.

The Miniature Schnauzer has a rectangular-shaped head with long, triangular arched eyebrows and a full beard. See "Rectangular Heads" on page 427 for instructions on grooming this head type.

See important information on "Carding" on page 30 and "Hand Stripping" on page 32.

Photo courtesy of Jumpstart Imagery

Quoted in part with permission from the American Miniature Schnauzer Club, Inc., Approved July 10, 2012:

He is sturdily built, nearly square in proportion of body length to height with plenty of bone, and without any suggestion of toyishness.

The backline is straight; it declines slightly from the withers to the base of the tail. The withers form the highest point of the body. The overall length from chest to buttock appears to equal the height at the withers.

Body: Short and deep, with the brisket extending at least to the elbows. Ribs are well sprung and deep, extending well back to a short loin. The underbody does not present a tucked up appearance at the flank.

Forelegs are straight and parallel when viewed from all sides. The sloping shoulders are muscled, yet flat and clean. They are well laid back, so that from the side the tips of the shoulder blades are in a nearly vertical line above the elbow. Both the shoulder blades and upper arms are long, permitting depth of chest at the brisket. Feet short and round (cat feet).

The hindquarters have strong-muscled, slanting thighs. They are well bent at the stifles. There is sufficient angulation so that, in stance, the hocks extend beyond the tail. The rear pasterns are short and, in stance, perpendicular to the ground and, when viewed from the rear, are parallel to each other.

Head: Ears – When cropped, the ears are identical in shape and length, with pointed tips. They are in balance with the head and not exaggerated in length. They are set high on the skull and carried perpendicularly at the inner edges, with as little bell as possible along the outer edges. When uncropped, the ears are small and V-shaped, folding close to the skull. Head – strong and rectangular, its width diminishing slightly from ears to eyes, and again to the tip of the nose. The topskull is flat and fairly long. The foreface is parallel to the topskull, with a slight stop, and it is at least as long as the topskull. The muzzle is strong in proportion to the skull; it ends in a moderately blunt manner, with thick whiskers which accentuate the rectangular shape of the head.

Coat: Double, with hard, wiry, outer coat and close undercoat. The head, neck, ears, chest, tail, and body coat must be plucked. When in show condition, the body coat should be of sufficient length to determine texture. Close covering on neck, ears and skull. Furnishings are fairly thick but not silky.

The Miniature Schnauzer

"The typical Miniature Schnauzer is alert and spirited, yet obedient to command. He is friendly, intelligent and willing to please."

Available on DVD: "The Miniature Schnauzer - Pet Trim"

TERRIER-LIKE PATTERN LINES

Recommended Blade Lengths, Snap-On Comb Lengths and Techniques **Bold Print** = Preferred Choices for Pet Trims							
10 15	10 7F	**7F** 5F carding	7F **5F** **4F** carding	thinning shears scissor	**7F**	

Otterhound

The Otterhound is a scent Hound that originated in England. Unlike other hounds, they have a rough double-coat and webbed feet. They were used primarily to hunt otters that began preying on fish in the rivers, streams and stocked ponds. Even though otter hunting has now been banned, the Otterhound is still used as a tracking dog due to its intense scenting abilities.

The Otterhound is shown in a <u>natural state without over-trimming</u>. This coat should be maintained by carding and hand stripping for the show ring. The pattern falls under this pattern group; however, it should appear <u>very subtle and natural</u>. The Otterhound body structure changes the profile from others in this group; however, the pattern is enhanced in the same manner.

If requested by the pet owner, various lengths of snap-on combs may be used for a short tidy trim. Carding and thinning shear techniques should be done in addition to clipping for a natural appearance. A Coat King may also be used on the back coat to help remove undercoat and help preserve the color and texture of the coat.

See important information on "Carding" on page 30 and "Hand Stripping" on page 32.

Quoted in part with permission from the Otterhound Club of America, Approved October 10, 1995:

The Otterhound is slightly rectangular in body; the length from point of shoulder to buttocks is slightly greater than the height at the withers. The Otterhound has good substance with strongly boned legs and broad muscles, without being coarse.

Shoulders are clean, powerful, and well sloped with moderate angulation at shoulders and elbows. Legs are strongly boned and straight, with strong, slightly sprung pasterns. Both front and rear feet are large, broad, compact when standing, but capable of spreading. They have thick, deep pads, with arched toes; they are web-footed (membranes connecting the toes allow the foot to spread).

Thighs and second thighs are large, broad, and well muscled. Legs have moderately bent stifles with well-defined hocks. Hocks are well let down, turning neither in nor out. Legs on a standing hound are parallel when viewed from the rear. Angulation front and rear must be balanced and adequate to give forward reach and rear drive.

The topline is level from the withers to the base of tail. The chest is deep reaching at least to the elbows on a mature hound. Forechest is evident.

The tail is set high, and is long reaching at least to the hock. The tail is thicker at the base, tapers to a point, and is feathered (covered and fringed with hair).

The head is large, fairly narrow, and well covered with hair. The head should measure 11 to 12 inches from tip of nose to occiput in a hound 26″ at the withers, with the muzzle and skull approximately equal in length. This proportion should be maintained in larger and smaller hounds.

The ears, an essential feature of this breed, are long, pendulous, and folded (the leading edge folds or rolls to give a draped appearance). They are set low, at or below eye level and hang close to the head, with the leather reaching at least to the tip of the nose. They are well covered with hair.

The skull is long, fairly narrow under the hair, and only slightly domed. The stop is not pronounced. The muzzle is square, with no hint of snipiness; the jaws are powerful with deep flews. From the side, the planes of the muzzle and skull should be parallel.

The coat is an essential feature of the Otterhound. The outer coat is dense, rough, coarse and crisp, of broken appearance. Softer hair on the head and lower legs is natural. The outer coat is two to four inches long on the back and shorter on the extremities. A naturally stripped coat lacking length and fringes is correct for an Otterhound that is being worked. A proper hunting coat will show a hard outer coat and woolly undercoat. The Otterhound is shown in a natural coat, with no sculpturing or shaping of the coat.

The Otterhound

"The Otterhound is amiable, boisterous and even-tempered."

DOG GROOMING SIMPLIFIED: STRAIGHT TO THE POINT

TERRIER-LIKE PATTERN LINES

	Recommended Blade Lengths, Snap-On Comb Lengths and Techniques **Bold Print** = Preferred Choices for Pet Trims					
10 15				thinning shears scissor	leave natural thinning shears carding	define with thinning shears carding

Tip To Remember:

The more natural breeds like the Otterhound and Wirehaired Pointing Griffon, for example, should be groomed keeping the unkempt appearance that is described in their breed standards. This can be done with the use of a Coat King, stripping knife and thinning shears to define the structure of the dog. For shorter trims, a variety of snap-on combs can also be used. Over trimming of these breeds should be avoided in order to keep the essence of the breed.

Petit Basset Griffon Vendeen

The name Petit Basset Griffon Vendeen means: Petit—small; Basset—low to the ground; Griffon—rough- or wire-coated; and Vendéen—the area of France from which this breed originated. This is a scent Hound that was bred to hunt small game, rabbit and hare.

The PBGV falls under this pattern group; however, it should appear <u>very subtle and natural</u>. It has a rough unrefined profile. This coat should be maintained by carding and hand stripping for show. If clipping is preferred, various lengths of snap-on combs may be used following the breed profile.

The natural "tousled" appearance of this breed should be kept in mind when using snap-on combs. Carding and thinning shear techniques should be used in addition to clipping for a natural appearance. A Coat King may also be used on the back coat to help remove undercoat and help preserve the color and texture of the coat.

The head, ears and throat are left natural.

See important information on "Carding" on page 30 and "Hand Stripping" on page 32.

Key points to remember when grooming the PBGV according to the breed standard:

The PBGV is slightly longer than it is tall. The neck is long and flows into a level topline. There is a slight rise over the loin that flows into a high-set tail. The tail is of medium length and is wider at the base, tapering to the tip. The tail is well furnished and is said to appear like "the blade of a saber".

The shoulders are well laid back and are equal in length to the upper arm. This sets the elbow in line with the withers. The PBGV has a deep chest with a prominent sternum, or forechest. The ribs are moderately rounded. When viewed from profile there appears to be very little tuck-up.

The front legs should appear straight and column-like. The feet can range between a hare and cat foot. The rear legs are muscular with well-bent stifles. The hocks are short and perpendicular to the ground.

The PBGV has a friendly expression with long eyebrows, beard and mustache. The skull is domed with a prominent occiput. The muzzle is slightly shorter than the skull. The ears are oval in shape and are covered with long hair. The ears are set to the level of the eyes.

The PBGV has a rough coat that has a harsh texture. For the show ring the PBGV should appear natural without the appearance of being sculpted.

The Petit Basset Griffon Vendeen

"The PBGV is bold and vivacious in character; compact, tough and robust in construction. He has an alert outlook, lively bearing and a good voice freely and purposefully used."

TERRIER-LIKE PATTERN LINES

Recommended Blade Lengths, Snap-On Comb Lengths and Techniques **Bold Print** = Preferred Choices for Pet Trims							
10 15				thinning shears scissor	leave natural thinning shears carding	define with thinning shears carding	

Spinone Italiano

The Spinone Italiano is a Sporting dog that originated in Italy. It is an all-purpose hunting dog, a pointer and an excellent retriever by nature. The Spinone has a wiry, dense coat and thick skin that protect this hunter from underbrush and cold water.

The Spinone should be maintained by carding and hand stripping for the show ring. Its pattern falls under this pattern group; however, it should appear <u>very subtle and natural</u>. The Spinone body structure changes the profile from others in this group; however, the pattern is enhanced in the same manner.

Various lengths of snap-on combs may be used for a shorter trim if requested by the pet owner. Carding and thinning shear techniques should be done in addition to clipping for a natural appearance. A Coat King may also be used on the back coat to help remove dead coat and to help preserve the color and texture of the coat.

The Spinone should present a natural appearance without being over-trimmed.

See important information on "Hand Stripping" on page 32 and "Carding" on page 30.

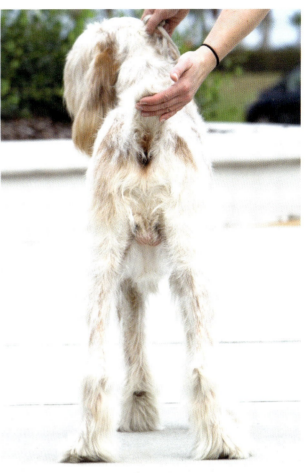

Quoted in part with permission from the Spinone Club of America, Approved February 11, 2000:

His build tends to fit into a square. The length of the body, measured from sternum to point of buttocks, is approximately equal to the height at the withers.

The distance from ground to the elbow is equal to 1/2 the height at the withers. The topline consists of two segments. The first slopes slightly downward in a nearly straight line from the withers to the 11th thoracic vertebrae, approximately 6 inches behind the withers. The second rises gradually and continues into a solid and well-arched loin. The underline is solid and should have minimal tuck-up.

The forelegs are straight when viewed from the front angle with strong bone and well-developed muscles; elbows set under the withers and close to the body.

The hipbones fall away from the spinal column at an angle of about 30 degrees, producing a lightly rounded, well filled-out croup. Tail: Follows the line of the croup, thick at the base, carried horizontally or down. The tail should lack fringes.

Thighs are strong and well muscled, stifles show good function angulation. The hock, with proportion of 1/3 the distance from the hip joint to foot being ideal, is strong, lean and perpendicular to the ground. Feet are slightly more oval than the forefoot with the same characteristics.

The profile of the Spinone is unique to this breed. Expression is of paramount importance to the breed. It should denote intelligence and gentleness. Skull of oval shape, with sides gently sloping. With occipital protuberance well developed, medial-frontal furrow is very pronounced. Muzzle: Square when viewed from the front. Muzzle length is equal to that of backskull. The planes of the skull and muzzle are diverging, downfaced. Its width measured at its midpoint is a third of its length. Stop is barely perceptible. Bridge of the muzzle is preferably slightly Roman, however, straight is not to be faulted.

Ears: Practically triangular shape. Set on a level just below the eye, carried low, with little erectile power.

The leather is fine, covered with short, thick hair mixed with a longer sparser hair, which becomes thicker along edges. Length, if measured along the head would extend to tip of nose and no more than 1 inch beyond the tip. The forward edge is adherent to the cheek, not folded, but turned outward; the tip of the ear is slightly rounded.

A Spinone must have a correct coat to be of correct type. The ideal coat length is 1 1/2 to 2 1/2 inches on the body, with a tolerance of 1/2 inch over or under the ideal length. Head, ears, muzzle and front sides of legs and feet are covered by shorter hair. The hair on the backsides of the legs forms a rough brush, but there are never any fringes.

The eyes and lips are framed by stiff hair forming eyebrows, mustache and tufted beard, which combine to save foreface from laceration by briar and bush. The coat is dense, stiff and flat or slightly crimped, but not curly, with an absence of undercoat. The Spinone is exhibited in a natural state. The appearance of the Spinone may not be altered. The dog must present the natural appearance of a functional field dog.

TERRIER-LIKE PATTERN LINES

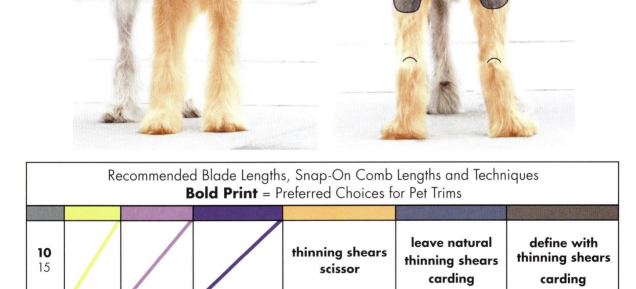

Recommended Blade Lengths, Snap-On Comb Lengths and Techniques **Bold Print** = Preferred Choices for Pet Trims						
10 15				thinning shears scissor	leave natural thinning shears carding	define with thinning shears carding

265

Welsh Terrier

The Welsh Terrier is a Terrier breed that originated in Wales. It was used to work in packs to hunt otter, fox and badger.

This coat should be carded and hand stripped for show. If clipping is preferred, blades ranging from 4F, 5F to 7F are recommended. Carding and thinning shear techniques should be done in addition to clipping for a natural appearance. A Coat King may also be used on the back coat to help remove undercoat and help preserve the color and texture of the coat.

The Welsh Terrier has a rectangular-shaped head with small triangular eyebrows, beard and goatee. See "Rectangular Heads" on page 427 for instructions on grooming this head type.

See important information on "Carding" on page 30 and "Hand Stripping" on page 32.

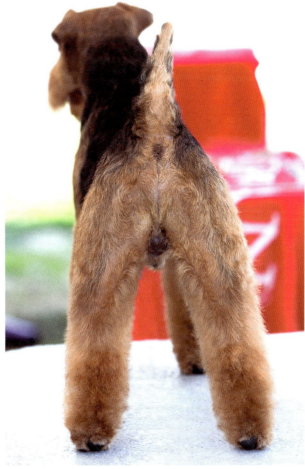

Quoted in part with permission from the Welsh Terrier Club of America, Inc., Approved August 10, 1993:

The Welsh Terrier is a sturdy, compact, rugged dog of medium size with a coarse wire-textured coat. The topline is level.

The neck is of moderate length and thickness, slightly arched and sloping gracefully into the shoulders.

The body shows good substance and is well ribbed up. There is good depth of brisket and moderate width of chest. The tail is docked to a length approximately level (on an imaginary line) with the occiput, to complete the square image of the whole dog. The root of the tail is set well up on the back. It is carried upright.

The front is straight. The shoulders are long, sloping and well laid back. The legs are straight and muscular. The feet are small, round, and catlike.

The hindquarters are strong and muscular with well-developed second thighs and the stifles well bent. The hocks are moderately straight, parallel and short from joint to ground. The feet should be the same as in the forequarters.

The entire head is rectangular. The ears are V-shaped, small, but not too thin. The fold is just above the topline of the skull. The ears are carried forward close to the cheek with the tips falling to, or toward, the outside corners of the eyes when the dog is at rest.

TERRIER-LIKE PATTERN LINES

Skull–The foreface is strong with powerful, punishing jaws. It is only slightly narrower than the backskull. There is a slight stop. The backskull is of equal length to the foreface. They are on parallel planes in profile. The backskull is smooth and flat (not domed) between the ears. The cheeks are flat and clean (not bulging). The muzzle is one-half the length of the entire head from tip of nose to occiput. The furnishings on the foreface are trimmed to complete without exaggeration the total rectangular outline.

Coat: The coat is hard, wiry, and dense with a close-fitting thick jacket. There is a short, soft undercoat. Furnishings on muzzle, legs, and quarters are dense and wiry.

The Welsh Terrier

"The Welsh Terrier is a game dog-alert, aware, spirited-but at the same time, is friendly and shows self control. Intelligence and desire to please are evident in his attitude."

Available on DVD: "The Welsh Terrier - Pet Trim"

TERRIER-LIKE PATTERN LINES

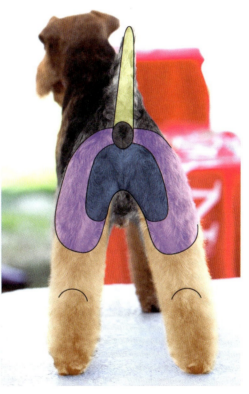

Recommended Blade Lengths, Snap-On Comb Lengths and Techniques **Bold Print** = Preferred Choices for Pet Trims							
10 15	**10** 7F	**7F** 5F carding	7F **5F** **4F** carding	thinning shears scissor	**7F**		

Wirehaired Pointing Griffon

The Wirehaired Pointing Griffon is a Sporting dog that originated in Holland. It is a pointer in the field and a retriever in the water. Its hard, coarse coat protects the WPG from briars, underbrush and cold water. It should have an unkempt appearance and should not appear overly groomed.

Photos courtesy of Catherine Lynch Carey

The WPG has a very natural coat that should be maintained by carding and hand stripping for the show ring. The pattern falls under this pattern group; however, it should appear <u>very subtle and natural</u>. The body structure changes the profile from others in this group; however, the pattern is enhanced in the same manner.

For pet trims, thinning shears can be used to tidy the appearance. A Coat King may also be used on the body to help remove undercoat and help preserve the color and texture of the coat. The throat is left natural. The ears, cheeks and topskull can be neatened using carding and thinning shear techniques.

Various lengths of snap-on combs may be used for a shorter trim if requested by the pet owner, keeping the natural untidy appearance in mind.

See important information on "Carding" on page 30 and "Hand Stripping" on page 32.

Quoted in part with permission from the American Wirehaired Pointing Griffon Association, Approved October 8, 1991:

Proportion: Slightly longer than tall, in a ratio of 10 to 9. Height from withers to ground; length from point of shoulder to point of buttocks.

Topline: The back is strong and firm, descending in a gentle slope from the slightly higher withers to the base of the tail.

Neck: Rather long, slightly arched. The chest must descend to the level of the elbow, with a moderate spring of rib. The chest must neither be too wide nor too narrow, but of medium width to allow freedom of movement. The loin is strong and well developed, being of medium length. The croup and rump are stoutly made with adequate length to favor speed. The tail extends from the back in a continuation of the topline. It may be carried straight or raised slightly. It is docked by one-third to one-half length.

Shoulders are long, with good angulation, and well laid back. The forelegs are straight and vertical from the front and set well under the shoulder from the side. Pasterns are slightly sloping. Feet are round, firm, with tightly closed webbed toes.

The thighs are long and well muscled. Angulation in balance with the front. The legs are vertical with the hocks turning neither in nor out. The stifle and hock joints are strong and well angulated.

The skull is of medium width with equal length from nose to stop and from stop to occiput. The skull is slightly rounded on top, but from the side the muzzle and head are square. The stop and occiput are only slightly pronounced. The required abundant mustache and eyebrows contribute to the friendly expression.

The coat is one of the distinguishing features of the breed. It is a double coat. The outer coat is medium length, straight and wiry, never curly or woolly. The harsh texture provides protection in rough cover. The obligatory undercoat consists of a fine, thick down, which provides insulation as well as water resistance.

The head is furnished with a prominent mustache and eyebrows. These required features are extensions of the undercoat, which gives the Griffon a somewhat untidy appearance. The hair covering the ears is fairly short and soft, mixed with longer harsh hair from the coat. The overall feel is much less wiry than the body.

The legs, both front and rear, are covered with denser, shorter, and less coarse hair. The coat on the tail is the same as the body; any type of plume is prohibited. The breed should be exhibited in full body coat, not stripped short in pattern. Trimming and stripping are only allowed around the ears, top of head, cheeks and feet.

TERRIER-LIKE PATTERN LINES

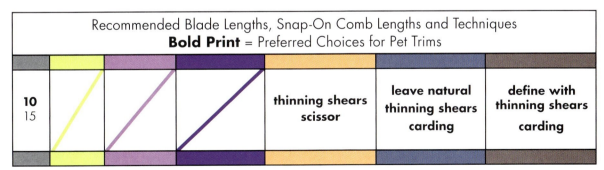

Recommended Blade Lengths, Snap-On Comb Lengths and Techniques **Bold Print** = Preferred Choices for Pet Trims							
10 15				thinning shears scissor	leave natural thinning shears carding	define with thinning shears carding	

WIRE FOX TERRIER

The Fox Terrier is a Terrier breed that originated in England. They were bred to control vermin and fox on the farm. They were extremely good at driving foxes from their hole due to their intense eyesight and highly developed sense of smell. There are two varieties, the Wire Fox Terrier and the Smooth Fox Terrier.

This coat should be carded and hand stripped for show. If clipping is preferred, blades ranging from 4F, 5F to 7F are recommended. Carding and thinning shear techniques should be done in addition to clipping for a natural appearance. A Coat King may also be used on the back coat to help remove undercoat and help preserve the color and texture of the coat.

The Wire Fox Terrier has a rectangular-shaped head with small triangular eyebrows, beard and goatee. See "Rectangular Heads" on page 427 for instructions on grooming this head type.

See important information on "Carding" on page 30 and "Hand Stripping" on page 32.

Quoted in part with permission from the American Fox Terrier Club, Approved February 9, 1991:

The back should be short and level with no appearance of slackness—the loins muscular and very slightly arched.

Shoulders when viewed from the front should slope steeply downwards from their juncture, with the neck towards the points, which should be fine. When viewed from the side they should be long, well laid back, and should slope obliquely backwards from points to withers, which should always be clean-cut. A shoulder well laid back gives the long forehand which, in combination with a short back, is so desirable in Terrier or Hunter. The elbows should hang perpendicular to the body. Viewed from any direction the legs should be straight. Feet should be round, compact.

Hindquarters should be strong and muscular; the thighs long and powerful; the stifles well curved and turned neither in nor out; the hock joints well bent and near the ground; the hocks perfectly upright and parallel with each other when viewed from behind.

Head: In a well balanced head there should be little apparent difference in length between skull and foreface. Ears should be small and V-shaped and of moderate thickness, the flaps neatly folded over and dropping forward close to the cheeks. The topline of the folded ear should be well above the level of the skull. The topline of the skull should be almost flat, sloping slightly and gradually decreasing in width toward the eyes.

Coat: The best coats appear to be broken, the hairs having a tendency to twist, and are of dense, wiry texture—like coconut matting—the hairs growing so closely and strongly together that, when parted with the fingers, the skin cannot be seen. At the base of these stiff hairs is a shorter growth of finer and softer hair—termed the undercoat. The coat on the sides is never quite so hard as that on the back and quarters. Some of the hardest coats are "crinkly" or slightly waved, but a curly coat is very objectionable. The hair on the upper and lower jaws should be crisp and only sufficiently long to impart an appearance of strength to the foreface. The hair on the forelegs should also be dense and crisp. The coat should average in length from 3/4 to one inch on shoulders and neck, lengthening to 1 1/2 inches on withers, back, ribs, and quarters.

The Wire Fox Terrier

"The Terrier should be alert, quick of movement, keen of expression, on the tip-toe of expectation at the slightest provocation."

TERRIER-LIKE PATTERN LINES

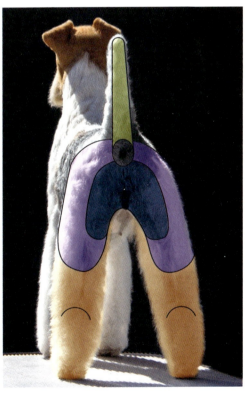

				Recommended Blade Lengths, Snap-On Comb Lengths and Techniques **Bold Print** = Preferred Choices for Pet Trims			
10 15	**10** 7F	**7F** 5F carding	7F **5F** **4F** carding	thinning shears scissor	**7F**		

TERRIER-LIKE PATTERN LINES
Subtle in Nature

Terrier-Like pattern lines can also be of a Subtle nature. "Subtle" means that the pattern line is not set tight, yet the Terrier-Like pattern is still visible. In addition, the difference between "Distinct" and "Subtle" Terrier-Like patterns is the fact that the Distinct Terrier-Like patterns do not carry long furnishings off the back of the rear legs. The breeds that will be discussed here carry longer furnishings than the Distinct pattern group.

The pattern lines of the West Highland White Terrier, as an example, are the same general pattern lines of many other breeds. Many of these breeds should be hand stripped and carded for show. However, on pet trims these patterns may be set with a 4F blade or preferably by using snap-on combs.

A #2, #1 or #0 comb would be ideal for these breeds. Setting these patterns with snap-on combs will give a more natural look that is more true to the breed profile. A Coat King may be used prior to clipping to remove undercoat and dead top coat.

You will see from this example that this show dog's body pattern is hand stripped from the back of the skull (occiput) to the tail. The pattern falls from the topline over the lower part of the ribcage to the area just below the elbow. The line slightly rises from just below the elbow to the loin.

When clipping these breeds, skim off with the clipper to lightly blend the clipped area into the furnishings. The pattern line should be well blended into the longer furnishings of the underline showing no evident transition line. Use thinning shears to blend the transition lines to mimic the show trim.

The length of underline will vary depending on the breed. The length of the furnishings may be modified according to the preference of the pet owner.

The shoulder and upper arm are set tighter than the body. The rear thigh muscle is tighter than the body to show the muscle tone.

It is recommended to use a stripping knife after clipping these breeds to remove undercoat, which will help promote healthy skin and coat. Using a stripping knife to card the coat will also allow the coat to lie down and look more natural even though the back coat is clipped. Clipping Terriers will often cause the coat to lighten in color and soften in texture. Depending on the breed, using carding techniques will help keep some texture and color of the coats.

Tip To Remember:

Clipping a Terrier coat shorter than a 7F blade can be detrimental to the skin. It also makes blending into longer furnishings very difficult. Using longer blades will assist in giving a seamless appearance and will also emulate the breed profile.

The throat should be clipped tight. The pattern starts at the throat latch on breeds with full heads (i.e., Westie, Cairn) or at the back of the lower lip on breeds with beards. Clip down to the breastbone using a #2 comb, 4F, 5F, 7F or 10 blade depending on the breed, density of the coat and sensitivity of the skin. These blades may also be used against the lay of coat (from the breastbone up toward the head) which will give a shorter appearance than clipping with the lay of coat. Continue to clip from the base of the ear, creating a U shape to the breastbone.

The throat is defined by a natural cowlick in the hair that runs from the base of the ear to the breastbone. When setting the front of these breeds imagine a W pattern (see page 285). The upper arm should be set tight to where the upper arm joins the lower arm (at the elbow line). A #2 comb, 4F, 5F or 7F blade is recommended. The chest furnishings start at the cowlick of hair under the breastbone and cover the prosternum. Once these lines are set, use thinning shears to blend all clipped areas together and to blend into leg and chest furnishings.

The skeletal structure of these breeds varies. The Sealyham Terrier and Scottish Terrier have a pronounced forechest, where the West Highland White Terrier presents a straighter front. The furnishings that fall beneath the breastbone will naturally enhance the forechest.

The front legs should be scissored in a column, leaving more coat on the front of the legs. The back of the front leg can be scissored tighter. Leaving the coat on the front of the leg will eliminate a visible foot and will give a more column-like appearance.

The front legs should appear parallel when viewed from the front. The legs should form a straight line from the side of the upper arm down to the side of the foot.

Since these breeds carry longer furnishings, the chest furnishings are left as long as the client prefers. The length of chest furnishings will be determined by the amount of side coat that is left. The two lengths should meet between the front legs and flow nicely, presenting a nice profile.

Tip To Remember:

Brush through Terrier furnishings after the bath to remove tangles and excess undercoat. This technique will speed up the drying process as well as facilitate in straightening the furnishings while drying. When brushing a longer coat, whether it is a Sporting dog, Terrier, drop-coat or even ears and tails, always brush from the end of the hair shaft working up to the mat. Brushing over a mat or tangle can damage the coat. A damaged coat can be attributed to matting.

The side of the neck and shoulders should be set tighter than the body pattern, yet longer than the throat. A 4F or 5F blade or #2 snap-on comb is recommended for the sides of the neck, shoulder and upper arm area. The pattern should fall over the side of the upper arm muscle where it meets the lower arm (at the elbow line).

When using different blade lengths, i.e., 5F or 7F blade on the throat, 4F or 5F on the shoulders and #2 snap-on comb on the body pattern, the coat should blend nicely together. Use thinning shears to enhance a well-blended trim.

If a shorter trim is preferred, adjusting the blade lengths accordingly should still give this end result, just tighter.

The thigh should be well defined to show the muscle. This can be done by using a blade or snap-on comb which is one blade length longer than what was used on the shoulder. This area can also be clipped with the same blade/snap-on comb that was used on the body; however, thinning shears should then be used to define the muscle to the desired length and to blend into the furnishings. While clipping, skim off with the clipper at the transition line where the pattern meets the furnishings. This will begin the blending process.

The furnishings fall off the stifle from the muscle of the thigh. The stifle should be trimmed to show proper bend/angulation and should line up approximately with the croup.

The hocks are trimmed perpendicular to the ground. The feet should be trimmed round and tight at the base.

If the pet owner requests shorter furnishings, using various lengths of snap-on combs will help set the desired length. Using thinning shears to tidy up the furnishings will help remove any lines that were left from the snap-on comb/scissors.

A 4F, 5F or #2 comb may be used to set the rear.

The pattern follows the contour of the muscle to the back of the thigh. There is a natural part directly below the anus. The coat falls to both sides of the part, creating a "mustache". This area should be clipped or set tight using thinning shears. The coat below this part will fall between the legs similar to a curtain. This coat is part of the rear furnishings.

The rear furnishings start below the "mustache" and naturally fall toward the inside of the rear legs. The furnishings should be trimmed in an inverted V.

When viewed from the rear the legs should appear parallel, falling into a straight line from the outer thighs to the side of the foot.

Use thinning shears to blend the clipped areas into the furnishings for a well-blended natural look.

TERRIER-LIKE PATTERN LINES

Pattern Placement Diagrams

				Recommended Blade Lengths, Snap-On Comb Lengths and Techniques **Bold Print** = Preferred Choices for Pet Trims			
10 15	**7F** 5F	7F **5F** 4F carding	5F 4F **#2** carding	thinning shears scissor			

285

Tip To Remember:

All patterns can be modified to different lengths based on the pet owner's preference. All furnishings can also be modified. Use good judgment to execute a manageable trim for the pet owner keeping the breed standard in mind.

TERRIER-LIKE PATTERN LINES

Subtle in Nature

Common Breeds

The following are common breeds that have Subtle Terrier-Like pattern lines. Minor deviations from the described pattern will be noted as well as recommended tools and techniques for each breed. Important breed standard information will be quoted in part from participating breed clubs. When grooming these breeds, refer back to the guidelines of setting this pattern on page 278.

Cairn Terrier

The Cairn Terrier is a Terrier breed that originated in Scotland. It originally was referred to as one of the "Skye Terrier" breeds of Scotland until the early 1900s, when it was given the name Cairn Terrier. It was used to hunt fox and badger that lived throughout the rock dens referred to as "cairns". The Cairn Terrier would slip through the rock dens and hold its prey by barking to alert the farmer.

This coat should be carded and hand stripped for show. If hand stripping is not desired by the pet owner, it is recommended to use a Coat King to remove the undercoat and dead coat following the pattern lines as described. Clipping may be done with various lengths of snap-on combs, preferably a #2, #1, or #0. Carding and thinning shear techniques should be done in addition to clipping for a seamless appearance.

The Cairn Terrier has a more natural appearance than the other breeds described. The pattern is evident, although the lines are invisible. The throat is not as tight as other breeds in this group; however, it should be set tighter than the body coat pattern.

The furnishings may be trimmed to present the proper profile of the breed. The length of furnishings may vary according to the preference of the pet owner.

TERRIER-LIKE PATTERN LINES

See "Round Heads" on page 434 for instructions on grooming this head type.

See important information on "Carding" on page 30 and "Hand Stripping" on page 32.

Key points to remember when grooming the Cairn Terrier according to the breed standard:

The body of the Cairn Terrier is well muscled with a level topline. The tail is set off the topline and is well furnished. The shoulders are well laid back. The ribs are well sprung. The front legs are straight but the feet may be slightly turned out. The rear legs appear muscular. The rear feet are slightly smaller than the front feet.

The head has a round appearance and is well furnished with hair. The ears are small and carried erect. The coat on the tips of the ears should be short.

The coat of the Cairn Terrier is weather-resistant. It consists of a harsh outer coat and short soft undercoat. This should be hand stripped for show.

TERRIER-LIKE PATTERN LINES

Dog Grooming Simplified: Straight To The Point

				Recommended Blade Lengths, Snap-On Comb Lengths and Techniques **Bold Print** = Preferred Choices for Pet Trims			
10 15	4F **#2** #1	4F #2 **#1** carding	#2 #1 **#0** carding	thinning shears scissor			

290

Tip To Remember:

Tipping ears: Instead of clipping the outside top portion of a Westie or Cairn Terrier ear, for example, comb all the coat to the side of the ear tip and scissor the edge of the ear tight. Comb the coat to the opposite edge of the ear and scissor that edge tight. This will give a nice tight ear tip without the look of a sharp clipped line. The inside tip of the ear can be clipped with a 15 or 40 blade for a neat appearance.

Norfolk Terrier

The Norfolk Terrier is one of the smallest working Terrier breeds. It originated in England and was referred to as "the barnyard ratter" and was also used to hunt fox. It comfortably works alone or in packs. The Norwich Terrier and the Norfolk Terrier were considered one breed until 1979, when they were separated by ear type and other slight differences.

This coat should be carded and hand stripped for show. If hand stripping is not desired by the pet owner, it is recommended to use a Coat King to remove the undercoat and dead coat following the pattern lines as described. Clipping may be done with various lengths of snap-on combs, preferably a #2, #1, or #0 comb. Carding and thinning shear techniques should be done in addition to clipping for a seamless appearance.

The Norfolk Terrier has a mane on the neck and shoulders which is characteristic of this breed. This area should be carefully blended with thinning shears and should not be removed. Removing this mane will take away from the breed profile.

For pet trims the ears can be clipped with a 7F or 10 blade for a smooth appearance. The topskull can be tightened by using thinning shears, leaving a slight brow. See important information on "Carding" on page 30 and "Hand Stripping" on page 32.

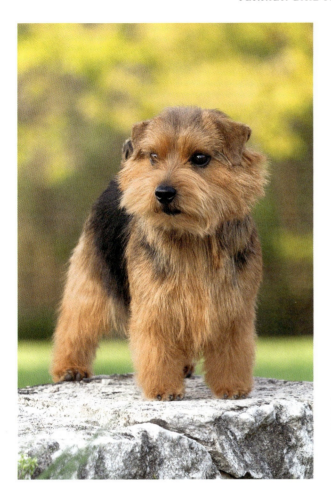

Key points to remember when grooming the Norfolk Terrier according to the breed standard:

The Norfolk Terrier is slightly longer than it is tall. The shoulders are well angulated. The neck is of medium length. The ribs are well sprung with a moderately deep chest. The topline is level. The tail is docked and is set high and level with the topline.

The front legs are straight and parallel with round feet.

The rear legs have muscular thighs and have well-bent stifles. The hocks are well let down and parallel to the ground. The back feet are round.

The skull of the Norfolk Terrier is wide and slightly rounded. The muzzle is wedge-shaped and appears strong. The stop is well defined. The muzzle, when measured from the nose to stop, measures 1/3 less than the skull when measured from the stop to occiput. The head should have a smooth appearance with small triangular eyebrows and short beard or whiskers.

The ears fold at the skull line and are carried close to the cheek. They have a V-shaped appearance with rounded tips. The ears should have a smooth appearance.

The outer coat is hard, wiry and straight with a definite undercoat. The coat lies close to the body and should be approximately 1 1/2″ to 2″ in length. The furnishings are of moderate length.

TERRIER-LIKE PATTERN LINES

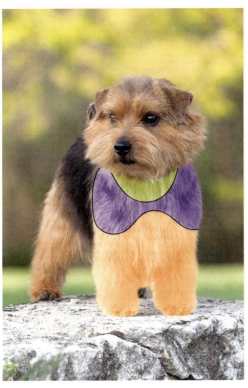

10 15	4F **#2** #1	4F #2 **#1** carding	#2 #1 **#0** carding	thinning shears scissor			

Recommended Blade Lengths, Snap-On Comb Lengths and Techniques
Bold Print = Preferred Choices for Pet Trims

Norwich Terrier

The Norwich Terrier is one of the smallest working Terrier breeds. It originated in England and was referred to as "the barnyard ratter" and was also used to hunt fox. It comfortably works alone or in packs. The Norwich Terrier and the Norfolk Terrier were considered one breed until 1979, when they were separated by ear type and other slight differences. The Norwich Terrier is known for its "foxy" expression.

This coat should be carded and hand stripped for show. If hand stripping is not desired by the pet owner, it is recommended to use a Coat King to remove the undercoat and dead coat following the pattern lines as described. Clipping may be done with various lengths of snap-on combs, preferably a #2, #1, or #0 comb. Carding and thinning shear techniques should be done in addition to clipping for a seamless appearance.

The Norwich Terrier has a mane on the neck and shoulders which is characteristic of this breed. This area should be carefully blended with thinning shears and should not be removed. Removing this mane will take away from the breed profile.

For pet trims the ears can be clipped with a 7F or 10 blade for a smooth appearance. The topskull can be tightened by using thinning shears, leaving a slight brow.

See important information on "Carding" on page 30 and "Hand Stripping" on page 32.

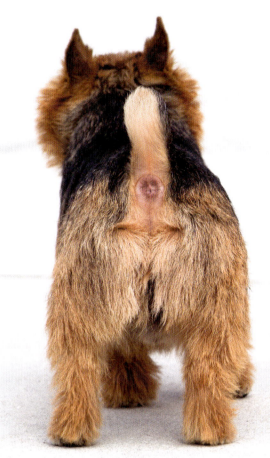

Quoted in part with permission from the Norwich Terrier Club of America, Approved October 13, 1981:

One of the smallest of the Terriers, the ideal height should not exceed 10 inches at the withers. Distances from the top of the withers to the ground and from the withers to base of tail are approximately equal. Level topline.

Neck of medium length, strong and blending into well laid back shoulders. Body moderately short. Compact and deep. Good width of chest. Well-sprung ribs and short loins. Tail medium docked. The Terrier's working origin requires that the tail be of sufficient length to grasp. Base level with topline; carried erect.

Forequarters: Well laid back shoulders. Elbows close to ribs. Short, powerful legs, as straight as is consistent with the digging Terrier. Feet round with thick pads.

Hindquarters: Broad, strong and muscular with well-turned stifles. Hocks low set and straight when viewed from the rear. Feet as in front.

A slightly foxy expression. Ears medium size and erect. Set well apart with pointed tips. Upright when alert. The skull is broad and slightly rounded with good width between the ears. The muzzle is wedge shaped and strong. Its length is about one-third less than the measurement from the occiput to the well-defined stop.

Coat: Hard, wiry and straight, lying close to the body with a definite undercoat. The coat on neck and shoulders forms a protective mane. The hair on head, ears and muzzle, except for slight eyebrows and whiskers, is short and smooth. This breed should be shown with as natural a coat as possible.

TERRIER-LIKE PATTERN LINES

Recommended Blade Lengths, Snap-On Comb Lengths and Techniques **Bold Print** = Preferred Choices for Pet Trims						
10 15	4F **#2** #1	4F #2 **#1** carding	#2 #1 **#0** carding	thinning shears scissor		

299

Scottish Terrier

The Scottish Terrier is a Terrier breed that originated in Scotland. It is commonly referred to as the "Scottie". It was bred to hunt and kill vermin on the farms of Scotland.

This coat should be carded and hand stripped for show. If clipping is preferred, a 4F blade, #2 or #1 snap-on comb are recommended. A Coat King can be used to remove the undercoat and dead coat following the pattern lines as described. Carding and thinning shear techniques should be done in addition to clipping for a natural appearance.

The Scottish Terrier has a well-developed, muscular and powerful rear. The rear should extend well beyond the tail-set. The Scottie should also have a well-developed forechest that extends well in front of the legs. These structure points change the profile of the Scottie compared with other breeds in this group; however, the pattern is set in the same manner.

The furnishings may be trimmed to present the proper profile of the breed. The length of furnishings may vary according to the preference of the pet owner.

A small tuft of hair is left in front of the ear canal. This hair hides the opening of the ear canal, which softens the extreme look of a completely shaved ear. This tuft should not be longer than half the height of the ear. It should be trimmed with thinning shears on an angle from the outside corner of the ear base up to the inside edge of the ear leather. The highest point of this angle should not exceed half the height of the ear. If the ears are set too far apart, more hair can be left on the inside tufts between the ears to give the illusion of a proper ear set. This tuft is very important to the expression of the Scottie. The Scottish Terrier has a rectangular-shaped head with long, arched triangular eyebrows and full beard.

See "Rectangular Heads" on page 427 for instructions on grooming this head type.

See important information on "Carding" on page 30 and "Hand Stripping" on page 32.

Quoted in part with permission from the Scottish Terrier Club of America, Approved October 12, 1993:

Height at withers for either sex should be about 10 inches. The length of back from withers to set-on of tail should be approximately 11 inches. The topline of the back should be firm and level.

The neck should be moderately short, strong, thick and muscular, blending smoothly into well laid back shoulders. The body should be moderately short with ribs extending well back into a short, strong loin, deep flanks and very muscular hindquarters. The ribs should be well sprung out from the spine, forming a broad, strong back, then curving down and inward to form a deep body that would be nearly heart-shaped if viewed in cross-section.

The forechest should extend well in front of the legs and drop well down into the brisket.

The tail should be set on high and carried erectly. The tail should be thick at the base, tapering gradually to a point and covered with short, hard hair.

The thighs should be very muscular and powerful for the size of the dog with the stifles well bent and the legs straight from hock to heel. Hocks should be well let down and parallel to each other.

The forelegs should be very heavy in bone, straight or slightly bent with elbows close to the body, and set in under the shoulder blade with a definite forechest in front of them. Scottish Terriers should not be out at the elbows. The forefeet should be larger than the hind feet, round, thick and compact with strong nails. The front feet should point straight ahead, but a slight "toeing out" is acceptable.

The head should be long in proportion to the overall length and size of the dog. In profile, the skull and muzzle should give the appearance of two parallel planes. The skull should be long and of medium width, slightly domed and covered with short, hard hair. In profile, the skull should appear flat. There should be a slight but definite stop between the skull and muzzle at eye level, allowing the eyes to be set in under the brow, contributing to proper Scottish Terrier expression.

The skull should be smooth with no prominences or depressions and the cheeks should be flat and clean. The muzzle should be approximately equal to the length of skull with only a slight taper to the nose. The muzzle should be well filled in under the eye, with no evidence of snipiness. The eyes should be set wide apart and well in under the brow.

The ears should be small, prick, set well up on the skull and pointed, but never cut. They should be covered with short velvety hair. From the front, the outer edge of the ear should form a straight line up from the side of the skull.

Coat: The Scottish Terrier should have a broken coat. It is a hard, wiry outer coat with a soft, dense undercoat. The coat should be trimmed and blended into the furnishings to give a distinct Scottish Terrier outline. The dog should be presented with sufficient coat so that the texture and density may be determined. The longer coat on the beard, legs and lower body may be slightly softer than the body coat but should not be or appear fluffy.

Available on DVD: "The Scottish Terrier - Pet Trim"

TERRIER-LIKE PATTERN LINES

	Recommended Blade Lengths, Snap-On Comb Lengths and Techniques **Bold Print** = Preferred Choices for Pet Trims						
10 15	**10** 7F	7F **5F** 4F carding	5F 4F **#2** carding	thinning shears scissor			

303

Sealyham Terrier

The Sealyham Terrier is a Terrier breed that originated in Wales. It was bred to hunt badger, fox and otter. Its white coat made the dog easy to see when it went to ground to capture vermin.

This coat should be carded and hand stripped for show. If hand stripping is not desired by the pet owner, it is recommended to use a Coat King to remove the undercoat and dead coat following the pattern lines as described. Clipping may be done with a 4F blade or various lengths of snap-on combs, preferably a #2 or #1 comb. Carding and thinning shear techniques should be done in addition to clipping for a seamless appearance.

The furnishings may be trimmed to present the proper profile of the breed. The length of furnishings may vary according to the preference of the pet owner.

The Sealyham Terrier has a rectangular-shaped head with a fall and full beard. See "Rectangular Heads" on page 427 for instructions on grooming this head type.

See important information on "Carding" on page 30 and "Hand Stripping" on page 32.

Quoted in part with permission from the American Sealyham Terrier Club, Approved February 9, 1974:

Length from withers to set-on of tail should be approximate height at withers, or 10 1/2 inches. Topline is level.

Neck: Length slightly less than two-thirds of height of dog at withers. Muscular without coarseness, with good reach, refinement at throat, and set firmly on shoulders.

Shoulders: Well laid back and powerful, but not over-muscled. Sufficiently wide to permit freedom of action. Forelegs strong, with good bone; and as straight as is consistent with chest being well let down between them. Hind legs longer than forelegs and not so heavily boned. Feet – Large but compact. Forefeet larger, though not quite so long as hind feet.

Body: Strong, short-coupled and substantial, so as to permit great flexibility. Brisket deep and well let down between forelegs. Ribs well sprung.

Hindquarters – Very powerful, and protruding well behind the set-on of tail. Strong second thighs [the part of the hindquarters from the stifle to the hock, corresponding to the human shin and calf].

Head: Long, broad and powerful, without coarseness. It should, however, be in perfect balance with the body, joining neck smoothly. Length of head roughly, three-quarters height at withers, or about an inch longer than neck. Skull – Very slightly domed, with a shallow indentation running down between the brows, and joining the muzzle with a moderate stop. Cheeks – Smoothly formed and flat, without heavy jowls. Jaws – Powerful and square.

Coat: Weather-resisting, comprised of soft, dense undercoat and hard, wiry top coat.

The Sealyham Terrier

"The Sealyham should be the embodiment of power and determination, ever keen and alert, of extraordinary substance, yet free from clumsiness."

TERRIER-LIKE PATTERN LINES

10 15	**7F** 5F	7F **5F** 4F carding	5F 4F **#2** carding	thinning shears scissor			

Recommended Blade Lengths, Snap-On Comb Lengths and Techniques
Bold Print = Preferred Choices for Pet Trims

307

WEST HIGHLAND WHITE TERRIER

The West Highland White Terrier, often referred to as the "Westie", is a Terrier breed that originated in Poltalloch, Scotland. Years ago it was called the Poltalloch Terrier but soon became the West Highland White Terrier in the early 1900s. This is a good little hunter, full of spunk and very intelligent.

This coat should be carded and hand stripped for show. If hand stripping is not desired by the pet owner, it is recommended to use a Coat King to remove the undercoat and dead coat following the pattern lines as described. Clipping may be done with a 4F blade or various lengths of snap-on combs, preferably a #2 or #1 comb. Carding and thinning shear techniques should be done in addition to clipping for a seamless appearance.

The furnishings may be trimmed to present the proper profile of the breed. The length of furnishings may vary according to the preference of the pet owner.

See "Round Heads" on page 434 for instructions on grooming this head type. See important information on "Carding" on page 30 and "Hand Stripping" on page 32.

Quoted in part with permission from the West Highland White Terrier Club of America, Approved December 13, 1988:

The Westie is a compact dog, with good balance and substance. The body between the withers and the root of the tail is slightly shorter than the height at the withers.

Topline: Flat and level.

Neck: Muscular and well set on sloping shoulders. The length of neck should be in proportion to the remainder of the dog. Ribs deep and well arched in the upper half of rib, extending at least to the elbows, and presenting a flattish side appearance. Chest very deep and extending to the elbows. Loin short, broad and strong. Tail–Relatively short, with good substance, and shaped like a carrot. It is covered with hard hair without feather, as straight as possible.

Shoulder blades are well laid back and well knit at the backbone. The shoulder blade should attach to an upper arm of moderate length, and sufficient angle to allow for definite body overhang. Forelegs are muscular and well boned, relatively short, but with sufficient length to set the dog up so as not to be too close to the ground. The legs are reasonably straight, and thickly covered with short hard hair. They are set in under the shoulder blades with definite body overhang before them. Height from elbow to withers and elbow to ground should be approximately the same.

Forefeet are larger than the hind ones, are round, proportionate in size.

Thighs are very muscular, well angulated, with hock well bent, short, and parallel when viewed from the rear. Rear legs are muscular and relatively short and sinewy. Hind feet are smaller than front feet.

Head is shaped to present a round appearance from the front. Should be in proportion to the body. Looking from under heavy eyebrows, they give a piercing look. Ears–Small, carried tightly erect, set wide apart, on the top outer edge of the skull. The hair on the ears is trimmed short and is smooth and velvety, free of fringe at the tips. Skull–Broad, slightly longer than the muzzle, not flat on top but slightly domed between the ears. It gradually tapers to the eyes. There is a defined stop, eyebrows are heavy. Muzzle–Blunt, slightly shorter than the skull, powerful and gradually tapering to the nose.

Coat: Very important and seldom seen to perfection. Must be double-coated. The head is shaped by plucking the hair, to present the round appearance. The outer coat consists of straight hard white hair, about two inches long, with shorter coat on neck and shoulders, properly blended and trimmed to blend shorter areas into furnishings, which are longer on stomach and legs.

The ideal coat is hard, straight and white, but a hard straight coat which may have some wheaten tipping is preferable to a white fluffy or soft coat. Furnishings may be somewhat softer and longer but should never give the appearance of fluff.

The West Highland White Terrier

"The West Highland is all terrier - a large amount of Scotch spunk, determination, and devotion crammed into a small body."

Available on DVD: "The West Highland White Terrier - Pet Trim"

TERRIER-LIKE PATTERN LINES

Recommended Blade Lengths, Snap-On Comb Lengths and Techniques **Bold Print** = Preferred Choices for Pet Trims							
10 15	**7F** 5F	7F **5F** 4F carding	5F 4F **#2** carding	thinning shears scissor			

Tip To Remember:

Many long-coated breeds—including the Bearded Collie, Shih Tzu, Yorkshire Terrier, Maltese and Havanese—are shown in full coat. However, these long coats can be difficult for pet owners to maintain. The techniques and pattern placements discussed in "Sculpted Body Trims" can be used for shorter stylized pet trims on longer-coated breeds.

Sculpted Body Trims

Bedlington Terrier

Bichon Frise

Black Russian Terrier

Bouvier des Flandres

Irish Water Spaniel

Kerry Blue Terrier

Lagotto Romagnolo

Poodle

Portuguese Water Dog

Soft Coated Wheaten Terrier

Tip To Remember:

There are countless styles of scissors available for groomers. Shears range in length, shank size, metal quality, cutting edge, weight, etc. Selecting the right shear is a personal choice. Using the correct edge for a particular coat type will help make scissoring seem effortless. A German style shear has a serrated edge to remove length of coat. A serrated edge will grab the coat and is capable of cutting volume. A Japanese style shear has a convex edge. This type of edge is very sharp and is not designed to remove volume. This shear is used to tip the ends of the coat to put a crisp scissor finish on the trim.

Sculpted Body Trims

Several breeds have a curly dense coat or a longer drop-coat that are scissored following the body structure. Unlike the other two pattern groups, when grooming coated breeds, the pattern is hand scissored instead of hand stripped or clipped. This pattern group is very similar to the Distinct Terrier-Like patterns. The difference is the length of coat, coat type and bone structure, which change the appearance of these breeds, making each breed unique.

The topline, shoulder angulation, rear angulation, correct underline, tuck-up, and other features are set based on the bone structure of each breed. This is done in the same manner as for the other groups. The only difference is — different coat types require different techniques and tools.

Many long-coated breeds—including the Bearded Collie, Shih Tzu, Yorkshire Terrier, Maltese and Havanese—are shown in full coat. However, these long coats can be difficult for pet owners to maintain. The techniques and pattern placements discussed in "Sculpted Body Trims" can be used for shorter stylized pet trims on longer-coated breeds.

Snap-on combs can be used to set the initial length and pattern on these breeds. Scissoring and/or thinning shear techniques are required to define the pattern and to finish the trim for a well-blended, seamless appearance.

The tail styles vary from breed to breed that fall under "Sculpted Body Trims". The Bedlington Terrier and Irish Water Spaniel, for example, have a rat tail. The Bouvier des Flandres and Black Russian Terrier, on the other hand, have docked tails. See "Tail Styles" on page 447 for instructions on grooming various tail styles.

See "Point-to-Point Scissoring" on page 37 for scissoring techniques.

The Lagotto Romagnolo, for example, has a curly dense coat and is scissored following the structure of the breed to create the proper profile.

Various lengths of snap-on combs can be used to set the initial length and pattern. Scissoring and/or thinning shear techniques are required to define the pattern and to finish the trim for a well-blended, seamless appearance.

You will see from this example that the body pattern on this show dog is hand scissored from the back of the skull (occiput) to the tail. The crest of neck should be left long enough in order to smoothly transition over the withers into the level topline.

The pattern falls from the topline over the lower part of the ribcage to the area just below the elbow. The widest part of the ribcage is located midway between the topline and the underline. This area should be scissored to create the proper spring of ribs. When clipping this pattern, leave the coat below the elbow line so it can be scissored in showing the proper underline and tuck-up.

The shoulder and upper arm are set tighter than the body to show the angulated shoulder blade. This can be achieved by using a shorter snap-on comb than was used on the body pattern. The pattern should fall off the upper arm and transition into a straight line down the side of the front leg.

The rear thigh muscle is scissored to show the muscle tone, leaving the coat longer on the front of the back leg to show the correct bend of stifle. This can be done by using a snap-on comb which is one length longer than what was used on the shoulder. This area can also be clipped with the same snap-on comb that was used on the body, however, the thigh area should then be scissored tighter to define the muscle.

The transition area from the tighter thigh muscle to the longer coat off the stifle should be well blended for a seamless appearance. The stifle should be trimmed to show the proper bend and should fall in line with the croup.

The chest is scissored to display the correct forechest. When scissoring the forechest on curly-coated breeds, follow the line of the prosternum from the breastbone. If too much coat is left on the front of the front leg, the forechest will be diminished. To show forechest, the front of the front leg should be trimmed as close to the front of the toes as possible, maintaining the column-like appearance.

The front legs are scissored to appear column-like. To achieve a column-like appearance, more coat is left on the front of the front leg than the back. For a point of reference, the elbow should fall in line with the withers.

The circumference of the front leg should be equal to the back leg when measured from the stifle to the back of the bend of stifle for a well-balanced trim. See "Leg Circumference" on page 42.

Tip To Remember:

Determining the length of coat for pet trims should be based on the pet's grooming schedule. Modifying the schedule or changing the length of the trim should be the choices to eliminate unnecessary matting.

The Soft Coated Wheaten Terrier, for example, has a drop-coat and should be trimmed solely with thinning shears for the show ring following the structure of the breed to create the proper profile. When grooming a drop-coated breed, think of a layered trim. The coat is trimmed the shortest on the topline and should gradually become longer as it rolls over the ribcage to the underline.

For pet trims this coat can be trimmed using snap-on combs and thinning shears. Scissoring and/or thinning shear techniques are required to define the pattern and to finish the trim for a well-blended, seamless appearance.

Snap-on combs can either be used close to the skin, leaving the coat true to the comb size, or they can be used with a "skimming off" technique. Using the comb with a light hand will help to blend drop-coats, creating a layered appearance. For example, when trimming the topline, the comb can be used against the skin. While transitioning over the ribcage, the comb can be used to skim over the ribcage with a light hand, blending the shorter coat of the topline into the longer coat of the ribcage.

This technique is demonstrated on the "The Soft Coated Wheaten Terrier - Pet Trim" and "Snap-On Combs: Theory & Techniques" DVDs.

You will see from this example that the body pattern on this show dog is trimmed with thinning shears from the back of the skull (occiput) to the tail. The crest of neck should be left long enough in order to smoothly transition over the withers into the level topline. On drop-coats it may be necessary to leave the coat slightly longer over the withers to achieve a smooth transition.

The pattern falls from the topline over the lower part of the ribcage to the area just below the elbow. The widest part of the ribcage is located halfway between the topline and the underline. This area should be scissored to create the proper spring of ribs. When clipping this pattern, leave the coat below the elbow line so it can be scissored in showing the proper underline and tuck-up.

The shoulder and upper arm are set tighter than the body to show the angulated shoulder blade. This can be achieved by using a shorter snap-on comb than was used on the body pattern. The pattern should fall off the upper arm and transition into a straight line down the side of the front leg.

The rear thigh muscle is trimmed to show the muscle tone, leaving the coat longer on the front of the back leg to show the correct bend of stifle. The thigh area can be set using a snap-on comb which is one length longer than what was used on the shoulder. The same snap-on comb that was used on the body can also be used to set the thigh; however, it should then be scissored tighter to define the thigh muscle.

The transition area from the tighter thigh muscle to the longer coat of the stifle should be well blended for a seamless appearance. The stifle should be trimmed to show the proper bend and should fall in line with the croup.

The chest is scissored to display the correct forechest.

The front legs are scissored to appear column-like. To achieve a column-like appearance, more coat is left on the front of the front leg than the back. The elbow should fall in line with the withers.

When comparing these two breeds, it is apparent that the pattern is set in the same manner. The coat type and structure of the dog are what change the appearance, making each one unique.

Tip To Remember:

It can be very difficult to blend drop-coated breeds. The coat is not very forgiving when it comes to scissoring and using snap-on combs. Lifting the coat with a comb and tipping the ends with thinning shears will even out the appearance.

The throat is set tight to the breastbone.

On curly-type coats, the chest is scissored from the breastbone following the prosternum, showing the correct forechest. On drop-coated breeds the coat falls with a more layered look. The shoulders are trimmed to show the angulated shoulder blade.

The pattern should fall off the upper arm and transition into a straight line down the side of the front leg. This can be achieved by using a shorter snap-on comb than was used on the body pattern.

The legs are parallel and appear column-like.

The rear pattern is set in the same manner on both coat types. The rear angulation is set the tightest at the back of the bend of knee.

When viewed from the rear, the legs present parallel lines. The inner thighs should be set tight. The inside parallel lines fall from the inner thighs. The outside parallel lines fall off the outer thigh muscle.

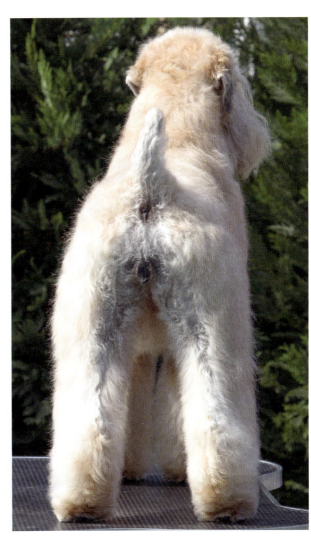

The patterns of the following breeds are all set in the same manner. There may be minor deviations from the pattern, which will be noted for each breed.

Bedlington Terrier

The Bedlington Terrier is a Terrier breed that originated in England. The name Bedlington comes from the mining shire where this breed originated. It is a ratting Terrier and a hunter of badgers and vermin. The Bedlington is quite the hunter despite its soft lamb-like appearance. It has "the head of a lamb and the heart of a lion".

The Bedlington carries a soft stand-up type coat which presents a subtle and seamless appearance of the pattern. The topline and underline should mimic one another.

Various lengths of blades and snap-on combs may be used to achieve this outline. The body coat should not exceed 1 inch in length. The entire trim should flow without sharp angles.

Quoted in part with permission from the Bedlington Terrier Club of America, Approved September 12, 1967:

Chest deep. Flat-ribbed and deep through the brisket, which reaches to the elbows. Back has a good natural arch over the loin, creating a definite tuck-up of the underline. Body slightly greater in length than height. Well-muscled quarters are also fine and graceful.

Legs and Feet: Lithe and muscular. The hind legs are longer than the forelegs, which are straight and wider apart at the chest than at the feet. Slight bend to pasterns which are long and sloping without weakness. Stifles well angulated. Hocks strong and well let down, turning neither in nor out. Long hare feet. Tail: Set low, scimitar-shaped, thick at the root and tapering to a point which reaches the hock.

Photo courtesy of Catherine Lynch Carey

Head: Narrow, but deep and rounded. Shorter in skull and longer in jaw. Covered with a profuse topknot which is lighter than the color of the body, highest at the crown, and tapering gradually to just back of the nose. There must be no stop and the unbroken line from crown to nose end reveals a slender head without cheekiness or snipiness.

Ears: Triangular with rounded tips. Set on low and hanging flat to the cheek in front with a slight projection at the base. Thin and velvety in texture, covered with fine hair forming a small silky tassel at the tip.

Coat: A very distinctive mixture of hard and soft hair standing well out from the skin. Crisp to the touch but not wiry, having a tendency to curl, especially on the head and face. When in show trim must not exceed 1 inch on body; hair on legs is slightly longer.

The pattern appears very subtle and seamless due to the coat type. The Bedlington carries a soft stand-up type coat.

Various lengths of blades and snap-on combs may be used to achieve this outline. The body coat should not exceed 1 inch in length. The entire trim should flow without sharp angles.

The topline has a natural arch over the loin called a "roach." A 1/2-inch area over the withers, or slightly behind the withers, should be scissored very tight or clipped with a 5F which will accentuate the length of neck and the structure of the topline.

The highest point of the tuck-up should fall in line with the highest point of the roach. The underline is scissored to show the extreme tuck-up which mimics the roach of the topline. The tuck-up can be skimmed with a 40 blade tight to the skin to accentuate the extreme tuck-up. The shape of the body from the shoulders to the point of rump should resemble the letter S.

The Bedlington is a flat-ribbed breed, which should be taken into consideration when setting the length of coat over the ribcage.

The shoulders are scissored tighter than the body to show the shoulder layback. This can be done using a 5F or 7F blade.

The thighs can be clipped with a blade/snap-on comb which is one length longer than what was used on the shoulder. The thigh can also be clipped the same length as the body; however, it should then be scissored tighter to accentuate the muscle.

The front legs should appear straight with a slight bend at the pastern. The Bedlington has hare feet and should be scissored to show this shape.

The rear legs are well angulated. The stifles are well bent and should fall in line with the croup.

The throat is clipped in a V shape set very tight using a 10 or 15 blade with or against the grain of coat. The chest is clipped or scissored tight over the prosternum. Drop off with the clipper before the prosternum curves under the dog. The undercarriage, between the front legs, can be scissored into a subtle V shape. This area should not extend below the elbow.

The front legs are straight; however, they are naturally wider apart at the chest creating a keyhole between them. The front feet stand close together and slightly toe out.

The head of the Bedlington should have a narrow rectangular appearance when viewed from the front. When viewed from profile the top of the muzzle should be scissored with a very slight arch as it reaches the occiput.

The cheeks, underjaw and neck can be clipped very tight using a 10 or 15 blade against the grain for pet trims. The clipped line starts approximately one finger width or 1/4" above the top of the ear ridge and runs to the corner of the eye. The line continues from the corner of the eye to the corner of the mouth or slightly in front of the corner of the mouth. The lip area under the front of the nose can be clipped with a 40 blade for a clean appearance.

The ears are carefully clipped against the grain using a 40 blade, leaving approximately one third of the ear at the tip with hair to create a tassel. The clipped tassel line should appear as an inverted V. The ear is clipped approximately one finger width or 1/4" over the ridge where the ear meets the skull. Caution should be taken around the fine flap of skin of the ear leather. This flap is located on the inside and outside back portion of the ear and can be easily cut.

The bottom of the tassel can be trimmed with a slight U shape or a straight line. When the ear is pulled forward, the length of the tassel should not extend past the tip of the nose.

Once the head is trimmed, the highest point of the occiput should transition into the crest of neck which then flows tight over the withers.

The rear, from the point of rump to the back of the bend of stifle, should be clipped tight with a 5F blade. The rear legs are scissored to accentuate the muscle of the thigh.

When viewed from the rear the legs should present parallel lines. The rear legs stand wider apart than the front legs. Therefore, the inside parallel lines should be scissored tighter than the outside parallel lines to set the legs apart.

The Bedlington has a rat tail. See "Tail Styles" on page 451 for instructions on grooming this tail type.

SCULPTED BODY TRIMS

Recommended Blade Lengths, Snap-On Comb Lengths and Techniques
Bold Print = Preferred Choices for Pet Trims

10 15	**10**	**5F** 7F	5F 4F **#2**	scissor		

327

Bichon Frise

The Bichon Frise is a member of the Non-Sporting group. It originated in the Mediterranean areas and descends from the Barbet or Water Spaniel. It was known as the Barbichon, which eventually was shortened to Bichon. These dogs are known for their merry disposition, which made them very desirable for sailors to use for bartering. The Bichon Frise is now a companion dog and is an extremely popular breed.

Groomed by Lindsey Dickens

The Bichon Frise is known to have a "powder puff" appearance. It should be scissored so all aspects of the trim are rounded off with subtle curves and flowing lines. The Bichon should never look extreme with sharp angles. This trim may be modified by using various lengths of blades and/or snap-on combs for a manageable pet trim following the body structure.

> Quoted in part with permission from the Bichon Frise Club of America, Inc., Approved October 11, 1988, Effective November 30, 1988:
>
> The Bichon Frise is a small, sturdy, white powder puff of a dog whose merry temperament is evidenced by his plumed tail carried jauntily over the back and his dark-eyed inquisitive expression.

Proportion: The body from the forward-most point of the chest to the point of rump is ¼ longer than the height at the withers. The body from the withers to lowest point of chest represents ½ the distance from withers to ground.

The arched neck is long and carried proudly behind an erect head. It blends smoothly into the shoulders. The length of neck from occiput to withers is approximately 1/3 the distance from forechest to buttocks. The topline is level except for a slight, muscular arch over the loin. The chest is well developed and wide enough to allow free and unrestricted movement of the front legs. The lowest point of the chest extends at least to the elbow. The rib cage is moderately sprung and extends back to a short and muscular loin. The forechest is well pronounced and protrudes slightly forward of the point of shoulder. The underline has a moderate tuck-up. Tail is well plumed, set on level with the topline and curved gracefully over the back so that the hair of the tail rests on the back.

The shoulder blade, upper arm and forearm are approximately equal in length. The shoulders are laid back to somewhat near a forty-five degree angle. The upper arm extends well back so the elbow is placed directly below the withers when viewed from the side. Legs are of medium bone; straight, with no bow or curve in the forearm or wrist.

The hindquarters are of medium bone, well angulated with muscular thighs and spaced moderately wide. The upper and lower thigh are nearly equal in length meeting at a well bent stifle joint. The leg from hock joint to foot pad is perpendicular to the ground.

A properly balanced head is three parts muzzle to five parts skull, measured from the nose to the stop and from the stop to the occiput. Ears are drop and are covered with long flowing hair. When extended toward the nose, the leathers reach approximately halfway the length of the muzzle. They are set on slightly higher than eye level and rather forward on the skull, so that when the dog is alert they serve to frame the face. The skull is slightly rounded, allowing for a round and forward looking eye. The stop is slightly accentuated.

A line drawn between the outside corners of the eyes and to the nose will create a near equilateral triangle.

Coat: When bathed and brushed, it stands off the body, creating an overall powder puff appearance. Trimming–The coat is trimmed to reveal the natural outline of the body. It is rounded off from any direction and never cut so short as to create an overly trimmed or squared off appearance. The furnishings of the head, beard, moustache, ears and tail are left longer. The longer head hair is trimmed to create an overall rounded impression. The topline is trimmed to appear level. The coat is long enough to maintain the powder puff look which is characteristic of the breed.

The Bichon Frise has a "stand off the body" coat type which can be hand scissored. The lines are very subtle and seamless due to the coat type and length of coat.

A variety of snap-on combs ranging from a #2, #1 or #0 can be used to achieve this outline. The legs should be scissored longer than the body for a well-balanced trim. The length of coat chosen will depend upon the pet owner's preference.

The crest of neck should be left long enough in order to smoothly transition over the withers into the level topline.

The shoulders are trimmed tighter than the body to show the shoulder layback. This can be achieved by using a shorter snap-on comb than was used on the body pattern.

The body is trimmed to show the spring of ribs.

The rear legs are trimmed to show rear angulation and to accentuate the muscle of the thigh. The stifles are well bent and should fall in line with the croup.

The thighs can be clipped with a snap-on comb which is one length longer than what was used on the shoulder. The thigh can also be clipped the same length as the body; however, it should then be scissored tighter to accentuate the muscle.

The hocks are perpendicular to the ground.

The front legs are scissored to appear column-like. The elbow should fall in line with the withers.

The underline is scissored to show the moderate tuck-up.

The throat is set tight to the breastbone. The front is scissored to present the proper forechest.

When grooming the head of the Bichon Frise, the ears should be invisible and should be scissored as part of the circle. The Bichon has a distinct "snake shaped" visor. This is achieved by using curved shears with the bend of the shear in front of the eye. The curve of the shear should be reversed between the eyes, which creates this shape. The front of the upper lip can be clipped with blades ranging from 10, 15 or 40 which prevents hair from entering the mouth. This also gives a clean appearance and shows the dark pigment in the skin. See "Round Heads" on page 434 for further instructions on grooming this head type.

When looking at the Bichon from the rear, the shape should resemble an inverted U. The rear should be well angulated with parallel lines. The rear angle should be set tightest at the bend of knee.

The Bichon should have a plumed tail. See "Tail Styles" on page 454 for instructions on grooming this tail style.

Available on DVD: "The Bichon Frise - Show Trim" and "The Bichon Frise - Pet Trim"

Dog Grooming Simplified: Straight To The Point

Sculpted Body Trims

Recommended Blade Lengths, Snap-On Comb Lengths and Techniques						
Bold Print = Preferred Choices for Pet Trims						
10 15	5F 4F **#2**	#2 #1 **#0**	#1 #0 **#A**	scissor	4F **#2** #1	

334

Tip To Remember:

It is very important to have a system while grooming any breed. Always start in the same place and end in the same place on every dog. This will improve efficiency while grooming. Point-to-point scissoring is a methodical way of scissoring. It is similar to "connect the dots". This method will assist the groomer in scissoring body parts in an efficient manner.

Black Russian Terrier

The Black Russian Terrier is a Working dog that originated in Russia. It was used to perform guard work.

The Black Russian has a wide chest with well-sprung ribs. It has a pronounced forechest. This breed displays strength and power. The BRT has somewhat of a drop-coat which is slightly wavy with a dense undercoat.

Various lengths of snap-on combs should be used to present the proper breed profile. The length of coat chosen should be based on the pet owner's preference as well as grooming schedule. If there is an excess of undercoat, the use of a Coat King will aid in reducing the density. However, if too much undercoat is removed the coat will fall and will lose the substance.

> Quoted in part with permission from the Black Russian Terrier Club of America, Approved May 12, 2009:
>
> The desired height to length ratio of the Black Russian Terrier is approximately 9.5 to 10. Thus the dog is slightly longer than tall.

The neck should be thick, muscular and powerful. The length of the neck and the length of the head should be approximately the same. The neck is set at an approximate 45-degree angle to the line of the back.

The whole structure of the body should give the impression of strength. The chest is oval shaped, deep and wide with well-sprung ribs. The forechest is pronounced. The withers are high, well developed and more pronounced in the male than in the female. There is a slight slope from the top of the withers into a straight, firm back.

Shoulders are well laid-back with blades broad and sloping. There is good return of upper arm so that the angle between the shoulder blade and the upper arm is approximately 100 degrees. Upper arms are muscular. The forelegs are straight, thick, of medium length, and parallel when viewed from the front. Length of the foreleg to the elbow is approximately 50% of dog's height at the withers. Pasterns are short, thick, and almost vertical. Feet are large, compact, and round in shape.

Viewed from the rear the legs are straight and parallel, set slightly wider than the forelegs. The hindquarters are well boned and muscular with good angulation to be in balance with the front shoulder angulation. Thighs are muscular and broad when viewed from the side. The hocks are moderately short and vertical when standing.

The Black Russian Terrier

"The Black Russian Terrier was initially bred to guard and protect. He is alert and responsive, instinctively protective, determined, fearless, deeply loyal to family, is aloof and therefore does not relish intrusion by strangers into his personal space."

The head must be in proportion to the body and give the appearance of power and strength. It is approximately equal to the length of neck and not less than 40% of the height of the dog at the withers. The ears are medium in size, triangularly shaped, set high, but not above, the level of the skull. The ear leather is dense, rounded at the bottom, hanging with the front edge lying against the head and terminating at approximately mid-cheek. The skull is moderately wide with round, but not too pronounced cheek bones. The supraorbital arches and occiput bones are moderately expressed. The back skull is flat. The stop is moderate. The back skull is slightly longer than the muzzle measured from the stop to the occiput and stop to end of nose, an approximate ratio of 5:4. The muzzle is broad with a slight tapering towards the nose. A moustache and beard emphasize volume and give the muzzle a square shape. Viewed in profile, the topline of the muzzle is parallel to the topline of the backskull.

Coat: The coat is a double coat. The natural untrimmed coat length varies from 1 1/2" to 6". While the outer guard hair is coarser than the softer undercoat, it is not wiry or curly. The body coat has a slight to moderate wave. The furnishings on the head form a fall over the eyes and a moustache and beard on the muzzle. The legs are covered and protected by long, dense coat.

The pattern appears very subtle and appears seamless due to the coat type and length. The BRT has somewhat of a drop-coat with a dense undercoat.

This breed can be trimmed using a #0, #1, #2 or various lengths of snap-on combs to achieve this outline.

The coat over the occiput should be transitioned into the crest of neck flowing over the withers. There is a slight slope over the withers to the level topline.

The shoulders are trimmed tighter than the body to show the shoulder layback. This can be achieved by using a shorter snap-on comb than was used on the body pattern.

The upper arm should appear muscular. Scissor the upper arm with a slightly rounded appearance to accentuate the muscle.

The Black Russian Terrier has a pronounced forechest and should be scissored to reflect that. The body is trimmed to show the well-sprung ribs.

The stifles are well bent and should fall in line with the croup.

The rear legs are trimmed to show rear angulation and to accentuate the muscle of the thigh.

The thighs can be clipped with a snap-on comb which is one length longer than what was used on the shoulder. The thigh can also be clipped the same length as the body; however, it should then be scissored tighter to accentuate the muscle.

The front legs are scissored to appear column-like. The elbow should fall in line with the withers.

The underline is scissored from just below the elbow to the loin showing a slight tuck-up.

The hocks are perpendicular to the ground.

The throat is clipped very tight using a 10 blade from the underjaw to the breastbone. The side of the neck is also clipped with a 10 blade. The line starts from the back of the base of the ear and continues on a slight angle, pointing toward the elbow, ending where the neck meets the shoulder.

The line continues around to meet the line on the throat. This line is very distinct. The appearance of the clipped neck is referred to as a "shirt front" or "tuxedo". The throat can also be clipped against the grain with a 7F blade if preferred.

The forechest is pronounced and should be scissored to reflect that.

The head of the BRT should be rectangular in shape. The head is broad and massive and displays strength. The ears of the BRT are clipped short from the fold to the tip with a 10 blade, leaving longer coat at the top of the ear to blend into the skull.

There is a square patch that is clipped on the plane of the topskull creating a flat appearance. This patch starts behind the brow, which is behind the fall area. This area is clipped with either a 5F or 7F blade with the lay of the coat. The patch extends to the area of the topskull where the front of the ear sets into the skull.

The area of the skull just beyond the square patch should be scissored to the occiput to accentuate the length of skull.

The length of the head should be equal to the length of neck. Leave just enough coat off the occiput to balance with the length of neck.

The area of the cheek just in front of the ear can be clipped with a 7F starting from the zygomatic arch.

The line continues to the underjaw meeting the clipperwork of the neck. The remainder of the cheek can be neatened with thinning shears to present the broad rectangular shape of the head. The BRT carries a full beard with a full fall covering the eyes.

Shape the cheeks and the side of the beard with thinning shears to complete the rectangle.

The rear angulation is clipped with a 7F blade against the grain or a 10 blade from the point of rump to two finger widths above the hock bone. This line is set lower than the other breeds in this group. The clipped line continues slightly inside the rear legs and inside thigh muscle. The clipped area should be well blended into the longer coat of the inside and outside parallel lines of the leg.

The underside of the tail and the area around the anus should also be clipped with the same blade.

When setting the inside parallel lines of the back legs, it is important to use the inside stifle coat to create the parallel line.

SCULPTED BODY TRIMS

Recommended Blade Lengths, Snap-On Comb Lengths and Techniques **Bold Print** = Preferred Choices for Pet Trims							
10 15	10	#2 **#1** #0	#1 **#0** **#A**	scissor			

343

Bouvier des Flandres

The Bouvier des Flandres is a Working breed that originated in Belgium. It was owned by farmers, butchers and cattle merchants and was used primarily for cattle driving.

The Bouvier is hand stripped for show; however, a #0, #1, #2 or various lengths of snap-on combs may be used on pet trims to achieve this outline. The length of coat chosen should be based upon the pet owner's preference as well as the grooming schedule.

The Bouvier has somewhat of a drop-coat with a dense undercoat. When grooming this breed think of a layered trim. The coat is trimmed the shortest on the topline and should gradually become longer as it rolls over the ribcage to the underline. This can be achieved by using snap-on combs.

A Coat King may be used on pet trims to remove excessive undercoat. Using a Coat King will also help the coat to fall and blend nicely.

Quoted in part with permission from the American Bouvier des Flandres Club, Inc., Approved January 10, 2000:

The Bouvier des Flandres is a powerfully built, compact, short-coupled, rough-coated dog of notably rugged appearance.

Proportion: The length from the point of the shoulder to the tip of the buttocks is equal to the height from the ground to the highest point of the withers.

The neck is strong and muscular, widening gradually into the shoulders. When viewed from the side, it is gracefully arched with proud carriage. Back short, broad, well muscled with firm level topline. The chest is broad, with the brisket extending to the elbow in depth. The ribs are deep and well sprung. The abdomen is only slightly tucked up.

Forearms viewed either in profile or from the front are perfectly straight, parallel to each other and perpendicular to the ground.

Hindquarters: They should be parallel with the front legs when viewed from either front or rear. Legs moderately long, well muscled, neither too straight nor too inclined. Thighs wide and muscular. There is moderate angulation at the stifle. Hocks strong, rather close to the ground. When standing and seen from the rear, they will be straight and perfectly parallel to each other.

The Bouvier des Flandres

"The Bouvier is agile, spirited and bold, yet his serene, well behaved disposition denotes his steady, resolute and fearless character. His gaze is alert and brilliant, depicting his intelligence, vigor and daring. By nature he is an equable dog."

Head: The head is impressive in scale, accentuated by beard and mustache. It is in proportion to body and build. Ears placed high and alert. If cropped, they are to be a triangular contour and in proportion to the size of the head. The inner corner of the ear should be in line with the outer corner of the eye. Skull well developed and flat, slightly less wide than long. When viewed from the side, the top lines of the skull and the muzzle are parallel. It is wide between the ears, with the frontal groove barely marked. The stop is more apparent than real, due to upstanding eyebrows. The proportions of length of skull to length of muzzle are 3 to 2. Muzzle broad, strong, well filled out, tapering gradually toward the nose without ever becoming snipy or pointed.

Coat: A tousled, double coat capable of withstanding the hardest work in the most inclement weather. The outer hairs are rough and harsh, with the undercoat being fine, soft and dense. The coat may be trimmed slightly only to accent the body line. Overtrimming which alters the natural rugged appearance is to be avoided. Topcoat must be harsh to the touch, dry, trimmed, if necessary, to a length of approximately 2½ inches. On the skull, it is short, and on the upper part of the back, it is particularly close and harsh always, however, remaining rough. Mustache and beard very thick, with the hair being shorter and rougher on the upper side of the muzzle. The upper lip with its heavy mustache and the chin with its heavy and rough beard gives that gruff expression so characteristic of the breed. Eyebrows, erect hairs accentuating the shape of the eyes without ever veiling them.

The pattern is very subtle and appears seamless due to the coat type and length of coat. The Bouvier has a drop-coat with a dense undercoat. Various lengths of snap-on combs ranging from a #0, #1 to #2 may be used on pet trims to achieve this outline.

The back of the skull should transition into the crest of neck which then flows over the withers to smoothly blend into the level topline. The coat should be left slightly longer over the withers for a smooth transition.

The shoulders are trimmed tighter than the body to show the shoulder layback. This can be achieved by using a shorter snap-on comb than was used on the body pattern.

The rear legs are scissored to show rear angulation and to accentuate the muscle of the thigh. The thighs can be clipped with a snap-on comb which is one length longer than what was used on the shoulder. The thigh can also be clipped the same length as the body; however, it should then be scissored tighter to accentuate the muscle.

The stifles are moderately bent and should fall in line with the croup. The hocks are perpendicular to the ground.

The front legs are scissored to appear column-like. The elbow should fall in line with the withers.

The underline is scissored to show the slight tuck-up.

The throat can be clipped with a 4F blade or a #2 comb. Clip throat from the back corner of the jaw to just above the breastbone. Blend this area well into the chest and side of the neck for a well-blended appearance

The front is trimmed to present the proper forechest.

The ears can be clipped with a 10 or 15 blade. The topskull is clipped tight using a 4F or 5F blade. The clipped line begins just behind the brow. The area that is clipped should include the area just above the zygomatic arch. The Bouvier has a full beard and a fall over the eyes which begins behind the brow.

The rear legs are trimmed to show rear angulation and to accentuate the muscle of the thigh. When viewed from the rear the legs should present parallel lines.

See important information on "Carding" on page 30 and "Hand Stripping" on page 32.

Available on DVD: "Snap-On Combs: Theory & Techniques"

Dog Grooming Simplified: Straight To The Point

Sculpted Body Trims

	Recommended Blade Lengths, Snap-On Comb Lengths and Techniques **Bold Print** = Preferred Choices for Pet Trims						
10 15	5F 4F **#2**	#2 #1 **#0 carding**	#1 #0 **#A carding**	scissor	4F #2 **#1**		

350

Tip To Remember:

Snap-on combs are a fabulous tool that no groomer should be without. These combs attach over the clipper blade, allowing the groomer to leave more length on a dog than what a blade allows. They can be used to set lines quickly to prepare the trim for a scissor finish. These combs are available in lengths from 1/8" to 1". They are a great time saver. They can also be used to skim the drop-coated breeds to help the coat blend and fall nicely. The techniques that can be used with snap-on combs are endless.

Irish Water Spaniel

The Irish Water Spaniel is the tallest of the Spaniel breeds in the Sporting group. This breed originated in Ireland, where they were once referred to as Rat-Tail Spaniels or Whip-Tail Spaniels. The Irish Water Spaniel is often referred to as the "clown" of the Spaniels due to its energetic personality. The IWS is used to hunt upland game and waterfowl. It is a water retriever with webbed feet and a rat tail that acts like a rudder in the water to help the dog swim efficiently.

This breed has a dense curly coat. The length of coat as well as the coat type presents a very subtle appearance of the pattern. Various lengths of snap-on combs can be used to mimic the breed profile. The length of coat chosen should be based on the pet owner's preference as well as grooming schedule. This coat can be misted with water to bring back the loose curls in the coat once the grooming has been completed.

Key points to remember when grooming the Irish Water Spaniel according to the breed standard:

The Irish Water Spaniel is slightly longer than it is tall. The rear is equal to or slightly higher than the withers. The ribs are well sprung. The loin is considered deep, so it does not give a tucked-up appearance.

The front legs are straight and are placed under the withers. The rear legs are strong and muscular, which gives this breed strength while swimming. The stifles and hocks are moderately bent. The hips are wide. The croup drops off to a low tail-set.

The tail is a "rat tail" and almost reaches the point of hock. The tail is thicker at the base and tapers to a point.

The coat on the face and throat is short and smooth and can be clipped with a 10 blade. The IWS has a small V-shaped patch of long curls at the back lower jaw covering the Adam's apple. This tuft of hair is left to protect the throat.

The topknot is the hallmark of this breed. It consists of loose, long curls that cover the skull. The topknot falls gently over the top of the ears and over the occiput. The ears are long and covered with long loose curls.

The coat of the IWS is dense with tight crisp curls and should be trimmed to enhance the structure of the dog.

The pattern is very subtle and appears seamless due to the coat type and length of coat. The Irish Water Spaniel has a dense curly coat.

For pet trims, the Irish Water Spaniel can be trimmed using a #0, #1, #2 or various lengths of snap-on combs following the structure of the dog.

The back of the skull should transition into the crest of neck which then flows over the withers to smoothly blend into the topline. The rear is slightly higher than the withers.

The shoulders are trimmed tighter than the body to show the shoulder layback. This can be done by using a shorter snap-on comb than was used on the body pattern.

The body is trimmed to show the spring of ribs.

The rear legs are scissored to show rear angulation and to accentuate the muscle of the thigh.

The thighs can be clipped with a snap-on comb which is one length longer than what was used on the shoulder. The thigh can also be clipped the same length as the body; however, it should then be scissored tighter to accentuate the muscle.

The stifles are moderately bent and should fall in line with the croup. The hocks are perpendicular to the ground.

The front legs are scissored to appear column-like. The elbow should fall in line with the withers.

Because the loin is deep, the underline does not present an evident tuck-up.

The front is trimmed to present the proper forechest.

The cheeks are clipped from the cowlick in front of the ear canal, to the corner of the eye with a 10 blade. The line continues to the corner of the mouth. The entire muzzle is clipped with the same blade. The throat is clipped with a 10 blade from the base of the ear, creating a V or U shape to the breastbone. The IWS has a small patch of long curls at the back lower jaw covering the Adam's apple. This tuft of hair is left to protect the throat.

It is optional to leave a beard and sideburns. If this is preferred, do not clip the cheek to the cowlick in front of the ear. Leave a strip, a sideburn, from the topknot down in front of the ear canal. The sideburn continues down the cheek to the base of the jaw. The line follows the underjaw to the Adam's apple. The patch of longer coat on the Adam's apple remains.

The topknot is the hallmark of this breed. It consists of loose, long curls that cover the skull. The topknot falls gently over the eyes and over the top of the ears and the occiput.

The IWS should have a bevel over the eyes extending approximately over a third of the muzzle. This bevel should be scissored in a U shape from the outside corner of the eye to the opposite outside corner of the eye with a "peak" or slight V shape between the eyes.

The side of the topknot, at the outside corner of the eye, should be blended into the front upper portion of the ear leather to appear as one piece. It is important not to separate the topknot from the ear like the Poodle. The ears are long and covered with long loose curls.

The rear legs are trimmed to show the rear angulation and the muscle of the thigh and to reflect the wide hips.

When viewed from the rear the legs should present parallel lines.

The Irish Water Spaniel has a rat tail. See "Tail Styles" on page 451 for instructions on grooming this tail type.

SCULPTED BODY TRIMS

Recommended Blade Lengths, Snap-On Comb Lengths and Techniques **Bold Print** = Preferred Choices for Pet Trims							
10 15	**10**	#2 **#1**	#1 **#0 #A**	scissor	4F #2 **#1**		

Kerry Blue Terrier

The Kerry Blue Terrier is a Terrier breed that originated in Ireland in the county of Kerry. It was used as an all-around working Terrier who could hunt small game from land as well as water. The Kerry Blue was also used to herd sheep and cattle. Unlike other Terriers, the Kerry Blue has a beautiful soft, dense, curly-wavy coat.

The Kerry is scissored to show the Terrier-Like profile, which presents a subtle and seamless appearance of the pattern.

The body pattern can be set with a #2, #1, or #0 comb. This trim may also be modified by using various lengths of blades and/or snap-on combs for manageable pet trims following the body structure.

After grooming this breed, the body coat can be misted with water to bring back the marcel waves in the coat.

Quoted in part with permission from the United States Kerry Blue Terrier Club, Inc., Approved October 10, 2005:

The typical Kerry Blue Terrier should be upstanding, well knit and in good balance, showing a well-developed and muscular body with definite Terrier style and character throughout.

Neck: Clean and moderately long, gradually widening to the shoulders upon which it should be well set and carried proudly. Back short, strong and straight (i.e., level).

Chest deep and of moderate breadth. Ribs fairly well sprung, deep rather than round. A slight tuck-up. Loin short and powerful. Tail should be set on high.

Shoulders fine, long and sloping, well laid back and well knit. The elbows hanging perpendicularly to the body and working clear of the side in movement. The forelegs should be straight from both front and side view. The pasterns short, straight and hardly noticeable. Feet should be strong, compact, fairly round and moderately small.

Hindquarters: Strong and muscular with full freedom of action, free from droop or crouch, the thighs long and powerful, stifles well bent and turned neither in nor out, hocks near the ground and, when viewed from behind, upright and parallel with each other.

The Kerry Blue Terrier

"The typical Kerry Blue Terrier should be upstanding, well knit and in good balance, showing a well-developed and muscular body with definite Terrier style and character throughout."

Head: Long, but not exaggerated, and in good proportion to the rest of the body. Ears–V-shaped, small but not out of proportion to the size of the dog, of moderate thickness, carried forward close to the cheeks with the top of the folded ear slightly above the level of the skull. Skull–Flat, with very slight stop, of moderate breadth between the ears, and narrowing very slightly to the eyes. Foreface full and well made up, not falling away appreciably below the eyes but moderately chiseled out to relieve the foreface from wedginess. Little apparent difference between the length of the skull and foreface. Jaws deep, strong and muscular. Cheeks–Clean and level, free from bumpiness.

Coat: Correct coat is important; it is to be soft, dense and wavy. In show trim the body should be well covered but tidy, with the head (except for the whiskers) and the ears and cheeks clear.

The lines are very subtle and seamless due to the coat type and length. The Kerry Blue has a dense wavy coat.

The body pattern can be set with a #2, #1, or #0 comb. This trim may also be modified by using various lengths of blades and/or snap-on combs for manageable pet trims.

The back of the skull should transition into the crest of neck which then flows over the withers to smoothly blend into the level topline.

The shoulders are trimmed tighter than the body to show the shoulder layback. This can be done by using a shorter snap-on comb than was used on the body pattern.

The body is trimmed to show the spring of ribs.

The rear legs are scissored to show rear angulation and to accentuate the muscle of the thigh.

The thighs can be clipped with a snap-on comb which is one length longer than what was used on the shoulder. The thigh can also be clipped the same length as the body; however, it should then be scissored tighter to accentuate the muscle.

The stifles are well bent and should fall in line with the croup. The hocks are perpendicular to the ground.

The front legs are scissored to appear column-like. The elbow should fall in line with the withers.

The legs should be scissored longer than the body for a well-balanced trim.

The underline is scissored to show a slight tuck-up.

The throat is clipped very close using a 10 blade with or against the grain depending on the sensitivity of the skin. The front is scissored to reflect the true "Terrier-Like" outline.

The Kerry Blue has a rectangular-shaped head with a fall, beard and goatee. See "Rectangular Heads" on page 427 for instructions on grooming this head type.

The underside of the base of the tail and the area on both sides of the anus to the testicles or vulva should be clipped with a 10 blade. The inner thighs should be clipped tight with either a 7F against the grain or a 10 blade.

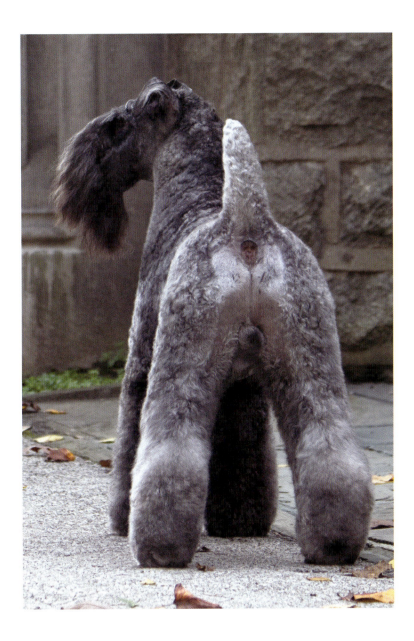

The inside parallel lines of the rear legs are scissored tighter than the outside of the rear legs. This sets the legs farther apart. When setting the inside parallel lines of the back legs, it is important to use the inside stifle coat to create the parallel line.

Dog Grooming Simplified: Straight To The Point

Sculpted Body Trims

10 15	**10**	4F #2 **#1**	#1 **#0** **#A**	scissor			

Recommended Blade Lengths, Snap-On Comb Lengths and Techniques
Bold Print = Preferred Choices for Pet Trims

364

Tip To Remember:

While scissoring, only use your thumb to open and close the shear. Keep your hand steady and glide over the coat without bouncing the shear. This will produce a flawless scissor finish. Using a scissoring spray while scissoring will help the coat to stand up for a nice even finish. Always comb the coat up away from the skin while scissoring Poodle-type coats.

Lagotto Romagnolo

The Lagotto Romagnolo is currently registered in the Miscellaneous class with the AKC, soon to be a Sporting breed. This is a small- to medium-sized dog with a dense, curly rustic coat. The Lagotto was originally bred to retrieve water fowl in the marshlands of Ravenna in Italy. Over the centuries the marshlands were drained and the Lagotto soon lost its original purpose. It is now used to search for truffles in Romagna, Italy. The Lagotto is a strongly built dog who displays strength and endurance to work all day in difficult and challenging terrain.

The Lagotto is known for its rustic appearance of tight ring-shaped curls which must cover the entire body and should not exceed 1.5 inches in its curly state. The coat on the head is not as tightly curled as on the body, yet it is just as dense with loose curls.

The length of coat and coat type will present a very subtle appearance of the pattern. It is important to keep the "rustic" look of this breed when grooming. For pet trims, the coat may be blown and brushed out in order to be scissored and/or clipped. After the grooming has been completed, the coat should be wet down thoroughly and allowed to dry naturally to bring back the tight curls that are the hallmark of this breed.

Various lengths of snap-on combs can be used to set the desired length. This coat has a dense undercoat which requires thorough brushing before using snap-on combs. The coat should never be clipped so short as to prevent the coat from curling.

Key points to remember when grooming the Lagotto Romagnola according to the breed standard:

The neck is approximately the same length as the length of the head when measured from the occiput to the nose. It is strong and muscular and is slightly arched as it reaches the occiput.

The topline is level and slightly slopes as it reaches the loin and tail-set. The tail, when at rest, should barely reach the hocks. The tail is wide at the base and tapers toward the end.

The Lagotto is a compact, strong dog. It is a squarely built dog, meaning that it is as long as it is tall.

The chest is well developed, reaching the elbow. The underline is a straight line from the elbow slightly rising to the loin with a slight tuck-up.

The shoulders are well angulated and are approximately the same length as the upper arm, which sets the elbow in line with the withers. The front legs are straight and parallel when viewed from the front.

The feet are rounded and compact with well-arched toes.

The rear legs are powerful and well angulated. The hocks are well let down and are perpendicular to the ground.

The head is moderately broad. The width of the skull is approximately the same length when measured from the occiput to the stop. The muzzle is shorter than the skull and wedge-shaped. The stop is not pronounced. The cheeks are somewhat flat.

The coat of the Lagotto has a woolly texture and consists of tight ring-shaped curls with a visible undercoat. This coat is waterproof. The length of the body coat should not exceed 1.5 inches when curly.

The coat on the head is considered "abundant" and consists of looser curls than on the body. The ears should be scissored to the edge of the ear leather with rounded tips.

The head is scissored round without showing distinct ears. The ears are part of the round head. The bottom of the ears should be scissored tight to the leather with rounded tips and gradually gain length as they become part of the topskull. The muzzle has a slight wedge shape as it transitions into the cheek. The coat on the cheeks should be slightly longer than on the muzzle and transition into the sides of the head. When trimming the topskull, a bevel should be left over the eyes.

The lines are very subtle and seamless due to the coat type and length.

Various lengths of snap-on combs ranging from a #2, #1 to #0 comb can be used to achieve this outline for pet trims. This coat has a dense undercoat which requires thorough brushing before using snap-on combs. The coat should never be clipped so short as to prevent the coat from curling.

The back of the skull should transition into the crest of neck which then flows over the withers to smoothly blend into the topline. The topline is level with a slight slope as it reaches the loin.

The shoulders are trimmed tighter than the body to show the shoulder layback. This can be done using a shorter snap-on-comb than was used on the body pattern

The body is scissored to show the spring of ribs.

The rear legs are scissored to show rear angulation and to accentuate the muscle of the thigh.

The thighs can be clipped with a snap-on comb which is one length longer than what was used on the shoulder. The thigh can also be clipped the same length as the body; however, it should then be scissored tighter to accentuate the muscle.

The stifles are well bent and should fall in line with the croup. The hocks are perpendicular to the ground.

The front legs are scissored to appear column-like. The elbow should fall in line with the withers.

The legs should be scissored longer than the body for a well-balanced trim.

The underline is scissored to show a slight tuck-up.

The throat is set tight to the breastbone.

The front is scissored to present the proper forechest.

The rear legs are scissored to show the rear angulation and to accentuate the muscle of the thigh. The rear angulation should be set tightest at the bend of knee.

When viewed from the rear the legs should present parallel lines.

Dog Grooming Simplified: Straight To The Point

Sculpted Body Trims

Recommended Blade Lengths, Snap-On Comb Lengths and Techniques						
Bold Print = Preferred Choices for Pet Trims						
10 15	5F 4F **#2**	#2 #1 **#0**	#1 #0 **#A**	scissor	4F #2 **#1**	

Tip To Remember:

Oftentimes pet owners will ask when to start the grooming process for their puppy. A good rule of thumb would be either approximately four months of age or after the puppy has received all required puppy vaccinations. Puppy sessions should consist of a bath/brush, nails and a short table training session. If it is a breed that requires facial clipping this should be done as well. Keep puppy sessions positive and fun.

POODLE

The Poodle is a member of the Non-Sporting group. It originated in Germany and was used as a water retriever. *Pudel* is German for Poodle; it comes from the verb *Pudelin*, meaning to splash in the water.

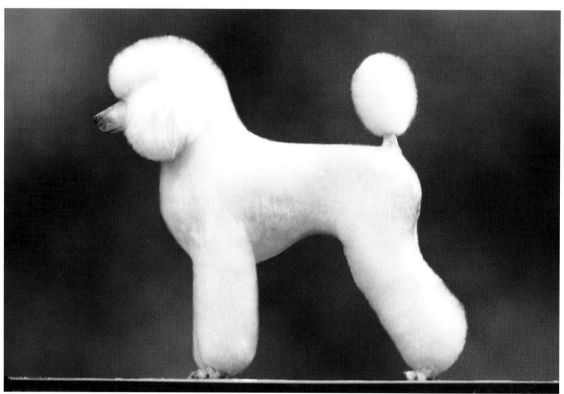

Sporting Trim

Groomed by Veronica Frosch

There are three varieties of Poodles: the Toy, the Miniature and the Standard. The Poodle can be trimmed for the dog show ring in either the Continental or English Saddle trim. A puppy, under a year old, may be shown in the Puppy trim. For information on show grooming the Poodle as well as various Poodle patterns, *Poodle Clipping and Grooming* by Shirlee Kalstone is highly recommended.

The Sporting Trim is a popular manageable pet trim. This traditional trim has long natural ears with a pom-pom tail.

The German trim is done by shaving the ears with blades ranging from 4F, 5F, 7F or 10. The tail is scissored in a carrot shape. The coat length of the tail should balance with the coat length of the ears. If a 10 blade is preferred on the ears, the tail should be scissored into a tighter carrot shape. Both trims are groomed in the same manner with the exception of the ears and tail.

For short pet trims, blades ranging from 5F, 4F to 3 3/4 can be used on the body pattern. A longer trim can be achieved by using a variety of snap-on combs ranging from a #2, #1 or #0 comb. The legs should be scissored longer than the body for a well-balanced trim.

The length of coat chosen will depend upon the pet owner's preference.

German Trim — Photo courtesy of Devin Murphy

Key points to remember when grooming the Poodle according to the breed standard:

The Poodle is square in outline, meaning that it is as tall as it is long. It has a level topline.

The shoulders are well laid back and are approximately the same length as the upper arm. This sets the elbow in line with the withers. The front legs should appear column-like and be parallel when viewed from the front.

The Poodle has a deep chest that should reach the elbows with well-sprung ribs which presents a high tuck-up.

The rear legs are well angulated and appear parallel when viewed from the rear. The stifles are well bent. The hocks are well let down and perpendicular to the ground.

The Poodle coat is curly and dense.

The pattern is seamless due to the coat type and length. The Poodle has a curly dense coat.

This outline can be achieved by using a variety of snap-on combs ranging from a #2, #1 to #0 comb. For short pet trims, blades ranging from 5F, 4F or 3 3/4 can be used on the body pattern.

Photo courtesy of Devin Murphy

The crest of neck should be left long enough in order to transition over the withers and blend smoothly into the level topline. The shape of the topknot to the topline resembles a question mark.

The shoulders are scissored tighter than the body to show the shoulder layback. This can be achieved by using a shorter snap-on comb than was used on the body.

The body is scissored to show the spring of ribs.

The rear legs are scissored to show rear angulation and to accentuate the muscle of the thigh.

The thighs can be clipped with a snap-on comb which is one length longer than what was used on the shoulder. The thigh can also be clipped the same length as the body; however, it should then be scissored tighter to accentuate the muscle.

The stifles are well bent and should fall in line with the croup. The hocks are perpendicular to the ground.

The front legs are scissored to appear column-like. The elbow should fall in line with the withers.

The underline is scissored to show the high tuck-up.

SCULPTED BODY TRIMS

Photo courtesy of Devin Murphy

The Poodle face, feet and tail-set may be clipped with a 10, 15 or 40 blade. The clipperwork on the cheek should start at the front corner of the ear creating a straight line to the outside corner of the eye. The entire cheek is clipped to the muzzle. The muzzle and lower jaw are also clipped with the same blade. The throat is clipped from the base of the ear creating a V or U shape at the base of the throat. The clipped line should end before the throat falls into the breastbone.

The feet are clipped against the grain to the ankle joint.

Groomed by Diane Betelak

The side of the Poodle topknot should be scissored over the top of the ear ridge. The line continues from over the ear to the outside corner of the eye, following the clipped line of the cheek. When scissoring the topknot it is desirable to have a bevel over the eyes. The top of the topknot should have a domed appearance and should transition into the crest of neck.

The front is trimmed to present the proper forechest.

See "Ear Styles" on page 441 and "Tail Styles" on page 455 for instructions on grooming this ear style and tail style.

Photo courtesy of Devin Murphy

The rear legs are scissored to show the rear angulation and to accentuate the muscle of the thigh. When viewed from the rear the legs should present parallel lines.

Available on DVD: "The Poodle" — a 4-hour DVD on Poodle pet trims

DOG GROOMING SIMPLIFIED: STRAIGHT TO THE POINT

SCULPTED BODY TRIMS

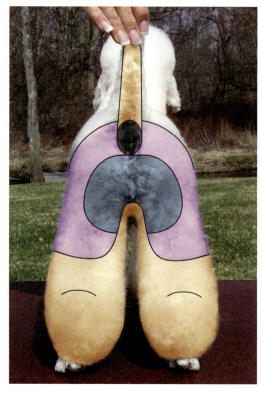

Recommended Blade Lengths, Snap-On Comb Lengths and Techniques **Bold Print** = Preferred Choices for Pet Trims								
10 15	10	#2 **#1**	#1 **#0** **#A**	scissor	4F #2 **#1**		

380

Tip To Remember:

Discourage clients from brushing their dog before their grooming appointment. Brushing a dirty coat will damage the coat and can cause future matting. If the client is brushing in between on a regular basis it can be an asset to the groomer. However, if they are trying to brush out a matted coat the night before, it can be damaging to the coat.

Portuguese Water Dog

The Portuguese Water Dog is a Working dog that originated in Portugal. It was used to herd fish into nets and to retrieve broken nets and tackle for fisherman. The Portuguese Water Dog is a natural swimmer and would act as a courier from both ship to ship and ship to shore.

Retriever Clip

The Portuguese Water Dog can be shown in two different clips: the Retriever clip or the Lion clip. This breed has two coat varieties: curly and wavy. The Lion clip is commonly seen on wavy coats.

The lines of the Retriever clip are very subtle and seamless due to the coat type. The shoulders are scissored tight to show the shoulder layback. The PWD has a forechest which should be scissored accordingly. The front legs should appear column-like. The rear legs are scissored to show rear angulation and to accentuate the muscle of the thigh. The underline is scissored to show a moderate tuck-up.

Lion Clip

The Lion clip carries a jacket which is left to the last rib. The area beyond the last rib is shaved with blades ranging from 7F, 5F to 4F. The rear and rear legs are completely shaved, leaving a lion-style tail. The jacket is tailored to accentuate the structure of the dog. The shoulders are scissored to show the angulation. The chest is scissored to show the proper forechest. The front legs are scissored to appear column-like.

Both clips have a lion tail. If the Lion clip is being executed, two thirds of the tail should be shaved with the same blade that was used on the rear of the dog. When executing the Retriever clip, two thirds of the tail is scissored following the natural shape of the tail. See "Tail Styles" on page 450 for instructions on grooming this tail style.

> Quoted in part with permission from the Portuguese Water Dog Club of America, Inc., Approved January 15, 1991:
>
> Proportion–Off square; slightly longer than tall when measured from prosternum to rearmost point of the buttocks, and from withers to ground.
>
> Neck–Straight, short, round, and held high. Strongly muscled.
>
> Topline–Level and firm.
>
> Chest is broad and deep, reaching down to the elbow. Ribs are long and well-sprung to provide optimum lung capacity. Abdomen well held up in a graceful line. Back is broad and well muscled. Loin is short and meets the croup smoothly. Croup is well formed and only slightly inclined with hip bones hardly apparent. Tail–Not docked; thick at the base and tapering; set on slightly below the line of the back; should not reach below the hock. When the dog is attentive the tail is held in a ring, the front of which should not reach

forward of the loin. The tail is of great help when swimming and diving.

Forelegs are strong and straight.

Hindquarters–Powerful; well balanced with the front assembly. Legs, viewed from the rear, are parallel to each other, straight and very strongly muscled in upper and lower thighs.

Head–An essential characteristic; distinctively large, well proportioned and with exceptional breadth of topskull. Ears–Set well above the line of the eye. Leather is heart shaped and thin. Tips should not reach below the lower jaw.

Skull–In profile, it is slightly longer than the muzzle, its curvature more accentuated at the back than in the front. When viewed head-on, the top of the skull is very broad and appears domed, with a slight depression in the middle. The forehead is prominent, and has a central furrow, extending two-thirds of the distance from stop to occiput. The occiput is well defined. Muzzle–Substantial; wider at the base than at the nose.

Coat–A profuse, thickly planted coat of strong, healthy hair, covering the whole body evenly, except where the forearm meets the brisket and in the groin area, where it is thinner.

There are two varieties of coat:

Curly–Compact, cylindrical curls, somewhat lusterless. The hair on the ears is sometimes wavy. Wavy–Falling gently in waves, not curls, and with a slight sheen.

Wavy Coat

Groomed by Ann Martin

Two clips are acceptable:

Lion Clip–As soon as the coat grows long, the middle part and hindquarters, as well as the muzzle, are clipped. The hair at the end of the tail is left at full length. Retriever Clip–In order to give a natural appearance and a smooth unbroken line, the entire coat is scissored or clipped to follow the outline of the dog, leaving a short blanket of coat no longer than one inch in length. The hair at the end of the tail is left at full length.

The lines are very subtle and seamless due to the coat type and length. The Portuguese Water Dog has either a curly or a wavy coat.

The Retriever outline can be achieved by using a variety of snap-on combs ranging from a #2, #1 to #0 comb. Ideally, the coat should not exceed 1 inch on the body pattern.

The back of the skull should transition into the crest of neck which then flows over the withers to smoothly blend into the level topline.

The shoulders are trimmed tighter than the body to show the shoulder layback. This can be achieved by using a shorter snap-on comb than was used on the body pattern.

The body is trimmed to show the spring of ribs.

The rear legs are trimmed to show rear angulation and to accentuate the muscle of the thigh.

The thighs can be clipped with a snap-on comb which is one length longer than what was used on the shoulder. The thigh can also be clipped the same length as the body; however, it should then be scissored tighter to accentuate the muscle.

The stifles are well bent and should fall in line with the croup. The hocks are perpendicular to the ground.

The front legs are scissored to appear column-like. The elbow should fall in line with the withers.

The legs should be scissored longer than the body for a well-balanced trim.

The underline is scissored to show a moderate tuck-up.

The throat can be clipped with a 4F blade or a #2 comb. Clip the throat from the back corner of the jaw to just above the breastbone. Blend this area well into the chest and side of the neck for a well-blended appearance.

The front is trimmed to present forechest.

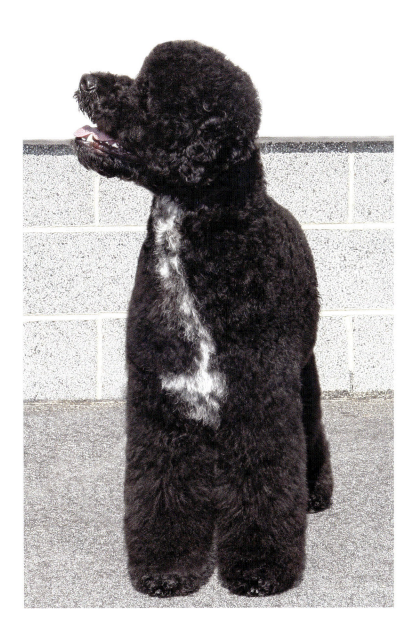

The head of the Portuguese Water Dog is very broad and should consist of a deep topskull that extends from the stop to just beyond the occiput. The topskull should be slightly flat, yet round. The bottom of the ears should present the shape of the bottom of a heart. The bottom of the ears should be scissored tight to the leather and gradually gain length as they become part of the topskull.

The two coat types give a slightly different appearance to the head. The wavy coat falls with a natural wave where the curly coat is dense and has more volume.

Curly Coat

Wavy Coat

When trimming over the eyes, scissor a U shape from the outside corner of the eye to the opposite outside corner of the eye. A bevel should be left over the eyes to give the eyes the deep-set appearance that the breed should have.

The muzzle should present a bottlebrush appearance which has a slight wedge shape as it transitions into the cheek. To achieve a bottlebrush appearance, comb all the muzzle coat forward. Hold the coat with your hand around the muzzle. With thinning shears, cut the coat flush with the front of the muzzle. Comb the muzzle coat back to the natural lay and neaten with thinning shears.

The cheeks should be slightly longer than the muzzle and transition into the sides of the head.

Once the head is trimmed, the back of the skull should transition into the crest which then flows over the withers.

The head on the Lion clip is done differently than the Retriever clip. The muzzle is clipped with blades ranging from 4F, 5F, 7F to 10. The structure of the muzzle will determine which blade to use. If the dog does not have a "substantial" muzzle, a longer blade should be used. If the dog has a nice strong muzzle, it can be shaved with a 10 blade to show off the beauty of the muzzle. The entire muzzle should be shaved back to the outside corner of the eye. The clipper line should fall from the outside corner of the eye, down the cheek and follow through to the throat latch. The cheek beyond the eye is not clipped. The cheeks and skull are trimmed in the same manner as the Retriever clip. The throat is clipped in the same manner as the Retriever clip.

The rear legs are scissored to show the rear angulation and to accentuate the muscle of the thigh. The rear angulation should be set tightest at the bend of knee. When viewed from the rear the legs should present parallel lines.

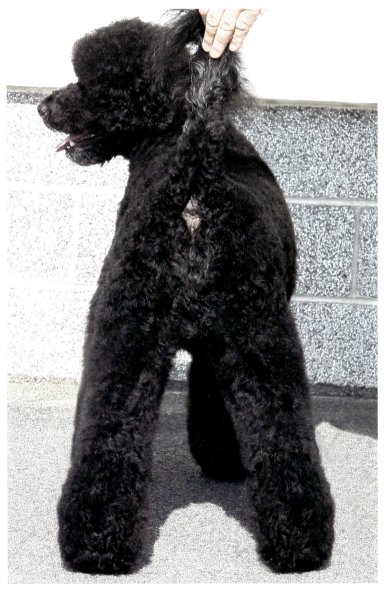

Available on DVD: "The Portuguese Water Dog - A Poodle in Disguise"

The dog used in this DVD is a Poodle trimmed like a PWD.

Dog Grooming Simplified: Straight To The Point

Sculpted Body Trims

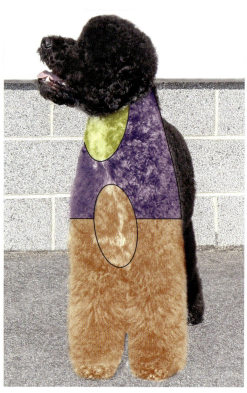

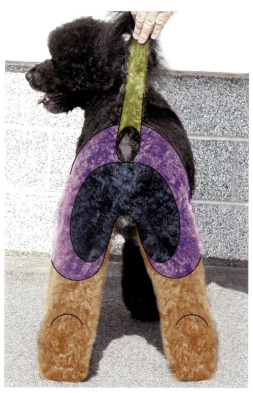

| Recommended Blade Lengths, Snap-On Comb Lengths and Techniques ||||||||
Bold Print = Preferred Choices for Pet Trims							
10 15	5F 4F **#2**	#2 #1 **#0**	#1 #0 **#A**	scissor	4F #2 **#1**		

390

Tip To Remember:

Many breeds have a natural marcel curl to their coat. The Portuguese Water Dog, Irish Water Spaniel and Kerry Blue Terrier have this type of coat. Misting the body coat with water after grooming will bring back the natural curl which is the essence of their breed.

Soft Coated Wheaten Terrier

The Soft Coated Wheaten Terrier is a Terrier breed that originated in Ireland. They were considered the poor man's all-purpose farm dog. They protected the farms, hunted vermin, served as guard dogs and herded sheep.

The Soft Coated Wheaten Terrier has a long, soft drop-coat. This breed should have a sufficient amount of coat for the show ring in order for the coat to flow when the dog is moving, trimmed solely with thinning shears. However, this coat is very soft and can be very difficult for pet owners to maintain if left too long.

For a pet trim, a #0, #1 or various lengths of snap-on combs may be used to achieve this outline. It is important to pick the right length and the proper grooming schedule for this breed to avoid excessive matting of the coat. Thinning shears should be used to blend scissor marks or snap-on comb lines for a seamless appearance.

Key points to remember when grooming the SCWT according to the breed standard:

The Soft Coated Wheaten presents a square outline; he is as tall as he is long. The neck is of medium length and gradually widens into the body. The shoulders are well laid back. The topline is level. The chest is deep with well-sprung ribs which presents a moderate tuck-up. The tail is set on high and is commonly docked.

The front legs are straight with round compact feet. The stifles should be well bent. The hocks are well let down and perpendicular to the ground.

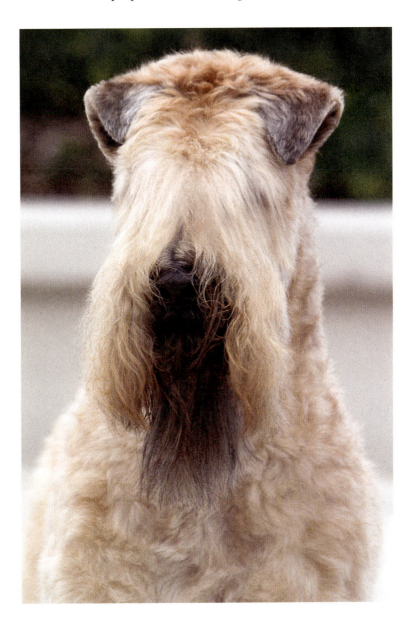

The head of the SCWT is rectangular in appearance and should appear powerful. The ears are small and should fold at the level of the skull. The ears are clipped short from the fold to the tip using blades ranging from 5F, 7F to 10. The skull and muzzle should be of equal length. The Wheaten should have a fall of hair covering the eyes. The eyes should never be fully exposed, only seeing through fringe.

The SCWT has a single coat that is soft with a slight wave.

The lines are very subtle and appear seamless due to the coat type and length. The Wheaten is a square-bodied dog, meaning that it is as long as it is tall.

The Soft Coated Wheaten has a soft drop-coat which is slightly wavy.

For a pet trim, a #0, #1 or various lengths of snap-on combs may be used to achieve this outline. When grooming this breed think of a layered trim. The coat is trimmed the shortest on the topline and should gradually become longer as it rolls over the ribcage to the underline.

The back of the skull should transition into the crest of neck which then flows over the withers and blends smoothly into the level topline. The coat should be left slightly longer over the withers for a smooth transition.

When clipping the pattern, skim off with the snap-on comb at the lower part of the rib cage. This will leave the coat longer on the underline, which can then be scissored in to the desired length and shape.

The shoulders are trimmed tighter than the body to show the shoulder layback. This can be done by using a shorter snap-on comb than was used on the body pattern.

The rear legs are scissored to show rear angulation and to accentuate the muscle of the thigh.

The thighs can be clipped with a snap-on comb which is one length longer than what was used on the shoulder. The thigh can also be clipped the same length as the body; however, it should then be scissored tighter to accentuate the muscle.

The stifles are well bent and should fall in line with the croup. The hocks are perpendicular to the ground.

The front legs are scissored to appear column-like. The elbow should fall in line with the withers. The underline is scissored to show a moderate tuck-up.

The throat can be clipped with a 4F or 5F blade. The side of the neck and shoulder may be clipped with a shorter snap-on comb than was used on the body, preferrably a #2 or #1 comb.

The Wheaten has a rectangular-shaped head with a full fall and full beard. See "Rectangular Heads" on page 427 for instructions on grooming this head type.

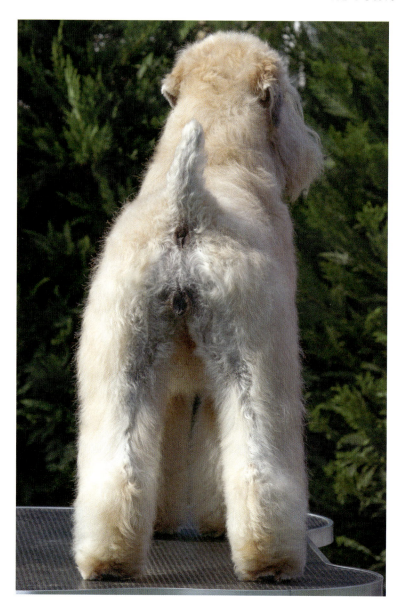

The inner thighs and rear angulation are set tight. The inner thighs can be clipped with a 4F or 5F blade. When viewed from the rear the legs should present parallel lines. When setting the inside parallel lines of the back legs, it is important to use the inside stifle coat to create the parallel line.

Available on DVD: "The Soft Coated Wheaten Terrier - Show Trim"

and "The Soft Coated Wheaten Terrier - Pet Trim"

SCULPTED BODY TRIMS

10 15	5F **4F** #2	#2 **#1**	#1 **#0** **#A**	thinning shears scissor			

Recommended Blade Lengths, Snap-On Comb Lengths and Techniques
Bold Print = Preferred Choices for Pet Trims

397

Tip To Remember:

Many people who own breeds that are required to be in full coat while being shown in the dog show ring, as in the Shih Tzu, Maltese, Yorkie, Havanese, etc., may prefer to keep their pet in a longer style trim. The techniques described for beveling the feet on the American Cocker Spaniel can also be applied to these breeds.

American Cocker Spaniel

Suburban Trim

Field Trim

American Cocker Spaniel

The Cocker Spaniel is the smallest of the Sporting dogs. It originated in England. The Cocker Spaniels and English Springer Spaniels were once born in the same litters. They were eventually divided by size and type and were then registered as individual breeds. The American Cocker Spaniel is a flushing Spaniel whose name derived from flushing woodcock.

The pattern of the American Cocker Spaniel does not fall into any of our pattern groups. This is an extremely popular breed with pet owners and can be very difficult to maintain if not groomed regularly. The show trim will be discussed as well as two different pet trims.

The American Cocker Spaniel's back coat should be hand stripped and carded for show. The hand stripped back coat flows into the longer furnishings of the side coat.

Since most pet trims are clipped, it can be difficult to achieve this look. However, using the techniques described here will assist in achieving a well-blended appearance.

When clipping the back pattern on a pet trim, it is recommended to use a 4F, 5F or 7F blade to achieve the most natural look possible. After clipping it is important to card the back coat using a stripping knife to remove the undercoat, which will promote healthy skin and coat. Carding techniques will also help blend the pattern lines and encourage the proper texture of the coat.

The body pattern on this show dog is hand stripped from the back of the skull (occiput) to the tip of the tail. The pattern flows from the topline over the top of the rib cage. Ideally, the short back work should blend into the longer furnishings approximately between the upper and mid portion of the ribs.

When clipping this pattern, skim off the top of the rib cage with the clipper, which will blend this part of the coat into the furnishings. Use thinning shears to blend the transition lines.

See important information on "Carding" on page 30 and "Hand Stripping" on page 32.

> Quoted in part with permission from the American Spaniel Club, Inc., Approved May 12, 1992:
>
> The Cocker Spaniel is the smallest member of the Sporting Group. He has a sturdy, compact body and a cleanly chiseled and refined head.
>
> The measurement from the breastbone to back of thigh is slightly longer than the measurement from the highest point of withers to the ground.
>
> The neck is sufficiently long to allow the nose to reach the ground easily, muscular and free from pendulous "throatiness." It rises strongly from the shoulders and arches slightly as it tapers to join the head. Topline–sloping slightly toward muscular quarters. The chest is deep, its lowest point no higher than the elbows. Ribs are deep and well sprung. Back is strong and sloping evenly and slightly downward from the shoulders to the set-on of the docked tail. The docked tail is set on and carried on a line with the topline of the back, or slightly higher.
>
> The shoulders are well laid back forming an angle with the upper arm of approximately 90 degrees which permits the dog to move his forelegs in an easy manner with forward reach. When viewed from the side with the forelegs vertical, the elbow is directly below the highest point of the shoulder blade. Forelegs are parallel, straight, strongly boned and muscular and set close to the body well under the scapulae. The pasterns are short and strong. Feet compact, large, round and firm with horny pads.
>
> Hips are wide and quarters well rounded and muscular. When viewed from behind, the hind legs are parallel when in motion and at rest. The hind legs are strongly boned, and muscled with moderate angulation at the stifle and powerful, clearly defined thighs. The hocks are strong and well let down.
>
> The skull is rounded but not exaggerated with no tendency toward flatness; the eyebrows are clearly defined with a pronounced stop. The bony structure beneath the eyes is well chiseled with no prominence in the cheeks. The muzzle is broad and deep, with square even jaws. To be in correct balance, the distance from the stop to the tip of the nose is one half the distance from the stop up over the crown to the base of the skull.
>
> Coat: On the head, short and fine; on the body, medium length, with enough undercoating to give protection. The ears, chest, abdomen and legs are well feathered, but not so excessively as to hide the Cocker Spaniel's true lines and movement or affect his appearance

and function as a moderately coated sporting dog. The texture is most important. The coat is silky, flat or slightly wavy and of a texture which permits easy care. Excessive coat or curly or cottony textured coat shall be severely penalized. Use of electric clippers on the back coat is not desirable. Trimming to enhance the dog's true lines should be done to appear as natural as possible.

The throat is clipped from the underjaw to approximately two finger widths above the breastbone using a 10 blade with or against the grain, depending upon the sensitivity of the skin.

Clip the entire throat from the base of the ear to approximately two finger widths above the point of shoulder. This area can be clipped with a 10 blade with the lay of coat. The front pattern should resemble a subtle W shape.

The throat is defined by a natural cowlick in the hair that runs from the base of the ear to the breastbone.

Clip the side of the neck, over the natural cowlick, using a 10 blade from under the ear down to approximately two finger widths past where the neck meets the shoulder blade.

Using a 7F blade, clip from just behind the ear, clipping over the shoulder. This will blend the 10 blade work on the side of the neck and the longer body coat together. Use thinning shears to blend the transition lines if needed.

The hip should be well defined to show a strong rear. On a hand stripped back coat this area can be tightened by carding with a stripping knife and by using thinning shears. For pet trims this area can be clipped with the same blade that was used on the body, or thinning shears may be used to tighten the hip.

When clipping, skim off with the clipper to blend the tight hip into the longer furnishings. Thinning shears can then be used to blend the lines.

The area around the anus should be clipped tight. The coat directly below the anus will part naturally and fall to both sides, similar to a "mustache". This coat is left natural and becomes part of the rear furnishings. The area above the pin bone should be tight into the hip.

Beveling the feet of a full-coated American Cocker Spaniel takes an artistic eye and practice. Every coat is different. Some bevels are easy to set while others are more of an effort.

The silky coats tend to show every scissor mark, while the heavier coats scissor beautifully. A beveled foot is tight at the base with a subtle V-shape appearance, as seen in this photo.

The back angle of the back foot should be set at a 30-degree angle.

Hold the hock hair between your fingers and cut a straight line to the back pad. This angle will determine the height of the back bevel. If this angle is lower than 30 degrees the bevel will be too low. A 30-degree cut is a perfect angle for a nice beveled foot.

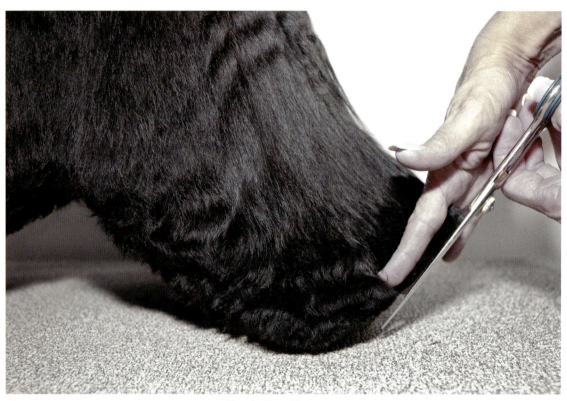

Photo by Renee Christensen

Hold the shear at a 30-degree angle and scissor around the base of the foot. Slowly bevel from the base of the foot to where the back angle of the hock flows into the side of the foot. This technique may be used on various long-coated pet breeds for a pretty beveled foot.

It is important to bevel the back feet before beveling the front feet. The back feet are not as heavily coated as the front feet and cannot always support as high a bevel as the front.

To bevel the front feet, hold the coat around the ankle and set the base of the foot round holding the shear at approximately a 30-degree angle. Release the longer coat and comb the coat down. Scissor the foot from the base of the bevel to the desired height. It is important that the height of the front bevels match the height of the back bevels for a well-balanced trim.

When setting the underline, locate the last rib of the dog. Set the tuck-up so it falls under the last rib by scissoring a notch in the coat at the desired height. Lifting the back leg up off the ground, draw the leg slightly back. Allow the stifle coat to fall naturally. Scissor a curved line from the ankle up to the tuck-up notch that was cut. This will set the stifle coat.

Photos by Renee Christensen

Place the foot down. Using straight shears, scissor a straight line from the tuck-up to the back pad of the front foot. These three steps should set a perfect underline. This process can be repeated with thinning shears to soften the lines.

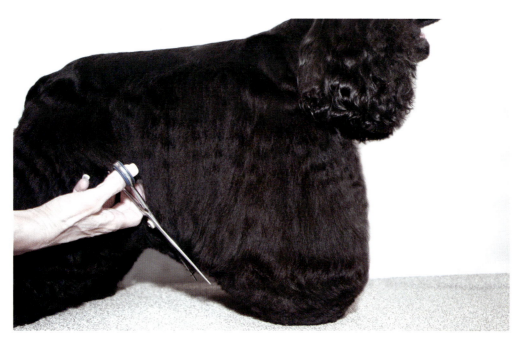

These techniques are shown in the "The American Cocker Spaniel - Show Trim" DVD. The entire bathing and drying process of the show dog is also included in the DVD.

AMERICAN COCKER SPANIEL

10 15	**10** 7F	**7F** 5F carding	7F **5F** 4F carding	thinning shears scissor		

Recommended Blade Lengths, Snap-On Comb Lengths and Techniques
Bold Print = Preferred Choices for Pet Trims

Suburban Trim

The American Cocker Spaniel is a heavily coated breed. Most pet owners are not able to maintain this coat type unless it is trimmed at a manageable length.

There are very nice modified pet trims that can be executed for this breed. The length of furnishings is the only difference between the various trims. It is very important to card the back coat after clipping the American Cocker, as with Setter-Like patterns and Terrier-Like patterns.

The Suburban trim is a very popular pet trim. This body pattern was clipped with a 5F blade and was blended into the longer furnishings. The legs were trimmed shorter with snap-on combs to a very manageable length. The side furnishings should also be trimmed using a snap-on comb to follow the contour of the ribs. The tuck-up can be set to fall under the last rib.

AMERICAN COCKER SPANIEL

The front legs were scissored to appear column-like. More coat was left on the front of the front leg, while the back and sides of the front leg were trimmed shorter. This gives a pretty column-like appearance.

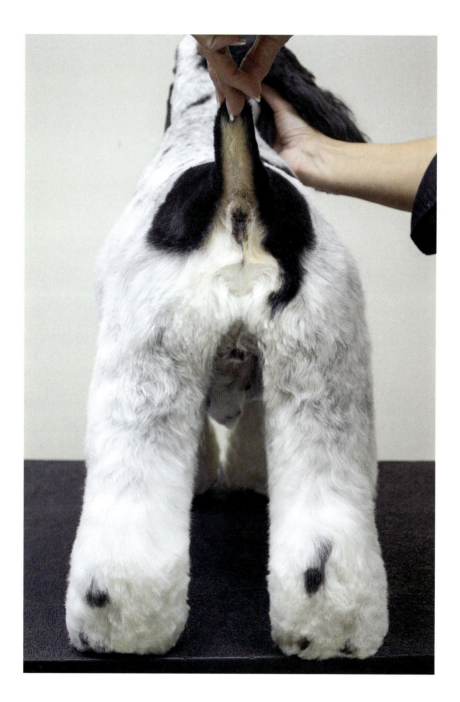

The rear legs can be trimmed with snap-on combs following the contour of the leg to show the angulation. Various sizes of snap-on combs can be used depending upon the dog's grooming schedule.

Field Trim

The Field trim is a sporty trim, with the entire body clipped with the same blade, preferably a 4F, 5F or 7F. This trim was clipped with a 5F blade. Clip the entire chest with the same blade, leaving only leg coat.

When viewed from the front and the rear the legs should be straight and parallel. The coat on the front legs should fall off the side of the upper arm smoothly. The coat on the rear legs should fall off the tight hip.

A small amount of coat should be left in the flank area to show a tuck-up which will transition the back legs into the short body. The tuck-up falls in the flank area instead of under the last rib, since the body is completely clipped. This is a very manageable and stylish trim for this breed.

Available on DVD: "The American Cocker Spaniel - Show Trim"

and "The American Cocker Spaniel - Pet Trims"

Tip To Remember:

Many pet owners may not want to spend the time or money it takes to keep up with a show trim for their pet. However, they do appreciate a well-groomed representation of their breed. Using a combination of the right tools and techniques will give pet trims the wow factor.

Show Trim Modified To Pet Trim

West Highland White Terrier

English Cocker Spaniel

Show Trim Modified To Pet Trim

Keeping show dogs in mind when grooming pets will help groomers achieve the proper look and balance of every breed. Whether the dogs are hand stripped or clipped, a groomer can achieve a beautiful trim using all the techniques that have been described in this text.

The breeds that have been discussed should have a seamless appearance. Most pet owners do not want to spend the time or the money to have their pet in a show trim. They do, however, appreciate a well-groomed representation of their breed. The length of furnishings can be modified for a shorter trim based on the pet owner's preference. However, the body pattern remains the same.

The following are examples of how a pet trim using clippers, various blades and thinning shears can give almost the same appearance as a hand stripped dog.

This is a Westie groomed for the show ring. The entire dog was hand stripped and carded. The results are seamless.

This is a pet Westie that was groomed using pet techniques. She was clipped using a #2 snap-on comb and the pattern was well blended using thinning shears and carding techniques.

Show Trim – Hand stripped rear

Pet Trim – Clipped rear

Show Trim – Hand stripped front

Pet Trim – Clipped front

Photo Courtesy of JC Photography

Grooming by Chereen Nawrocki

This is an English Cocker Spaniel in show coat which has been hand stripped and carded.

Photo and Grooming by Chereen Nawrocki

This is the same English Cocker Spaniel once he retired from the show ring and was groomed using pet techniques. He was clipped using a 5F blade and was well blended using thinning shear and carding techniques.

Tip To Remember:

Following the bone structure and reference points of the skull will help to set a rectangular shaped head. The orbital ridge (brow), zygomatic arch, corner of the eye, corner of the mouth and whisker nodules are all reference points to use when setting the lines of the head.

A spray gel or mousse can be used on Terrier eyebrows before drying to give them a straight appearance.

Head Styles

Rectangular Heads

Round Heads

Sporting Dog Heads

Head Styles

Several common head styles are seen by groomers on a daily basis: the round head, the rectangular head, and the Sporting dog head. These head styles can also be used on mixed breed dogs.

Rectangular Heads

This head style resembles a brick shape. The length of head from the occiput to the tip of the nose is longer than the width of the skull, which creates this shape. To achieve a rectangular head it is very important to set the sides of the skull very tight. The bony ridge that runs from the outside corner of the eye to the

front of the ear is called the zygomatic arch. This area as well as the cheeks should be set the tightest. The clipperwork on rectangular heads can be done with blades ranging from 4F, 5F, 7F to 10 used with or against the grain. The topskull is clipped against the grain from the occiput to the area behind the eye-socket bone of the brow. The blade chosen will be determined by what the dog needs to create the flat plane of the topskull.

The cheeks are clipped to the corner of the mouth or whisker nodule. The underjaw is clipped to the chin whisker nodule on breeds with full beards or the canine tooth on breeds with goatees.

The most common mistake in trying to achieve this head style is to pinch in the area where the cheek meets the muzzle. This results in an hourglass shape. When clipping the sides of the cheek into the muzzle, allow for transitioning by leaving coat from the clipper work into the beard and blend this area using thinning shears. This will help create a straight parallel line from the cheek to the beard.

Each breed with a rectangular head may have slight differences. Some may have a fall, while others may have long or short triangular eyebrows.

All falls and triangular eyebrows start from behind the eye socket bone of the brow. To set a triangular eyebrow, the outside corner of the brow should be set tight. A straight shear or a curved shear may be used to set the brow. Lay the scissor at the outside corner of the eye, just off the edge of the zygomatic arch, with the tip of the shear pointing to the center of the dog's nose and scissor a straight line. Breeds like the Schnauzers have a curved longer brow in which a curved shear would be used to make this cut. For a smaller triangular brow, as on the Wire Fox Terrier, the point of the shear may be angled in toward the bridge of the muzzle to tighten the triangle.

The eyebrows should be separated between the eyes. This can be done by using thinning shears, removing the coat between the brows.

Tip: Adjusting the length of beard and eyebrows can change the appearance of the length of the skull or muzzle. For example: If the dog has a shorter muzzle than desired, the brow can be shortened and the beard left longer to present a longer muzzle.

For breeds that require a fall, like the Kerry Blue Terrier and Lakeland Terrier, the fall starts from behind the eye socket bone of the brow. The fall covers the eyes flowing to the nose. The eyes should only be seen in profile. When viewed from the front, the eyes should not be exposed.

The side of the fall is set off the zygomatic arch. This area can be set with thinning shears or straight shears by cutting a straight line from the outside corner of the eye following the parallel line of the muzzle.

Use the zygomatic arch as the plane for tightening the fall on the outer corner of the eyes.

Some breeds, like the Wheaten Terrier, may not be as closely clipped but still should reflect a rectangular shape. In this case, longer blades and thinning shears should be used to achieve the correct shape. The side skull and cheeks can be clipped with a 4F or 5F blade. Thinning shears can be used to tighten this area to present the parallel lines of the sideskull. The topskull can be set with thinning shears.

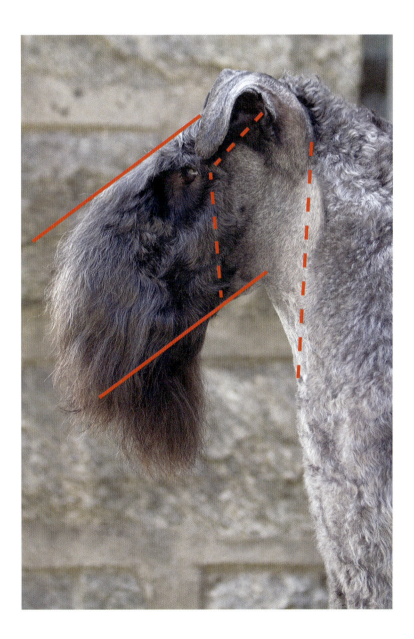

The Soft Coated Wheaten Terrier is the only breed with a rectangular head that has a crescent shape from the outside corner of the ear to the opposite outside corner of the ear. However, when viewing the head from the front and profile it is still a rectangle. The coat between the ears, over the backskull, is left longer to create the crescent and tapers shorter as it reaches the eyebrow ridge.

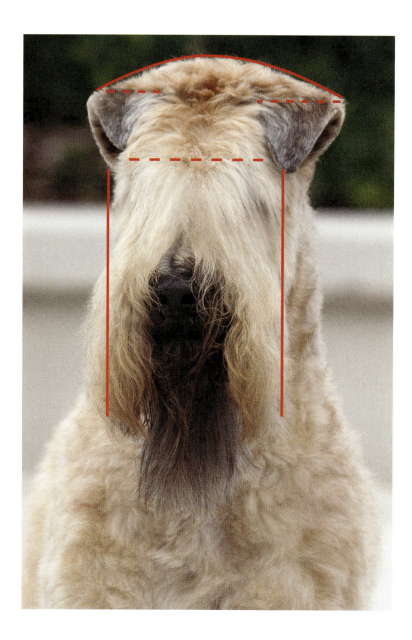

Beard lengths vary based on the particular breed. The wire-coated Terriers have a shorter beard than the breeds with more natural beards like the Wheaten, Scottie and Schnauzers. Some breeds may have goatees like the Airedale and Wire Fox Terriers. On these breeds, the entire lower jaw is clipped to the canine tooth. The coat left in front of the canine is the goatee. The upper jaw beard is left to the corner of the upper lip or whisker nodule to form the rectangle.

To remove bulk from beards several techniques can be used. On wire-coats, a Coat King may be used to thin the beard to present the rectangular appearance. The Coat King will pull the excess dead coat from the root which will help create the parallel lines of the side skull into the muzzle.

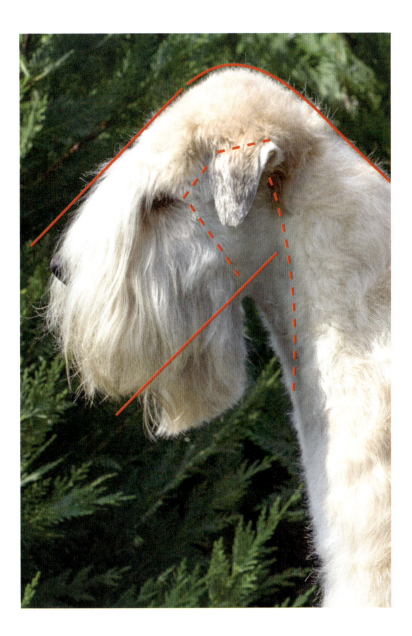

On silky type beards, like the Miniature Schnauzer and Soft Coated Wheaten Terrier, thinning shears can be used to shape the beard to create the parallel lines of the side skull into the muzzle.

Use the photos in *Straight to the Point* as a guide in determining the length of beard and eyebrows for pet trims.

Round Head

Numerous breeds require a round head style. Round heads are very popular with mixed breed dogs as well. When creating a round head, imagine the eyes being the center of the circle. A snap-on comb can be used to set the initial length of a round head. However, it is best to hand scissor this type of head, as using a snap-on comb can sometimes take the cheeks too flat, which will alter the round appearance.

It is important to remember that the coat should only encompass the skull. The head does not extend past the occiput or into the neck or throat.

Begin by setting the chin at approximately one inch in length. Once the bottom of the circle is set, the top can be set to the proper length. Scissor the sides of the circle by joining the top and the bottom with the shape of a semicircle. Combing and manipulating the coat is very important to create the circle. Using a scissoring spray is helpful to hold the coat in place while scissoring.

Using texturizing sprays/shampoos as well as spray gels/mousse before drying helps give the coat substance.

When grooming a round head, the muzzle coat should not be left as one length after setting the chin. If this coat is left as a blunt cut under the muzzle, the circle will not be complete. Comb up the muzzle coat and trim it with thinning shears to create a layered look. This will give the muzzle volume which will complement the roundness of the head.

Comb the muzzle coat forward and round the front of the upper lip coat to remove the corners, which will help finish off the circle.

Many breeds with round heads have prick ears. Many of these ears require the tips to be either hand stripped or clipped tight. This is often referred to as "tipping" the ears. On pet trims, the top part of the ears can be clipped short using a 10 blade on both the inside and outside of the ear leather. The edge of the ear leather should be tightened with small detail shears for a neat appearance. When creating a round head with erect or prick ears, imagine the ears are invisible. The ear tips that pop out of the circle should be clipped tight.

Sporting Dog Heads

Sporting dog heads can all be very similar. One type of head presents two level planes, which refers to the top of the skull and top of the muzzle. These planes are of equal length. The Setters, English Cocker Spaniel, English Springer Spaniel and several others have this head style.

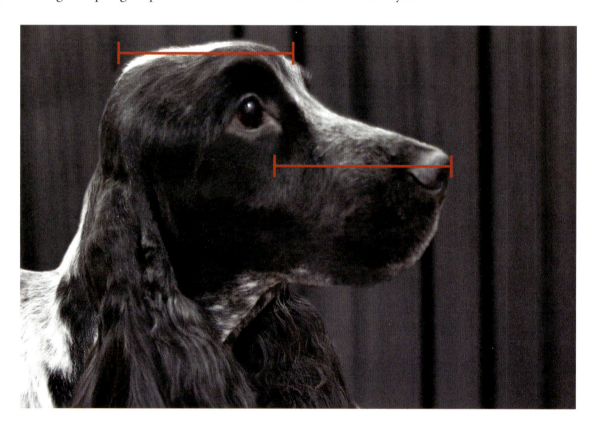

HEAD STYLES

The American Cocker Spaniel head has a round topskull with one part muzzle to two parts skull. This head style should resemble the number 8. The sideskull and width of the muzzle should be equal in width.

Several of these Sporting breeds require the top portion of the ear leather to be shaved with either a 10 or 15 blade with or against the grain. The blade length chosen will depend upon the density of the coat and sensitivity of the skin.

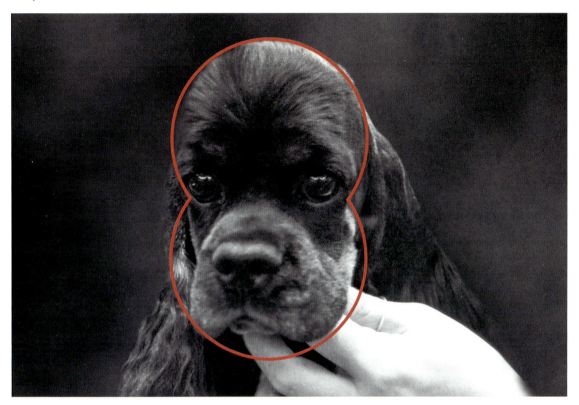

There is a fold of skin on the top front portion of the ear. The clipped line should end at the bottom of this skin fold.

The shaved pattern line can be set in either a U shape or a V shape. Setter ears are also clipped in the same manner; however, just the fold itself is often left fringed on both the inside and outside, which softens the dogs' expression. This is more of a personal preference. Both ear styles are acceptable.

The inside of the ears are clipped in the same manner as the outside, following the same pattern. If the outside of the ear is clipped with a U shape, the inside pattern should be set in the same manner.

Many of the Spaniel and Setter cheeks are clipped tight with a plush muzzle. The cheeks are clipped using a 10 blade with or against the grain. Starting from the cowlick in front of the ear canal, clip to the corner of the eye and to the corner of the lip. Using a light hand, skim the muzzle to remove longer coat or whiskers using a 10 blade. Thinning shears can also be used to neaten the muzzle, which will give the illusion of more substance.

Many Sporting dogs have a natural flat coat on their cheeks and may just require skimming with a 10 blade to tidy the appearance rather than clipping the cheek tight against the grain.

The topskull of these Sporting dogs should be groomed with thinning shears to create the proper shape and natural appearance of the skull. Sporting dogs should look natural and not extreme in any way. Using thinning shears preserves the natural appearance of these breeds. Carding techniques may be used on the top of the skull to remove fuzzy undercoat, which will facilitate in achieving the proper look.

The brows should be free of long hair and can be tidied with thinning shears.

There are also many Sporting dogs that have a more natural head and ear style. See "Ear Styles" on page 441. These breeds do not require clipping.

Tip To Remember:

Round heads can be difficult to achieve on coats that do not have the volume needed to create the ideal circle. Volumizing and texturizing products, mousse and spray gels are just some products that are available to give limp hair a little lift.

Tip To Remember:

Scissoring long ears to shorten the length will often leave scissor marks in the coat. This is due to the fact that ears tend to have a silky texture. Scissor the ear to the desired length and follow with thinning shears to texturize the ends of the coat. This will remove any marks the scissor may have left.

Ear Styles

Short Natural Ears

Long Natural Ears

Clipped Ears

Ear Styles

Several common ear styles are seen by groomers on a daily basis: the short natural ear, the long natural ear and the clipped ear. These ear styles can also be used on mixed breed dogs.

Short Natural Ears

Several breeds should not carry fringe on their ears. These include the Golden Retriever, Brittany, Welsh Springer Spaniel, Clumber Spaniel and Newfoundland among many others. These ear styles can be tidied with thinning shears for a more natural appearance. They are blended tighter at the bottom of the ear and are longer at the top in order to blend into the skull.

Long Natural Ears

Long natural ears are seen on various breeds. Examples include the Sussex Spaniel, Cavalier King Charles Spaniel, American Water Spaniel and Poodle. This ear style should be trimmed to the desired length and left as natural as possible. Ears should never fall past the point of shoulder. Trimming long ears with thinning shears will leave a natural appearance without scissor marks.

Clipped Ears

The clipped ear may vary from a prick ear to a folded ear. This is done on many breeds. The breeds that are hand stripped require the ears to be hand stripped as well. However, for pet trims these ears can be clipped. This ear style also looks nice on mixed breeds and other pet trims. Blades ranging from 10, 7F, 5F, to 4F can be used. A clipped ear can be a nice alternative for a breed that has difficulty with the ears matting when left long.

When clipping the ears with short blades, hold the ear leather over your fingers and clip from the inner portion of the ear leather clipping over the edge. Never clip from the edge into the ear as this area can easily be cut. After clipping, the ear leathers may be trimmed with detail scissors for a neat appearance.

TIP TO REMEMBER:

Tail styles are very similar from breed to breed. Numerous breeds have docked tails, flag tails, plume tails and carrot tails. The techniques used to trim these tail styles are consistent from breed to breed. The tools used may differ based on the coat type.

Tail Styles

Flag Tail

Lion Tail

Rat Tail

Carrot Tail

Docked Tail

Plumed Tail

Poodle Tail

Tail Styles

A variety of tail styles are seen on different breeds. For instance, the Setters have a flag tail, while many of the Terriers have a carrot or docked tail. This section shows the most common tails and gives quick grooming tips.

Various tail styles can be used on different breeds and on mixed breeds. Mixed breeds may have docked tails or long tails. Choosing a tail style that fits the trim is up to the groomer's creativity.

Just because the dog is a Poodle doesn't mean it has to be groomed like a Poodle with a Poodle tail. Poodles look very nice with carrot tails. Think outside the box when grooming mixed breeds and purebred dogs whose owners just "want something different".

Flag Tail

The flag tail, which is seen on all the Setters and many other breeds, can be easily mastered. Gather the hair from the base of the tail and slide your hand down to the tip. Hold all the hair of the tail to the tip and trim it to the desired length. This creates a flag effect. It may be necessary to trim the longest point of the tail, closest to the base of the tail, to sharpen the line.

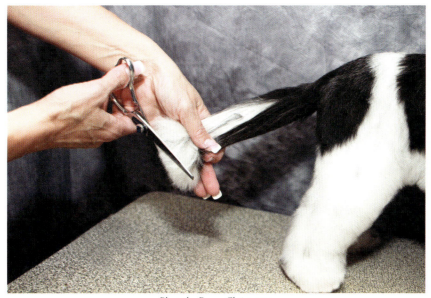

Photo by Renee Christensen

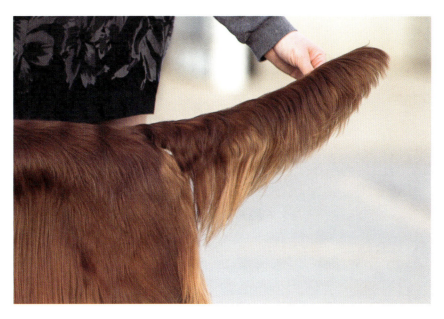

Lion Tail

A lion-style tail is seen on breeds like the Löwchen and Portuguese Water Dog. Two-thirds of this tail from the base is clipped or scissored, leaving the coat long and natural at the end. When the tail is carried over the back it should be short from the base of the tail to where the tail bends over the back.

Rat Tail

The Bedlington Terrier, Cesky Terrier and Irish Water Spaniel are examples of breeds with rat tails. Starting at the tip, carefully clip against the grain with a 10 or 15 blade, clipping two-thirds of the end of the tail. Shave the entire underside and sides of the tail with the same blade to the base. Hand scissor the top third of the tail to form a V shape. The widest part of the V should be at the base of the tail, where the tail meets the rear.

Carrot Tail

Carrot tails are seen on many Terrier breeds, including the Westie, Scottie and Cairn, to name a few.

On pet trims this tail is normally hand scissored, trimming the underside of the tail the shortest. The tail should appear to be a continuation of the topline without a break at the tail-set. The coat should be scissored the same length as the body pattern so it is properly balanced. The shape of this tail style is widest at the base and tapers at the tip.

Docked Tail

The docked tail is clipped at the same length as the body pattern. The underside of the tail is trimmed very tight. The tail should appear to be a continuation of the topline without a break at the tail-set. The only difference between a docked tail and a carrot tail is the natural shape of the tail. Grooming these two tail styles is similar.

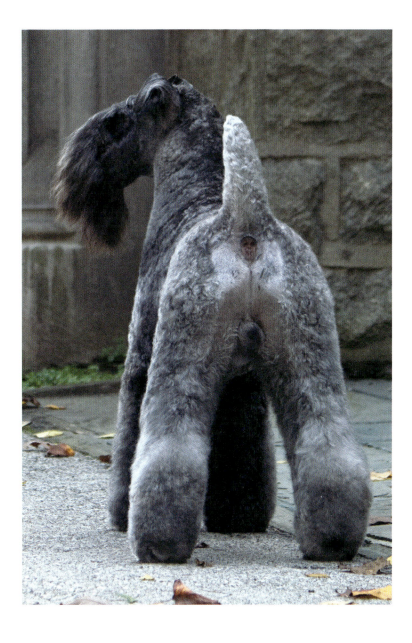

Plumed Tail

The plumed tail has a very natural appearance and is seen on the Bichon Frise, Shih Tzu, Maltese, Pomeranian, Lhasa Apso and Tibetan Spaniel, among others. This tail can be trimmed similar to the flag tail by holding all the coat from the base of the tail, sliding your hand down to the tip of the tail and trimming it to the desired length with thinning shears. Hold the tail over the back of the dog in its natural position and neaten the underside of the base of the tail with thinning shears for a neat appearance.

Photo by Renee Christensen

Poodle Tail

The Poodle tail has a shaved base and tail-set. Place the tail down over the anus. Mark with one finger the point of the tail that falls right beneath the anus. This is a good rule of thumb to follow when deciding where to clip the base of the tail to. Shave the base of the tail to that point with a 10 or 15 blade. A small triangle may be shaved where the tail sets into the croup.

The shape of the tail is going to depend upon the length of the tail bone itself. If the tail is docked very short it is going to be hard to make a nice pom-pom. If the tail is docked too long the pom-pom will look oblong instead of round.

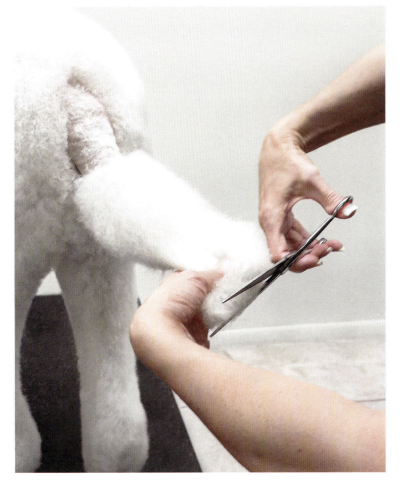

Diagram 1

Hold the coat to the end of the tail bone and scissor the hair off with a straight cut (Diagram 1).

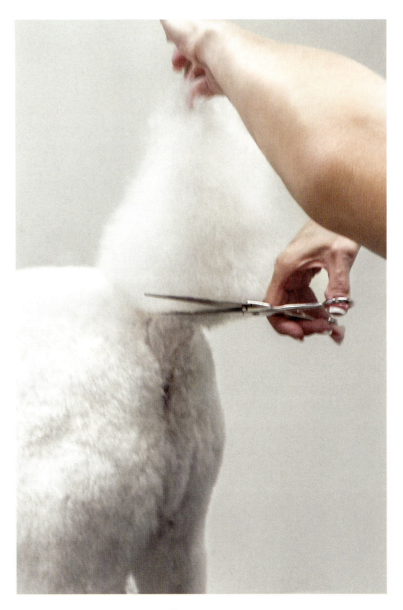

Diagram 2

Hold the tail up at the tip and comb the coat down toward the base of the tail. At the clipper line, scissor around the base with curved shears (Diagram 2).

Diagram 3

Once the top and bottom of the tail are set there should only be a ring around the middle that needs scissoring. Fluff the tail with a comb and neaten with scissors to present a round pom-pom (Diagram 3).

Tip To Remember:

Choosing a head style and ear style for a mixed breed dog is up to the creativity of the groomer. It takes an artistic eye to select the right style for these breeds. Select an ear style keeping the dog's ear-set in mind. For a clipped ear style, the ear should fold and fall nicely against the head. If the dog's ears tend to "fly-away", that particular ear style may not be the right choice. Check how the ears are falling once the dog is wet in the bath. This will give the groomer an idea of how the ears will look when clipped.

MIXING IT UP

**Using Sculpted Body Trims,
Terrier-Like and Setter-Like Patterns on Various Breeds**

    Bichonpoo "Bichon Frise"

    Cockapoo "Soft Coated Wheaten Terrier"

    Maltese "Setter-Like Pattern"

    Pompoo "Sculpted Body Trim"

    Poodle "Bedlington Terrier"

    Poodle "Kerry Blue Terrier"

    Shih Tzu "Terrier-Like Pattern"

    Yorkie "Terrier-Like Pattern"

MIXING IT UP

Using Sculpted Body Trims, Terrier-Like and Setter-Like Patterns on Various Breeds

Utilizing various pattern lines on different breeds for pet trims can be very stylish. Once the groomer understands where to set patterns based on the dog's structure, styling becomes fun and easy. Sculpted Body Trims, Terrier-Like patterns and Setter-Like patterns can be set on a variety of breeds and mixed breeds.

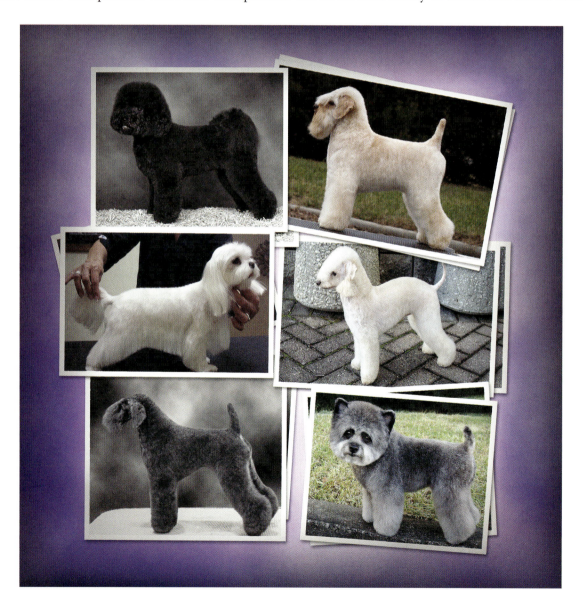

Groomers see a huge variety of mixed breeds on a daily basis. Many of these are Poodle mixes, e.g., Cockapoos, Goldendoodles, Labradoodles, Shihpoos, Maltipoos, Bichonpoos, Yorkipoos, Schnoodles and the list goes on. In addition to that, pet owners of purebred dogs often don't always want their dogs to look like the breed they actually own. For whatever the reason, groomers will get requests from time to time stating, "Don't make my Poodle look like a Poodle" or "We like the scruffy look".

This is when our creativity, as groomers, can come into play—thinking outside of the box. Once the groomer has an understanding of patterns and how to sculpt body lines to bring out the best attributes in a dog, selecting a pattern to put on various breeds becomes fun and easy.

The following are several examples of setting patterns on different breeds. Several of the trims go to the next level and actually imitate a specific breed in its entirety, which can also be fun.

Available on DVD:

"The Cockapoo with a Dandie Dinmont Expression"

"The Portuguese Water Dog: A Poodle in Disguise"

"The Goldendoodle"

"The Shag"

Many more to come!

Bichonpoo

"Bichon Frise"

Peanut, the Bichon-Poodle mix, was trimmed imitating the Bichon Frise.

Photo by Animalphotography-Ren Netherland   Groomed by Lisa Correia

Since this is a mixed breed and not a true Bichon Frise, camouflage grooming came into play. The groomer created the structure of a Bichon by sculpting the coat to present the proper profile. Leaving coat in the right places, as well as taking coat off in the right places, created this wonderful illusion of a Bichon Frise. This is a great alternative for pet owners who do not want their Poodles to look like Poodles.

Cockapoo

"Soft Coated Wheaten Terrier"

Charlie, the Cockapoo, was groomed imitating the Soft Coated Wheaten Terrier.

Groomed by Jodi Murphy

This trim was selected for Charlie because of his similar coat type and texture to the Wheaten Terrier.

Since this is a Cockapoo and not a true Soft Coated Wheaten Terrier, camouflage grooming came into play. The structure of a Wheaten was created by sculpting the coat to present the proper profile. The head structure of a Cockapoo is very different from the Wheaten. Leaving coat in the right places, as well as taking coat off in the right places, created this wonderful illusion of a Soft Coated Wheaten Terrier.

Maltese

"Setter-Like Pattern"

Chloe, the Maltese, was trimmed following the Setter-Like pattern.

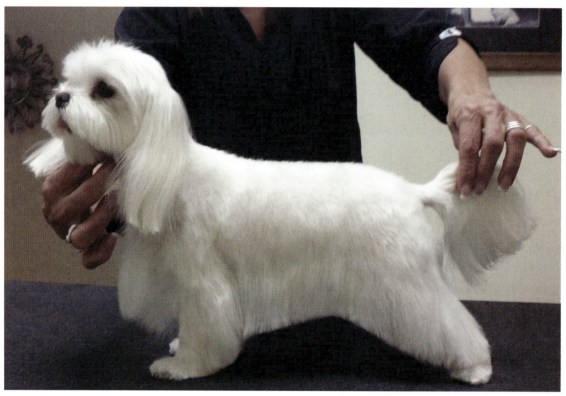

Groomed by Jodi Murphy

The pattern is well blended into the longer furnishings.

Due to minor surgery, the animal hospital shaved the front of Chloe's front leg for an IV catheter. After blending the shaved area of the leg to even things out, the Setter-Like pattern suddenly came to mind. This is a nice alternative when pet owners prefer a longer style, yet there is much less hair to maintain.

Pompoo

"Sculpted Body Trim"

Rudy, the Pomeranian-Poodle mix, was trimmed following the Sculpted Body Trim pattern.

Groomed by Jose Rojas

The front legs were scissored to have a column-like appearance. The rear legs were scissored to show a well angulated rear.

Since Rudy is a stout little girl, her body was scissored tight which gave her a slim appearance. Her legs were left longer than her body for a well-balanced trim.

Poodle
"Bedlington Terrier"

Sawyer, the Toy Poodle, was trimmed imitating the Bedlington Terrier.

Groomed by Mackensie Murphy

This trim on a Poodle is often called the "Poodlington" by groomers.

Since this is a Poodle and not a true Bedlington, camouflage grooming came into play. The groomer created the structure of a Bedlington Terrier, which can be extremely difficult. The head structure of a Poodle is very different from the Bedlington. Leaving coat in the right places, as well as taking coat off in the right places, created this wonderful illusion of a Bedlington Terrier.

Poodle
"Kerry Blue Terrier"

Gigi, the Miniature Poodle, was trimmed imitating the Kerry Blue Terrier.

Groomed by Jennifer Lee

Since this is a Poodle and not a true Kerry Blue, camouflage grooming came into play. The groomer created the structure of a Kerry Blue Terrier, which can be extremely difficult. The head structure of a Poodle is very different from the Kerry Blue. Leaving coat in the right places, as well as taking coat off in the right places, created this wonderful illusion of a Kerry Blue.

Shih Tzu

"Terrier-Like Pattern"

Curtis, the Shih Tzu, has been groomed following the Distinct Terrier-Like pattern.

Groomed by Jodi Murphy

The pattern was set using a 5F blade and was well blended into the legs and underline by using thinning shears. The front legs were scissored to appear column-like. The rear legs were scissored to show the angulation.

Yorkie

"Terrier-Like Pattern"

Chloe, the Yorkshire Terrier, has been groomed following the Subtle Terrier-Like pattern.

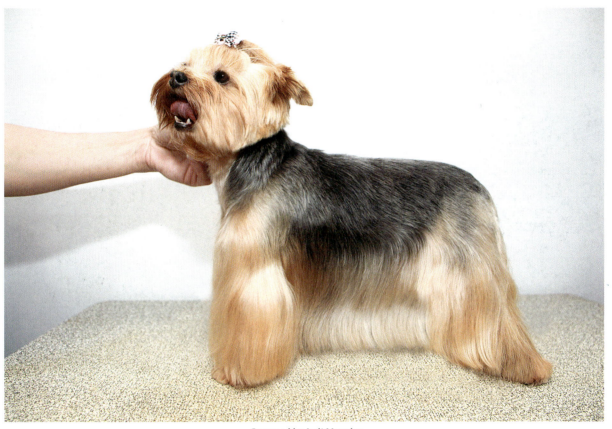

Groomed by Jodi Murphy

This Yorkie does not have as dense a coat as the dogs described in this group, which results in a tighter pattern. The pattern was set using a 5F blade and was well blended into the longer furnishings by using thinning shears. The front pattern was left higher because the coat is very fine. Setting the pattern lower would remove too much of the front furnishings, which would take away from the desired profile.

TIP TO REMEMBER:

Going the extra mile to camouflage structure faults while grooming pets will not go unnoticed. Pet owners may not know exactly what was done to their dog but what they do know is that their dog never looked better. Building a clientele is often based on word of mouth. Happy clients refer their groomer to their friends.

Grooming Tips To Correct Faults

Lack of Forechest

Short Neck

Long in Body

Up on Leg

Low on Leg

Dip in the Topline

Steep Shoulders

Slab-Sided

Straight in Rear

Toeing Out

Grooming Tips to Correct Faults

When working with coated breeds it is possible to correct minor faults by strategically grooming the coat to camouflage these areas. There are several tricks of the trade that will help to create the ideal profile. Different techniques must be used for curly-coated breeds vs. drop-coated breeds. Of course, the drop-coated breeds are trickier to correct. Leaving hair in the right places and taking hair off in the right places is the key to correcting faults.

Lack of Forechest

Curly coats

If a dog is lacking forechest, several things can be adjusted to create forechest. More coat can be left at the breastbone and over the prosternum to build a chest.

The front of the front legs can be trimmed shorter, leaving more coat on the back of the front leg. This will set the front leg farther back under the dog, which will show more forechest.

Drop-coats

On Setter-Like breeds the clipped line of the front can be raised higher than the breastbone. This will give the front furnishings more volume, which will help build the chest. The furnishings of the front chest can be angled higher, which will make the chest pop out.

Short Neck

Curly coats

Breeds like the Poodle and Bichon among many other breeds that have a topknot are the easiest to fix. Leaving more coat on the topskull will give the neck length. Tightening the topline as well as the sides of the neck will also present a longer neck.

Long in Body

Adjusting the position of the tuck-up will change the appearance in the length of the dog. Moving the tuck-up forward will shorten the appearance. Moving the tuck-up back past the last rib will give the appearance of a longer body.

Leaving more coat on the back of the front legs and front of the back legs will close in the space between the front and rear legs. This trick helps to shorten the length of the dog.

On curly-coated breeds it is important to set the front and rear as tight as possible without taking away from the forechest or rear angulation. Excess coat on the front and rear will lengthen the body of the dog.

The transition from the crest of neck over the withers can be moved slightly behind the withers to shorten the appearance of the back.

Up on Leg

If a dog appears taller than what the breed standard states, leaving the underline coat a bit lower will give the appearance of the correct height. The topline may have to be adjusted in order for the dog to appear balanced.

Low on Leg

Curly coats

Many breeds, especially pet dogs, tend to be low on leg. In this case, the underline should be set as tight as possible, which will lengthen the appearance of the leg.

Drop-coats

The furnishings of the underline can be taken shorter to lengthen the appearance of the leg.

Dip in the Topline

Curly coats

If a dog appears to have a swayback or dip, it can be easily fixed by scissoring the topline level allowing for fill coat in the dip area.

Drop-coats

On double-coated breeds, avoid carding in the dip area, leaving undercoat to fill in the low spot. Some dogs may appear high in the rear, for example. More carding over this area can be done to tighten the croup.

Steep Shoulders

Oftentimes the shoulder blades are not angled properly and are more upright. In this case the shoulder blades meet closer into the back of the neck than they should. This presents a short neck and a longer topline. On coated breeds the transition line from the neck over the withers can be adjusted. Moving the transition area behind the withers will give the appearance of correctly set shoulders.

Slab-Sided

When dogs lack the proper spring of ribs they can appear slab-sided. In this case scissoring the rib cage fuller at the centerline of the ribs will fill in this area.

Straight in Rear

Curly coats

If a dog is lacking rear angulation, leaving more coat on the point of rump and hock area will accentuate the rear angle. The bend of leg should be scissored tight. The stifle should be emphasized to show more bend. Sculpting the back and front of the rear leg in this manner can change the appearance of a straight rear.

Drop-coats

Set the rear angle at the bend of knee as tight as possible. On double-coated breeds, like the English Cocker, American Cocker and Setters for example, carding techniques can be done in the rear angulation to accentuate the bend of knee.

Toeing Out

Many dogs tend to toe out with their front feet. On coated breeds this can be easily fixed. The feet should be scissored as if they are pointing forward. This would mean that the outside of the front feet should be scissored tight, while leaving more coat on the inside of the feet to create the illusion that the foot is pointing forward.

Closure . . .

When I was a new groomer I attended dog shows on a regular basis to see how the dogs were being groomed. I had no other source of education, and this helped me tremendously. I chose to bring you these show dogs to learn from, as that is how I taught myself—by watching. Having a correct vision of these breeds will help you to recognize proper pattern placement and proper balance.

Correct pattern placement is the same whether it is a pet trim or a show trim. The technique used to set the pattern is the only difference. The length of the pattern and furnishings can be modified for a manageable pet trim.

Show trims should be our guide for making pets look like the breed they were bred to be. Using the techniques that have been discussed here will help your trims look natural and will also benefit the skin and coat of these breeds.

Over the years I have experimented with putting different patterns on different breeds and mixed breeds. I have shared here things that I have discovered over the years. I hope you will be able to utilize this information to become the best groomer you can be and give you the confidence of thinking outside of the box.

The AKC's *The Complete Dog Book* is a great form of reference. When in doubt . . . look it up. I have given you a taste of the AKC book with the quotes that I thought were important. The breed clubs offer even more information in their standards that will educate you, not only on the structure, but also about the dogs, i.e., the history of the breed, what they were bred for and how their physical characteristics match the aims of that breeding.

It is important to observe dog shows often, as the grooming styles of many of the breeds evolve over time. This is no different than our hair styles. Keeping up with the styling trends and the new breeds that become registered with the AKC will keep you abreast in the industry.

The breed standards remain; however, putting style and flair on breeds is what changes over the years. Looking back at breeds like the Poodle and Bichon Frise, for example, shows how the grooming evolved over the years and became more stylized.

Our skill level steadily increases with time and experience. Keep learning, ask questions, be patient and you will soon develop an eye for balance and correct breed profiles.

"Instruction ends in the school-room, but education ends only with life." — Frederick W. Robertson

"Knowledge leads to confidence, confidence leads to success." — Jodi Murphy

Glossary of Terms

Against the grain: Refers to clipping the coat in the opposite direction that the coat naturally lies.

Arched toes: Well-knuckled-up feet.

Breed standards: Individual breed descriptions written by the parent breed clubs which define the ideal dog based on correct structure, temperament, coat type, etc. The standard is considered a blueprint to the perfect animal of that particular breed. Having breed standards sets goals for breeders to improve their breeding programs. Standards slightly vary from country to country.

Brisket: Sternum; the eight bones that form the floor of the chest.

Camouflage grooming: Grooming techniques used to hide the flaws in a dog's structure to give the illusion of correct structure.

Canine teeth: The two upper and lower large pointed teeth.

Carding: Describes the technique of removing undercoat from the follicles by the use of a stripping knife or shedding rake.

Cat foot: A round, compact foot with arched toes.

Coat King: An undercoat rake manufactured by Mars.

Column-like: Refers to the front legs. To achieve this appearance the coat is left longest on the front of the leg. The rear and sides of the legs are trimmed shorter.

Croup: Rump of the dog. Muscular area just in front of the set of tail.

Depth of chest: Referring to the chest reaching to the level of the elbow, i.e., above, at the level or below.

Fill coat: Coat which is left longer in areas to fill in a low spot of the topline or tail-set.

Flank: The flap or webbing of skin below the loin between the last rib and the thigh.

Forechest: Part of the chest in front of the forelegs. This is often referred to as being "pronounced". A pronounced forechest is one that is very evident.

Go to ground: When vermin take refuge below the ground and the dogs pursue them in their underground burrows.

Griffon: Referred to as a rough- or wire-coated breed.

Hare foot: A foot on which the two center digits are longer than the inside and outside toes, creating the appearance of a long foot.

Hock: The bones of the rear leg that form the joint between the second thigh and the metatarsus.

Keel: The rounded outline of the lower chest, between the prosternum and the breastbone. A term commonly used when describing short-legged Terriers.

Layback: The angle of the shoulder blade.

Loin: The loin is the area between the last rib and the pelvis. Think of the human waistline when referring to the loin.

Low tail-set: A tail-set that is below the level of the spine.

Occiput: The posterior or back point of the skull.

Pin bone or Point of rump: The point of the pelvic bones adjacent to and slightly below the anus.

Prosternum: The projected front portion of the chest referred to as the forechest.

Rustic coat: A coat that looks natural with a somewhat unkempt appearance. It often appears to have tight ringlets of curls and/or cords with a woolly texture.

Saber tail: A tail carried in a semicircle.

Sinewy: Free from excessive muscle or fat.

Slab-sided: Flat-ribbed; lack of spring of ribs.

Spay coat: A coat that has changed in color and texture because the dog was spayed or neutered.

Spring game: Flush; to drive birds from cover, forcing them to fly or spring.

Spring of ribs: The curvature of the rib cage; the widest part of the rib cage located midway between the topline and the underline.

Stifle: The knee; the joint where the femur and tibia/fibula meet.

Stop: The area between the eyes where the top of the muzzle and skull meet.

Supraorbital ridge: The bony ridge located above the eye sockets; eyebrow.

Tail-set: The area where the tail meets the rump.

Throat latch: The area where the head and neck join directly under the lower jaw.

Topline: The area of the top of the back (spine) from behind the withers to the tail-set.

Tuck-up: The highest point of the underline as it comes into the flank—behind the last rib.

Undercoat: The short, soft, dense hair that supports the outer coat.

Underline: The contour of the brisket from behind the elbow to the loin.

Utility: The job that the dog was bred for.

Variety: Certain breeds are bred with a variety of size and/or coat type. For example, the Collie can be bred with one of two coat types, rough coat or smooth coat. The Poodle has three size varieties, Toy, Miniature and Standard. The Dachshund has three varieties of coat, longhaired, smooth and wirehaired. The Dachshund is also shown in two sizes, miniature and standard.

Webbed feet: Toes that are connected by membrane. Webbed feet are often seen in water-retrieving breeds.

Well laid back: Well-angulated shoulder blade.

Well let down: A short hock.

Withers: The ridge between the highest point of the shoulder blades located between the base of the crest of neck and topline.

Breed Index

Breed	Page
Affenpinscher	210
Airedale Terrier	214
American Cocker Spaniel	399
American Eskimo Dog	132
American Water Spaniel	84
Australian Shepherd	136
Australian Terrier	88
Bedlington Terrier	322
Bernese Mountain Dog	140
Bichon Frise	328
Black Russian Terrier	336
Border Collie	144
Bouvier des Flandres	344
Boykin Spaniel	94
Brittany	98
Brussels Griffon	218
Cairn Terrier	288
Cavalier King Charles Spaniel	102
Cesky Terrier	222
Clumber Spaniel	106
Collie	148
Dandie Dinmont Terrier	228
English Cocker Spaniel	56
English Setter	60
English Springer Spaniel	64
Field Spaniel	110
Flat-Coated Retriever	152
German Wirehaired Pointer	114
Giant Schnauzer	232
Glen of Imaal Terrier	236
Golden Retriever	156
Gordon Setter	68
Great Pyrenees	160
Irish Setter	72
Irish Terrier	240
Irish Water Spaniel	352
Japanese Chin	164
Keeshond	168
Kerry Blue Terrier	358
Lagotto Romagnolo	366
Lakeland Terrier	244
Longhaired Chihuahua	172
Longhaired Dachshund	118
Miniature Schnauzer	248
Newfoundland	176
Norfolk Terrier	292
Norwich Terrier	296
Otterhound	252
Papillon	180
Petit Basset Griffon Vendeen	258
Pomeranian	184
Poodle	374
Portuguese Water Dog	382

Samoyed	*188*
Scottish Terrier	*300*
Sealyham Terrier	*304*
Shetland Sheepdog	*192*
Soft Coated Wheaten Terrier	*392*
Spinone Italiano	*262*
Sussex Spaniel	*122*
Tibetan Spaniel	*196*
Welsh Springer Spaniel	*76*
Welsh Terrier	*266*
West Highland White Terrier	*308*
Wirehaired Dachshund	*126*
Wirehaired Pointing Griffon	*270*
Wire Fox Terrier	*274*

NOTES

AVAILABLE ON DVD

Breed Specific DVDs

The Airedale Terrier
The American Cocker Spaniel
The Bichon Frise
The Border Terrier
The Golden Retriever
The Havanese
The Lhasa Apso
The Maltese
The Miniature Schnauzer
The Poodle
The Scottish Terrier
The Shih Tzu
The Soft Coated Wheaten Terrier
The Welsh Terrier
The West Highland White Terrier
The Yorkshire Terrier

Technique DVDs

Before the Groom
Carding & Hand Stripping for Pets
Dematting: Theory & Techniques
Deshedding: Theory & Techniques
Scissoring: Theory & Techniques
Smooth Road to Shavedowns
Snap-On Combs: Theory & Techniques
Thinning Shears: Theory & Techniques

Show Trims

The American Cocker Spaniel
The Bichon Frise
The Irish Setter
The Soft Coated Wheaten Terrier

Mixing it Up

The Cockapoo: A Dandie Dinmont Expression
The Goldendoodle
The Portuguese Water Dog: A Poodle in Disguise
The Shag

Miscellaneous DVDs

Expressions
Fragile: Handle with Care
On the Same Page: One on One with a Vet
The Puppy Cut
Secrets of the Contest Ring

Mobile Grooming DVDs

The Business End
A Day in the Spa
A Day on the Road with Jodi & Danelle Part I
A Day on the Road with Jodi & Danelle Part II

The most complete instructional series available on DVD!

Everything You Need to Know!

The Complete Educational Package!

Over 40 DVD Volumes Available!

Educating Groomers Around the World!

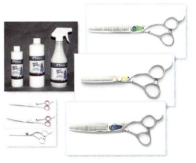

The Right Tools Get You The Right Results!

Finally A Reason to Say NO to Smocks!

Your Guides to Starting & Maintaining a Successful Business!

MASTER PET STYLIST

This Full Line of Jodi Murphy Products Available Now at **JodiMurphy.net**